BECOMING VEGETARIAN

THE COMPLETE GUIDE TO ADOPTING A HEALTHY VEGETARIAN DIET

VESANTO MELINA, R.D.

BRENDA DAVIS, R.D.

VICTORIA HARRISON, R.D.

BOOK PUBLISHING COMPANY
SUMMERTOWN, TENNESSEE

Book Publishing Company
P.O. Box 99
Summertown, TN 38483
1–888–260–8458

Design: Counterpunch
Cover illustration: Helen D'Souza

ISBN 1-57067-013-7

Melina, Vesanto, 1942–
    Becoming vegetarian : the complete guide to adopting a healthy vegetarian diet / Vesanto Melina, Brenda Davis, Victoria Harrison.
        p.   cm.
    Includes bibliographical references and index.
    ISBN 1-57067-013-7 (alk. paper)
    1. Vegetarianism. I. Davis, Brenda, 1959- . II. Harrison, Victoria, 1941- . III. Title.
    RM236.M44   1995
        613.2'62--dc20   95-30573
                                                      CIP

Printed in the United States

03 02 01 00 99   6 7 8 9 10

To our children,

Chris and Kavyo;
Leena and Cory;
Richard, Christina and Rachel.

*May each day of your life fill you with the inspiration
and courage to stand for what you believe.*

SELECTED REFERENCES

American Dietetic Association. 1993. Position of the American Dietetic Association: Vegetarian diets. *J. Am. Diet. Assoc.* Vol. 93:1317–1319.

Brown, M.L. *Present Knowledge in Nutrition.* Washington, D.C.: International Life Sciences Institute, Nutrition Foundation, 1990.

Chow, C.K., ed. *Fatty Acids in Foods and their Health Implications.* New York. Marcel Kekker Inc., 1993.

Committee on Diet and Health, Food and Nutrition Board, Commission on Life Sciences, National Research Council. *Diet and Health.* Washington, D.C.: National Academy Press, 1989.

Draper, A., Lewis, J., Malhota, N. et al. 1993. The energy and nutrient intakes of different types of vegetarian: a case for supplements? *Brit. J. Nutr.* 69:3–19.

Dwyer, J.T. Nutritional consequences of vegetarianism. 1991. *Annu. Rev. Nutr.* 11:61–91.

Erdman, J.W. and Fordyce, E.J. 1989. Soy products and the human diet. *Am. J. Clin. Nutr.* 49:725–737.

Geil, P.B. and Anderson, J.W. 1994. Nutrition and health implications of dry beans: a review. *J. AM. Coll. Nutr.* Vol. 13, 6:458–558.

Groff, J.L., Gropper, S.S. and Hunt, S.M. *Advanced Nutrition and Human Metabolism.* 2nd ed. West Publishing Co. St. Paul, 1995.

Hallas, T.J. and Walker, A.F., eds. Vegetarianism: the healthy alternative? pp. 210–247 in Walker, A.F. and Rolls, B., eds. *Issues in Nutritional Toxicology.* New York: Elsivier Applied Science, 1992.

Harland, B.F. and Morris, E.R. 1995. Phytate: A good or bad food component? *Nutrition Research.* Vol. 15. 5:733-754

Health and Welfare Canada. *Nutrition Recommendations: The Report of the Scientific Review Committee.* Ottawa: Supply and Services Canada, 1990.

Heaney, R. P., 1993. Protein Intake and the Calcium Economy. *J. Am. Diet. Assoc.* Commentary Vol. 93: 1250–1260.

Kitts, D.D. 1993. Bioactive substances in food. *Can. J. Physiol. Pharmacol..* Vol. 72:423–434.

Lee, K., Oilce Y., and Kanazawa T., eds. *The Third International Conference on Nutrition in Cardiovascular Diseases.* Annals New York Acd. Sci. Vol. 676, 1993.

Mangels, A.R. 1992. Vegetarian infants and children: a review of recent research. *Issues in Vegetarian Dietetics.* Vol. 1, No. 2: 4–6.

O'Connell, J.M., Dibley, M.J., Sierra, J. et al 1989. Growth of vegetarian children: The Farm study. *Pediatrics.* Vol. 84, No. 3: 475–481.

Pennington, J.A. *Bowes and Church's Food Values of Portions Commonly Used.* 16th ed. Philadelphia: Lippincott Company, 1993.

Sanders, T.A.B. 1988. Growth and development of British vegan children. *Am. J. Clin. Nutr.* 48:822–825.

Young, V. R. 1991. Soy Protein in Relation to Human Nutrition and Amino Acid Nutrition. *J.Am. Diet. Assoc.* 91: 828–835.

Wahle, K.W.J. and James, W.P.T. 1994. Isomeric fatty acids and human health. *Eur. J. Clin. Nutr.* 47:828–839.

Willet, W.C. 1994 Diet and Health: What should we eat? *Science.* Vol. 264:532–537.

World Health Organization Study Group on Diet, Nutrition and Prevention of Noncommunicable Diseases. *Diet, Nutrition and Prevention of Chronic Diseases.* Geneva, Switzerland: Technical Report Series No. 797. World Health Organization, 1991.

CONTENTS

ACKNOWLEDGEMENTS

To every person who made this book possible, through their unfailing enthusiasm, support, patience and advice, we offer our gratitude. We are especially indebted to the following people:

Our deepest thanks to:
Dr. Paul Harrison, Paul Davis and David Melina for thoughtful advice, invaluable assistance and encouragement. Cynthia and Bob Holzapfel, Michael Cook, Warren Jefferson and the rest of the wonderful staff at Book Publishing Company. It has been a privilege for us to work alongside people whose lives reflect compassion as well as professional expertise. Dietitian Suzanne Havala for her guidance, skill and clarity.

Many thanks to our professional reviewers and advisors for their assistance, support and advice:
Dr. R. G. Ackman, Dr. Susan Barr of the University of British Columbia, Dr. Tai C. Chen of Boston University Hospital, Lucia Crosson of Omega Nutrition, Dr. Rosalind Gibson of the University of Guelph, Kirsten Hanson of Macmillan Canada, Dr. Barbara Harland of Howard University, H. C. Hawthorne of Hoffman LaRoche Laboratories, Dr. Michael Klaper, Dr. William Lands of National Institute of Alcohol and Alcoholism, Dr. Alexander Leaf of Harvard Medical School, Dr. Joseph Leichter of the University of British Columbia, Dr. Edward Siguel of Boston University Hospital, Dr. Cristine M. Trahms of the University of Washington, Dr. Connie Weaver of Purdue University, Dr. Vernon Young of M. I. T. The following dietitians: Kyra Bartlett, Barbara Cheng, Hughette Cloutier, Susan Denton, Jeannie Dickie, Susan Ferris, Jean Freemont, Ketti Goudey, Laurie Hunter, Gerry Kasten, Sherry Kutynik, Vicki Lalari, Louise Lambert-Lagacé, Karin Litzcke, Sherry Ogasawara, Patty Pasinyk, Kathleen Quinn, Shefali Raja, Fiona Smith, Jane Swalling, Linda Watts.

Sincere thanks to those who provided thoughtful chapter reviews, hours of undaunted recipe testing and other help with recipes:
Chefs Joseph Forest and Michael Fisher, Ruth Sebastian; Ken and Susan Collerman, Sandra Lindstrom, Clare Daem and her students. Thanks also to Sunrise Tofu Company, Omega Nutrition and to the Red Star Yeast division of Universal Foods.

We also offer our heartfelt appreciation to:
Dr. E. S. and Aldona Goranson (Vesanto's father and stepmother) and John and Doreen Charbonneau (Brenda's parents) and Jean Harman (Victoria's mother) for setting the high standards by which we live and work, and for giving us the inspiration to follow our hearts.

FOREWORD

Becoming Vegetarian is a book about a topic whose time has come, . . . to stay. A 1992 Yankelovich survey, sponsored by *Vegetarian Times* magazine, found that nearly 7 percent of American adults are consciously reducing their meat intakes and describing themselves as vegetarians. Another study conducted the same year by the National Restaurant Association found that almost one out of five restaurant patrons is seeking a meatless meal. Just around the corner, your neighborhood supermarket is stocking a wide variety of vegetarian burgers, hot dogs and other meatless products.

Times have changed. When I was finishing college in 1981, doctors considered a cholesterol level of 300 mg/dl to be normal. Hospital coronary units fed heart attack victims bacon and eggs for breakfast. In one nutrition course, I learned about the Pritikin program and vegetarianism under the unit on "fad diets." No more.

The movement toward a plant-based diet accelerated over the last ten years as an increasing body of research associated vegetarian lifestyles with lower rates of many chronic, degenerative diseases and conditions. "Diseases of affluence," as they are sometimes called – coronary artery disease, some forms of cancer, high blood pressure, obesity and others – more commonly afflict people who eat the traditional "meat and potatoes" American diet.

Vegetarian diets are outside our culture and outside the personal experience of most American health professionals. Nevertheless, today there is growing acceptance of vegetarianism as a healthful alternative. The American Dietetic Association (ADA), in its 1993 position paper on vegetarian diets, states that "vegetarian diets are healthful and nutritionally adequate when appropriately planned." Members of the ADA have organized a dietetic practice group, or subgroup, within the Association, for dietitians who wish to specialize in or learn more about vegetarian diets. Some dietitians are even citing vegetarian diets as their primary area of expertise or practice.

Attitudes about vegetarian diets have changed, and so have the guidelines for planning them. Recommendations for planning vegetarian diets used to be accompanied by many cautionary notes, the implication being that in order to be healthy on a diet that excluded meat, painstaking care had to be taken in order to get it right. One false move and you were in big trouble. Foods had to be carefully combined lest protein deficiency result. Additional hand-wringing ensued if the diet excluded dairy products and eggs.

Fortunately, old attitudes and beliefs have given way to a better understanding of nutrition and the relationships between diet and disease, as well as to possibilities for alternative eating styles. The science of nutrition may be complicated, but eating well is a far simpler matter.

Vegetarian diets are one option, one that can easily meet nutritional needs while helping people avoid the dietary excesses that characterize the traditional American diet. Vegetarian meals can be easy to plan and prepare, and they do not require the meticulous planning that was once believed necessary.

Our increasingly multicultural society is exposing us to a wide range of foods and dishes from every corner of the world, many of them traditionally vegetarian. Some used to think that when one reduced or eliminated meat from the diet, the diet became more limited. Most vegetarians would say the opposite is true. Today, when people broaden their options to include vegetarian dishes, they discover the endless variety and sheer abundance of foods of plant origin.

Becoming Vegetarian is about making prudent food choices. It's about expanding the scope of your diet and enjoying the variety and abundance that come with plant-centered meals.

Becoming Vegetarian is a book for everyone – vegetarian or not – who wants to eat well and be well. Veteran vegetarians will find its pages full of the latest information about health and nutrition. For others who would like to take a first step in the direction of a plant-based diet, *Becoming Vegetarian* is a great place to begin.

Suzanne Havala, M.S., R.D., L.D.N., F.A.D.A.
Author, *Simple, Lowfat & Vegetarian* and *Shopping for Health*

INTRODUCTION

Becoming Vegetarian is an invitation to explore nutrition options that could well change the way you look at food. It is for the many people who find themselves adopting or moving toward a plant-based diet. Whether you are just beginning the transition or are fine tuning a vegan diet, this book will help to answer your most challenging questions.

You may wonder why three dietitians would write a book that encourages people to eliminate meat from their menu. We are often asked if we have been vegetarians all our lives. To the contrary: Vesanto followed the lead of her daughter some 17 years ago; Brenda has been a vegetarian for 6 years; Victoria for 4. We were all raised in traditional homes where meat was the focus of our meals. We went through mainstream universities and taught nutrition using the trusted four-food-group method. We told people to eat their meat for high-quality protein and iron, and drink their milk for calcium. But it became harder to ignore the evidence implicating the typical North American diet in chronic disease. We became aware of the powerful connection between our food choices, the environment and world hunger. We began to take a good look at the way our food arrives on the table and were deeply saddened by the conditions in which the animals people consume live and die. For us, the decision to become vegetarian was not difficult – it was the only option.

If you too find yourself moving in this direction, rest assured that you are not alone. Every year, more than a million North Americans become vegetarian, and many others take giant strides in that direction. But if you grew up on meat, you may feel at a loss as to what to do with tofu. You may be unsure of how to plan a meatless menu with a full complement of necessary nutrients. And you may wonder if this way of eating is healthy for your children. As nutrition professionals, we understand these concerns and have committed ourselves to easing your transition. During our years as vegetarians we have gained valuable insight from many people in the world who maintain excellent health without any significant reliance on meat or milk. Our experience has taught us that vegetarian eating can not only be healthy, but interesting and delicious.

Becoming Vegetarian will give you new confidence in your ability to put together wonderfully nutritious meals and provide guidance and encouragement as you make choices that support a healthier world.

Vesanto Melina, R.D.
Brenda Davis, R.D.
Victoria Harrison, R.D.
1995

WHAT IS A VEGETARIAN?

Over 15 million North Americans consider themselves "vegetarians." Of these, about a third completely eliminate meat, poultry and fish from their diets. The others generally include poultry or fish, but avoid red meat. It may strike you as rather odd that so many people who eat meat choose to identify themselves as vegetarians. Perhaps it is an indication that vegetarianism is being viewed as a positive step by many people.

Although vegetarians are by no means a homogeneous group, there are certain characteristics that are more prevalent in this population than in the rest of society. Perhaps the most obvious is a strong interest in health. They often select minimally processed foods and tend to use less salt, sugar and caffeine. Some prefer organically grown foods and avoid artificial colors, preservatives and additives.

But while vegetarians often share an interest in health and ecology, there is tremendous variety among their ranks, not only in their individual diets, but also in their reasons for becoming vegetarian. For some people vegetarianism is a way of achieving better health, while for others it is a matter of ethics, religion, ecology or animal rights. Indeed, some find themselves facing rather difficult questions regarding their degree of commitment to vegetarianism, questions such as: Do real vegetarians eat marshmallows? Am I still a vegetarian if I eat turkey at Christmas? But these kinds of issues are not important. It matters far more how comfortable you are with your choices and how well they fit into your life. Each one of us will make the transition towards vegetarianism in our own way and in our own time; one way is not necessarily any better than another.

TYPES OF VEGETARIAN DIETS

A "vegetarian" is someone who completely avoids animal flesh, whether it comes from cows, chickens or fish. In contrast, those who include both plants and animals in their diet are called "omnivores."

Vegetarians are sometimes further categorized according to the foods they are or are not willing to eat. There are many variations within each category, depending on the beliefs, traditions and experiences of each individual. When people become vegetarian for reasons of health, there may be some flexibility in their use of animal foods; however when the choice is made on the basis of ethics or religion, there is a greater tendency towards complete adherence to the diet.

LACTO-OVO VEGETARIAN

Lacto-ovo vegetarians avoid all animal flesh, but continue to use eggs (ovo) and dairy products (lacto). Approximately 90–95 percent of vegetarians in North America include dairy and/or eggs in their diets.

PURE VEGETARIAN OR VEGAN

The pure (total) vegetarian or vegan avoids all foods of animal origin, including eggs, dairy foods, gelatin and honey (the product of bees). Although the terms vegan and pure vegetarian are generally used interchangeably, there is a distinction between the two. Vegans go beyond diet, avoiding as much as possible products derived from animals. They may shun leather goods, wool and silk, tallow soaps and standard photography that requires gelatin. (Gelatin, used in making marshmallows, Jell-O and other confections, is made from the bones and connective tissue of animals.)

Others Choosing a Plant-Based Diet

There are many individuals who are "in transition" towards a vegetarian diet and are slowly reducing their intake of animal foods. Some of these people eat no red meat, but do include chicken and/or fish in their menu. Others eat meat occasionally but choose vegetarian food most of the time. People who consume near-vegetarian diets are sometimes referred to as "semi-vegetarians."

A number of people eat a plant-centered diet in keeping with the philosophy of a particular movement or religion. One of the most widely recognized philosophies of that type is macrobiotics, which emphasizes a simple life in harmony with nature. Followers of the macrobiotic diet advocate the use of locally grown whole foods such as grains, fresh vegetables, sea vegetables and beans. Sea salt and grain sweeteners such as rice syrup replace refined salt and sugar. Processed foods containing chemical additives are avoided, as are most concentrated fats. Animal foods (meat, poultry and dairy products) are not recommended except for small amounts of white fish.

There are many similarities between the macrobiotic way of eating and the current dietary goals for the United States which are intended to help reduce the incidence of chronic disease. The diet is low in fat and cholesterol, high in fiber and includes plenty of whole grains, vegetables and legumes. For adults, macrobiotic eating patterns can be expected to have very favorable consequences for health. On the other hand, macrobiotic diets have been shown to offer insufficient protein, energy, fat, vitamins and minerals to support the rapid growth and development of infants and young children (see page 35). When feeding an infant or child, the principles of macrobiotics must be carefully balanced with our current knowledge of infant and child nutrition (see Chapter 9) to insure all nutrient needs are met. This means providing sufficient calories, as well as protein, fat, and reliable sources of vitamin B12, vitamin D, zinc, iron and other vitamins and minerals that could potentially be lacking.

Nutritional concepts with Eastern origins, such as the macrobiotic system, offer valuable ideas on balancing food choices in a way that is quite different from our Western food group model. People can experience the benefits of both worlds when Western scientific concepts are used as the basis for building a nutritionally adequate diet and Eastern ideas of health and nutrition are added to this foundation. With this kind of approach, excellent nutrition can be achieved in people of all ages.

REASONS WHY PEOPLE BECOME VEGETARIAN

The reasoning that moves a person toward a vegetarian diet includes matters of both the heart and the head. Many believe that a vegetarian diet is more healthful. Many also believe that killing animals for food is wrong, particularly when the animals are mistreated during their lives. Almost 70 percent of North American vegetarians still cite one of these as being their primary reason for becoming vegetarian. The connection between the food that we choose and the state of the environment, human hunger and economics also moves people toward a plant-based diet.

The decision to become vegetarian is not one that is taken lightly, for it is a decision that is contrary to our culture, our tradition and what most of us grew up believing. Regardless of the hurdles, every year more and more people are making the switch, and others are beginning to sit up and take notice. Some of the more common reasons why include:

Health

Health is the number one reason people become vegetarian. There is a strong consensus that a vegetarian diet is healthier than a diet that emphasizes animal foods. The points most frequently cited are:

- A vegetarian diet reduces one's risk of chronic, degenerative diseases such as coronary artery disease, cancer, diabetes, obesity, osteoporosis, gallbladder disease and hypertension.
- A plant-based diet more commonly meets the current recommendations for percentages of fat, carbohydrate and protein than an omnivorous diet. We are told to cut back on fat, especially saturated fat, to emphasize grains, fruits and vegetables and to increase fiber. This is a fairly simple task for a vegetarian.
- There is less chance of contracting a bacterial infection such as *E. coli*, *Camphylobacter* or *Salmonella* on a meat-free diet.
- Vegetarian diets generally contain fewer pesticides. Many of these substances accumulate as we move up the food chain. Some pesticides are fat soluble, thus when animals eat contaminated plants and feed, the pesticide can become concentrated in their fat. When we eat the animals, these pesticides are deposited in our fat.
- Diseases such as bovine spongiform encephalopathy (BSE), bovine leukemia virus (BLV) and bovine immunodeficiency virus (BIV) found in animals could potentially affect human health.

Ethics and Animal Rights

For many people, vegetarianism is a statement against violence and cruelty. There is a feeling that taking the life of another creature is fundamentally wrong. Every year in the United States more than seven billion animals (not including fish) are slaughtered for food. People who choose to be vegetarian as a means of protest express their concerns as follows:

- Animals are feeling creatures with complex behavioral patterns and intense bonds to their offspring.
- Today's system of animal agriculture treats animals like inanimate objects. As our population and our food needs grow, incidences of overcrowding, confinement, isolation and brutality increase. The animals are

often robbed of the opportunity to behave in instinctive ways and can be driven insane.

• Animals are transported to slaughter in appalling conditions, often without food or water for extended periods of time. As a result, millions of animals die each year en route to slaughter.

• The actual slaughter is inhumane, primitive and violent. Stunning methods are sometimes unreliable, and many animals move in pain along the disassembly line toward becoming our food.

The Environment

There is an unprecedented reaction by our society to the state of the environment. People are beginning to realize that we cannot continue to consume the earth's resources at this rate if there is to be any hope for future generations. They make the choice to become vegetarian as a way of further reducing environmental destruction. Their arguments are as follows:

• The raising of livestock is a major contributor to desertification (loss of topsoil and drying-out of the land to such an extent that it cannot support the growth of any vegetation) and deforestation (loss of trees in many settings, including those of the precious rain forest).

• Animal agriculture demands tremendous amounts of fresh water. For example, it takes about 25 gallons of water to produce a pound of wheat and 390 gallons to produce a pound of beef. It takes less water to produce the food that a pure vegetarian needs for one year than to produce the food that a meat eater needs for a month.

• The earth's topsoil, which is essential for growth of plants, is being depleted more quickly than it is being formed. Animal agriculture contributes significantly to this critical situation.

• Animals raised for food require intensive use of fossil fuels. Fuel is needed to transport animal feed (grains and legumes), to heat animal shelters (often large buildings) and to transport animals to slaughter, meat packing plants and grocery stores. This heavy requirement for fossil fuels and, to a lesser extent, methane production by animals, contribute to global warming.

• Large amounts of pesticides, herbicides and fertilizers used to grow feed for animals contribute to pollution when they make their way onto the land and into the water supply, with far-reaching effects.

• The destruction of natural habitats to make room for animal agriculture contributes to the rapid rate of extinction of many plants and animals.

Human Hunger

World hunger is a problem of enormous proportion. Nearly one-quarter of the human population does not get enough to eat. Of these, 40–60 million die of starvation and related diseases each year. Many people who choose a vegetarian diet do so, at least in part, to make some contribution to the reduction of world hunger. Their rationales include the following:

• Animal agriculture is a very inefficient use of our food resources. It requires tremendous energy and produces little usable food, in comparison to plant yields.

• The demand for meat among the rich people of the world takes precedence over the need for grain and legume production among the poor in developing countries. Land owners frequently opt to grow or raise whatever brings in the greatest profit. That often means choosing to grow beef for the rich rather than beans for the hungry. The land, labor and resources of the poor are often exploited in the process.

• In developing countries, land desperately needed to grow indigenous foods is used to grow cash crops, animal feed and fodder, and livestock for export in order to service international debts.

• Two-thirds of the grain exported from North America to other countries goes to feed livestock. This livestock in turn goes to feed only those people who can afford it.

• One-quarter of the world's population uses 80–86 percent of the nonrenewable resources and 34–53 percent of the food. In the United States, 230 lbs of animals are consumed by each man, woman and child per year, while in India animal consumption is less than 5 lbs per person.

Economics

Many of the world's people exist on vegetarian or near-vegetarian diets simply because they cannot afford meat. Economics can mold political decisions and dictate food choices. For some people economics is yet another driving force toward a vegetarian diet. The arguments that they use to support this decision include:

• In many affluent countries meat is affordable only because it is subsidized by government. Without such subsidies, meat would be less affordable and more people would have to base their diets on grains and vegetables. These subsidies for meat make little economic sense when the very foods that are being subsidized are the primary dietary contributors to many chronic degenerative diseases. Our governments are in fact subsidizing the cost of meat three times over: first for its production, second for its environmental cost and third for the increase in health care costs.

• If farming policies favored grains and vegetables, the use of land would shift and populations could be fed more cheaply and efficiently.

• A plant-based diet is generally more affordable than a diet which is based on animal foods, especially when meat and dairy subsidies are considered.

Religion

Although it is important to mention religion as a reason why people become vegetarian, in most cases the rationale for a church recommending this dietary regime is based on health issues or a belief that killing is inherently wrong.

• Some Christian groups, including both the Trappist monks of the Catholic Church and the Seventh-Day Adventist Church, encourage a vegetarian diet.

• Many religions of the east, including Buddhism, Hinduism, and Jainism, adhere to a philosophy that promotes reverence for life and harmony with nature. The slaughter of animals is limited or prohibited within their following.

VEGETARIANISM STANDS THE TEST OF TIME

Vegetarianism has been a dietary option since the dawn of recorded time. Its origins remain somewhat of a mystery, though the mythologies of many cultures tell of a beginning without violence, where people lived off the plants of the earth. One of the most widely recognized records is that found in the Old Testament where Adam and Eve are told what is to be their food:

> And God said, behold, I have given you every herb-bearing seed, which is upon the face of all the earth, and every tree, in the which is the fruit of a tree yielding seed; to you it shall be for meat.
>
> *Genesis 1:29*

Throughout history, vegetarianism has been woven into cultures around the world. Many of the world's greatest philosophers and intellects refused meat in times when such a choice was contrary to dictates of the ruling class.

In the west, the first of these was Pythagoras, who is often considered "the father of vegetarianism." Until the late 19th century, when the word "vegetarian" was coined, people who lived on a meatless diet were referred to as "Pythagoreans." Pythagoras, born in approximately 580 B.C., was credited with the discovery of the Pythagorean theorem, many other mathematical and geometrical findings, the idea of planetary motion and the speculation that the earth moves around the sun. He also founded a society that pursued wisdom, believed in the transmigration of souls and practiced meditation. Among the Pythagoreans, materialism and meat-eating were taboo. Contrary to the general view of the time, women were considered equal to men. Pythagoras also believed that one's maximum philosophical potential could be reached only when the body was an efficient instrument. Thus, a strict exercise regime including gymnastics, running and wrestling was practiced.

Following Pythagoras, many influential thinkers through the centuries refused to eat meat:

> I have from an early age abjured the use of meat, and the time will come when men such as I will look on the murder of animals as they now look on the murder of men.
> *Leonardo da Vinci, 1452–1519*

> My refusing to eat flesh occasioned an inconvenience, and I was frequently chided for my singularity, but with this lighter repast I made the greater progress, from greater clearness of head and quicker comprehension.
> *Ben Franklin, 1706–1790*

> Flesh foods are not the best nourishment for human beings and were not the food of our primitive ancestors. There is nothing necessary or desirable for human nutrition to be found in meats or flesh foods which is not found in and derived from plant foods.
> *Dr. J. H. Kellogg, 1852–1943*

> It ill becomes us to invoke in our daily prayers the blessings of God, the compassionate, if we in turn will not practice elementary compassion toward our fellow creatures.
> *Mahatma Gandhi, 1869–1948*

> Whenever I injure any kind of life, I must be quite certain that it is necessary. I must never go beyond the unavoidable, not even in apparently insignificant things. That man is truly ethical who shatters no ice crystal as it sparkles in the sun, tears no leaf from a tree . . .
> *Albert Schweitzer, 1875–1965*

> Nothing will benefit human health and increase the chances for survival of life on earth as much as the evolution to a vegetarian diet.
> *Albert Einstein, 1879–1955*

The list goes on – Plato, Socrates, Plotinus, Plutarch, Newton, Voltaire, Shelley, Darwin, Emerson and Shaw, to name a few. It took great courage for these people to become advocates of vegetarianism in their times.

George Bernard Shaw (1856–1950) describes the reaction of his physician when he announced his decision to remove meat from his diet. The physician cautioned the young Shaw that if he continued to insist on this meat-free diet, he would surely die of malnutrition in short order. Shaw replied that he would sooner die than consume a "corpse." It's rather ironic when you read the words of Shaw as he approached his 85th year:

> The average age (life expectancy) of a meat eater is 63. I am on the verge of 85 and still work as hard as ever. I have lived quite long enough and I am trying to die; but I simply cannot do it. A single beef steak would finish me; but I cannot bring myself to swallow it. I am oppressed with a dread of living forever. That is the only disadvantage of vegetarianism.

In 19th-century England, the influence of those individuals with a compassion for all living things affected many people. They began to draw together for discussion and support. The modern world's first vegetarian society, formed in England in 1847, was followed by similar societies in many European countries and the United States. The growth in vegetarianism was slow. During the first half of the 20th century, movements were fueled by the ideals of health reformers and those defending the ethical principles of a vegetarian diet.

It is interesting to note that although meat was considered a symbol of social status and culture, it is only in the last century that anyone other than the very rich could afford to eat it in any quantity. Even in the 18th and 19th centuries, well-to-do families of many European countries such as France and Holland could seldom afford to eat meat more than once a week. The truth is that the vast majority of the world's population has existed on a near-vegetarian diet and still does, though not necessarily by choice.

A New Era for Vegetarianism

The late 1960s and early 1970s brought a new era for vegetarianism. Peace-loving "counterculture" groups sprang up with a message of ecology and natural living. Vegetarianism became synonymous with the hippie movement to many people. Health professionals often viewed the vegetarian diet as a dangerous fad which could lead to nutritional deficiencies.

In 1971, Frances Moore Lappé's book *Diet for A Small Planet* gave a tremendous boost to the vegetarian cause. Her work drew many supporters toward a vegetarian diet with a strong argument for the environment and world hunger issues.

John Robbins further strengthened the vegetarian movement with his books, *Diet for a New America*, 1987, and *May All Be Fed*, 1992. Robbins' arguments are based on issues that appeal to a mainstream audience – the environment, world hunger and the degenerative diseases of affluence. He also presents a strong voice for animal rights which has profoundly touched people as an idea whose time has come.

The 1980s also saw a push for vegetarianism from members of the health community. Dr. Colin Campbell spearheaded a huge epidemiological study of 6500 Chinese. Dr. Dean Ornish presented evidence for the reversal of atherosclerosis through a combination of diet and lifestyle changes. Both made a case for vegetarianism. The Physicians' Committee for Responsible Medicine, headed by Dr. Neal Barnard, also encourages a vegetarian diet (although under fire by more conventional health professionals). Many other outspoken physician-writers, including Dr. Michael Klaper, Dr. John McDougall and Dr. Benjamin Spock, have persuaded people to remove meat and milk from their diets.

THE FUTURE IS BRIGHT!

The old stereotype of the vegetarian flower-child is finally being laid to rest. Today we see people of every age and from every walk of life choosing vegetarianism and fewer people condemning that choice.

Although the diversity among vegetarians is considerable, there also seems to be a common bond that creates kinship among those who opt to exclude animal flesh from their diets. People are making this choice out of concern for health – the health of human beings, of the earth and of the animals with which we share this planet. As these concerns increase, the vegetarian alternative offers hope for a brighter future.

The growth in the vegetarian movement today is greater than at any other time in history. In response to this growth, vegetarian options are sprouting up everywhere: vegetarian convenience foods, meatless restaurant options, vegetarian magazines and books, and even vegetarian spas. Conferences, workshops, newsletters and journals for health professionals often feature materials on vegetarianism. There is little doubt that the dietary shift toward vegetarian foods is gaining momentum and there's no indication that it's going to slow down any time soon. The impact of these trends is potentially enormous. Perhaps someday soon veggie burgers will be a regular option on the menus of every hospital, school cafeteria and fast food restaurant in America. Perhaps the day will come when the sales of veggie burgers outnumber hamburgers at McDonald's.

THE EVIDENCE IS IN

Today's consumers are bombarded with messages that sell health through promises of good nutrition. Retailers no longer promote cooking oil on the basis of its performance or taste; rather we are sold on the product's lack of cholesterol or high concentration of poly- or monounsaturated fats. This emphasis on the nutritional value of food is a reflection of the growing interest in the relationship between diet and disease. That association has created a dramatic shift in the way people view food. A well-marbled steak is less highly esteemed in our society than it once was. Instead, we are turning to pasta and broccoli.

In this chapter we examine the evidence that links diet to disease. Why are people moving away from a diet centered on animal foods toward one centered on plant foods?

THE STANDARD AMERICAN DIET –
GUILTY AS CHARGED?

The Standard American Diet, which on occasion has been referred to as "SAD," has been "on trial" for its potential link to hundreds of millions of deaths in the United States. Scientists have acted as lawyers for both the prosecution and the defense. They have produced tens of thousands of pages of research examining the connection between diet and chronic degenerative diseases. In order to assess the strength of this evidence, the World Health Organization (WHO) commissioned a panel of nutrition experts from around the world. The result, a 200-page technical paper entitled "Diet, Nutrition and the Prevention of Chronic Diseases," was published in 1990 and an executive summary was published in 1991. They conclude:

> Medical and scientific research has established clear links between dietary factors and the risk of developing coronary artery disease, hypertension, stroke, several cancers, osteoporosis, diabetes, and other chronic diseases. This knowledge is now sufficiently strong to enable governments to assess national eating patterns, identify risks and then protect their populations through policies that make healthy food choices the easy choices.

The evidence is in and a verdict has been reached. The diet of affluence is found guilty as charged. The most fitting sentence, as seen by health authorities, is death by public education.

The Evolution of the "Affluent Diet"

In pre-agricultural, hunter-gatherer societies, the human diet consisted of approximately 20 percent of total calories from fat and a higher ratio of unsaturated to saturated fatty acids than present day Western diets. Daily fiber intake was approximately 40 grams per day, calcium intake was an estimated 1500 mg per day (none from dairy), and vitamin C intake was several times what it is today. Over many centuries, different populations varied the composition of this diet by consuming more or less plant and animal foods, depending largely on the availability of these items. In virtually all cases, plant foods were consumed in a fairly natural state, fats and sweets were minimal and the animals that were consumed were far leaner than domestic animals.

The development of agricultural societies, which began about 10,000 years ago, meant a significant improvement in food security. Gradually, agricultural techniques became more sophisticated, and people began to have a choice in the foods that they wanted to consume. The real changes in terms of the amount of fat, sugar and other nutrients that people received was surprisingly small. The most obvious changes were a slightly lower intake of fat and higher intake of starchy foods.

About 200 years ago, the industrial revolution brought about a dramatic shift in our food supply. As more people moved to urban centers, the pressure on the agricultural industry to produce safe and adequate food for this growing population was intensified. New methods of production, processing, storage and distribution were developed to satisfy these needs.

By the 1930s, governments were placing a greater emphasis on public health, and nutrition became recognized as a significant contributor to the overall health of the population. The elimination of deficiency diseases emerged as the nutritional challenge of the day. Animal products gained special status as foods rich in protein and minerals. Early studies showed that diets emphasizing animal foods reduced the risk of malnutrition, as evidenced by feeding trials on children. Governments responded by offering incentives to increase the production of meat and milk, and by educating the public about the importance of such foods in the diet.

In earlier days meat was generally found as an ingredient in stews, casseroles and soups. Now meat takes center stage on our dinner plates. Compared to the agriculturalists of 200 years ago, we now consume double the fat, half the carbohydrate and half the fiber. However, diseases of nutritional deficiencies were rapidly diminishing, and it appeared as though the job of improving the health of the nation through nutrition had been well accomplished.

But by the late 1940s, a new health picture emerged with coronary artery disease and cancer at the helm. These disorders presented a real challenge to researchers who could uncover no bacteria or virus on which to blame the latest "plagues." Scientists began to ponder the possibility of an environmental influence, and a massive investigation was underway.

Scientists had some good leads, based on laboratory research. As far back as 1913, Russian researchers Anitschkow and Chalatow noted a possible connection between dietary cholesterol and coronary artery disease. Numerous studies of varying sizes and designs were initiated in an attempt to determine the extent of the link between the foods we eat, and the diseases from which we suffer.

CORONARY ARTERY DISEASE

Many North Americans have come to think of coronary artery disease as a fact of life. Whether you are a man or a woman, there aren't too many things you can count on more than your odds of dying of coronary artery disease. It may seem as though it's just the luck of the draw, but in reality coronary artery disease is far from being a random killer. It preys on those who haven't built an adequate defense. Fortunately, people are beginning to realize that changes as simple as a morning walk and a bowl of oatmeal can go a long way to helping build that defense.

Coronary artery disease has been on the downward swing since the 1960s, when it accounted for over half the deaths in North America. Although some of the credit must go to advancements in medical care, we can't underestimate the value of our positive lifestyle changes. People are making a conscious effort to cut back on fat and increase dietary fiber. As a result, blood cholesterol levels are starting to come down. But don't start doing a victory dance quite yet. Coronary artery disease still manages to claim more lives than any other cause of death in North America.

It is important to realize that coronary artery disease is not the work of a single villain, but rather of a whole gang of offenders. The more evidence that accumulates, the more it becomes apparent that diet is a ring leader. For many years, the effects of diet on coronary artery disease were attributed solely to the potential for certain dietary constituents to increase or decrease blood cholesterol levels. While these effects on blood cholesterol levels are extremely important to our overall risk of coronary artery disease, recent evidence has demonstrated that diet can increase or decrease risk through mechanisms quite unrelated to blood cholesterol levels.

Epidemiological Studies

Epidemiological studies allow researchers to compare people living in one area with people living in another. They may study two or more groups of people within a single country or people from different countries. The rates of disease are generally examined, as well as the environment and lifestyle factors that could be contributing to the disease. Scientists may also follow people that move from a country with a low incidence of a particular disease to a country with a high incidence and evaluate the effects of the newly adopted lifestyle on the rates of the disease in these people.

Although epidemiological studies can help to provide clues as to what might be responsible for a particular disease, they don't establish a definitive cause and effect relationship.

STUDIES BETWEEN POPULATIONS

International comparisons of various populations have provided compelling evidence for a direct link between the food we eat and our risk of coronary artery disease. A classic work is Keys' Seven Countries Study, which followed over 12,000 men for 20 years. The participants were from 16 different regions of seven countries: Finland, United States, Netherlands, Italy, Greece, Yugoslavia and Japan (listed here according to their incidence of coronary artery disease from highest to lowest). Those countries with the highest intake of saturated fat also had the highest blood cholesterol levels and the highest incidence of coronary artery disease. These results provided a powerful incentive to delve more deeply into the connection between the foods that we eat and our risk for coronary artery disease.

Since Keys' study, numerous works have further confirmed these findings.

MIGRATION STUDIES

Although studies between countries provided some convincing evidence, researchers wondered how much of these findings could be due to genetic variations within different ethnic groups. If indeed the people of a given culture are blessed with a great resistance to coronary artery disease, changes in lifestyle practices should have little impact on their overall risk for the disease. In order to assess these possibilities, migration studies were carried out. These studies looked at groups who were moving to another country and adopting a new way of life.

The most widely recognized of the migration studies include those that took place between 1973 and 1975, looking at Japanese men who moved from Japan to Hawaii and San Francisco. As they gave up their traditional, low-fat eating patterns in favor of the high-fat American diet, they experienced progressively greater increases in their blood cholesterol, and their incidence of coronary artery disease became indistinguishable from that of Americans.

Good genes can offer some protection against coronary artery disease, but it seems as though the average person can neutralize their good genes by choosing a bad diet.

STUDIES WITHIN A SINGLE POPULATION

Within a given country interesting differences in risk have been noted according to lifestyle practices.

In 1949, a landmark study began in Framingham, Massachusetts. Over 5000 participants were followed for more than 30 years. The results provided powerful evidence for a link between coronary artery disease and high blood cholesterol levels. This study showed that people with an average cholesterol level of 260 mg/dl* suffered heart attacks three to five times more often than people with levels below 195. Blood cholesterol levels of 220 to 240, which were considered normal by most North American physicians, were also found to increase the risk for coronary artery disease. No one in the study who had a cholesterol level below 150 suffered a heart attack. It is interesting to note that the average blood cholesterol level of vegans is about 125.

A second important study, the Multiple Risk Factor Intervention Trial, followed 356,222 men from 1973 to 1985. This study demonstrated that the risk for coronary artery disease is increased even with blood cholesterol levels as low as 182. Study participants with higher levels experienced increases in fatal heart attacks (MI) as described in Table 2.1.

*People often refer to their cholesterol levels with just a number. This number is a measure of cholesterol concentration in mg cholesterol/deciliter of blood.

Table 2.1: Risk for Fatal Heart Attacks with Increasing Blood Cholesterol Levels

Blood Cholesterol Level (mg/dl)	% Increase in Fatal MI
182-202	29%
203-220	73%
221-244	121%
over 245	242%

Numerous epidemiological studies comparing groups of people have demonstrated that vegetarians, and particularly vegans, have lower blood cholesterol levels and are at a lower risk for coronary artery disease than the general population. One of the largest studies followed 25,000 vegetarian and omnivorous male Seventh-Day Adventists for over 20 years. Those who consumed meat four or more times per week had a fourfold increase in their risk of dying from coronary artery disease in their 40s and double the risk in their 60s than vegetarian participants. These figures included adjustment for smoking habits and activity levels.

WHAT WE LEARNED FROM THE EPIDEMIOLOGICAL STUDIES

These studies have served to present a powerful case regarding the relationship between dietary fat, blood cholesterol levels and coronary artery disease. The primary hypothesis from these investigations was that a diet high in total fat, saturated fat and cholesterol raises blood cholesterol levels, thereby increasing one's risk for coronary artery disease. The challenge that remained for researchers was to prove a cause and effect relationship between specific dietary components and coronary artery disease.

CLINICAL STUDIES

Clinical studies, sometimes referred to as intervention or controlled trials, help to confirm a hypothesis or prove a cause and effect relationship between a factor or group of factors and a disease. In these studies two or more groups of participants are compared. One receives a treatment (such as a specific diet or lifestyle change), and the other goes untreated or receives a placebo. Clinical studies are generally done on a smaller scale than epidemiological studies.

Many clinical studies have been carried out to help determine those dietary factors that have the potential to either increase or decrease blood cholesterol levels. Scientists have found that certain dietary components are powerful cholesterol-raising agents, while other dietary components actually lower our blood cholesterol levels.

Dietary Factors that Increase Risks of Coronary Artery Disease

Total fat and saturated fat

Significant cholesterol-lowering effects of diets with reduced total fat and saturated fat have been demonstrated consistently by many studies. The findings are so conclusive that the reduction of total fat and saturated fat in the diet is now recognized as the most effective dietary means of reducing blood cholesterol levels.

While saturated fats are powerful cholesterol-raising agents, some have greater potential for doing so than others. For example, dairy fats (high in myristic acid) strongly increase LDL levels, while cocoa butter (high in stearic acid) increases LDL only slightly.

Trans-fatty acids

Trans-fatty acids are largely a product of a commercial processing technique called hydrogenation (see page 111). These fats are used extensively in the food industry to make shortening, margarine and other hard fats for cookies, crackers, baked goods and other processed foods, and for deep frying in restaurants.

Trans-fatty acids have an unfavorable influence on blood cholesterol levels. Not only do they raise total cholesterol levels, but they increase LDL cholesterol ("bad cholesterol" which raises the risk of coronary artery disease), and reduce HDL cholesterol ("good cholesterol" which protects against coronary artery disease). In the excellent and timely book, *Good Fat, Bad Fat* by Lambert-Legacé and Laflamme (Stoddart Publishing, 1995), it has been suggested that these effects may explain the "French Paradox," the situation in which the French, who consume as much saturated fat as North Americans, experience lower rates of coronary artery disease. In France, the use of hydrogenated fats has largely been resisted, while butter, olive oil and other vegetable oils are the fats of choice.

Cholesterol

Dietary cholesterol raises blood cholesterol levels, regardless of dietary fat consumption. It is estimated that for every 100 mg of cholesterol consumed per 1000 calories, there is an average increase in blood cholesterol of approximately 12 mg/dl. There is also evidence that the oxidized forms of cholesterol in food have greater potential for damaging arteries than cholesterol itself. Cholesterol can be oxidized when it is exposed to high temperatures, light, storage, oxygen and a range of pro-oxidizing agents, particularly in the absence of sufficient antioxidants.

Although the influence of dietary cholesterol on blood cholesterol levels is very significant, many scientists feel dietary fat has a greater overall influence.

Animal protein

Animal protein has been shown to increase blood cholesterol levels, while plant protein reduces blood cholesterol levels. It has been estimated that animal protein can increase blood cholesterol levels by 5–20 percent, depending on the quantity of protein consumed.

WHAT WE LEARNED FROM THESE CLINICAL STUDIES

Carefully controlled scientific studies have confirmed that saturated fat, trans-fatty acids, cholesterol and animal protein raise blood cholesterol levels. Cholesterol and animal protein are found only in meat, poultry, eggs, seafood and dairy products. Saturated fats are found primarily in these. Trans-fatty acids are most concentrated in hydrogenated and partially hydrogenated vegetable oils.

Dietary Factors that Reduce Risk of Coronary Artery Disease

Polyunsaturated fat

Polyunsaturated fats lower LDL cholesterol and total cholesterol, however, they *may* lower protective HDL cholesterol as well. Saturated fats are about twice as effective at raising blood cholesterol levels as polyunsaturated fats are at lowering them. Although some increase in polyunsaturated fats may be beneficial, current thinking favors greater emphasis on reducing total fat, saturated fat, trans-fatty acids and cholesterol, and moderating consumption of polyunsaturated fats.

There are two "families" of polyunsaturated fats: the omega-6s and the omega-3s (see pages 104–8 in Chapter 6). It is important that we receive a good balance of fats from each of these two families, as they have considerable influence on the process of cardiovascular disease. For most people, there is a relative lack of dietary omega-3 fatty acids (found in flaxseeds and flax oil, fish, canola oil, soyfoods, walnuts, wheat germ and dark greens) and an excess of omega-6 fatty acids, particularly arachidonic acid (found in meat, eggs and dairy products).

Monounsaturated fat

Monounsaturated fats also lower LDL cholesterol, but *may* have the added advantages of not appreciably lowering beneficial HDL levels and of reducing triglyceride levels in adult onset diabetics. Some researchers have suggested the high intake of monounsaturated fats (mainly from olives and olive oil) in southern Italy and Greece is, at least in part, responsible for the relatively low incidence of coronary artery disease in spite of a fairly high total fat intake.

Soluble Fiber

Fiber, particularly soluble fiber, can also have a significant impact on blood cholesterol levels. Dr. James Anderson sparked considerable interest in this area in the 1970s, when he published studies that examined the effects of fiber on health. This work demonstrated that giving individuals with high levels of blood cholesterol (more than 260 mg/dl) approximately 17 grams of soluble fiber each day could produce a reduction in blood cholesterol of about 20 percent. This much soluble fiber can be obtained from 7 cups of cooked oatbran (2⅓ cups uncooked) *or* one bowl of oatbran, 7 or 8 servings of vegetables and fruits, a half cup of cooked beans plus 5 or 6 servings of whole grains (i.e., a variety of whole foods as outlined in the food guide in Chapter 8). For people with normal blood cholesterol levels, 17 grams of soluble fiber per day can be expected to lower blood cholesterol levels by about 6 percent.

Phytochemicals

Plants contain a vast array of phytochemicals that have potential for reducing our risk of coronary artery disease. The most well-recognized are *antioxidants,* including vitamin E, vitamin C, carotenoids, flavonoids and others. Antioxidants can help to protect against LDL oxidation in the body, thereby reducing coronary artery damage. One recent study found that people with the highest intakes of vitamin E (at least 100 IU's/day) had approximately 40 percent lower risk of heart attack compared to those with the lowest intakes.

Other phytochemicals have also been found to be of significant benefit. For example, terpenes (found in citrus fruits, caraway, dillweed, spearmint and green coffee beans) and organosulfur compounds (found in allium vegetables such as garlic and onion) can lower blood cholesterol levels.

Soy protein

Soy protein can reduce total cholesterol and LDL cholesterol. In patients with high cholesterol, substituting all or a large proportion of the dietary protein with soy protein resulted in a drop in total cholesterol of 23 to 30 percent. More modest cholesterol reductions were demonstrated in studies where a portion of the protein was replaced by soy protein. Potter and colleagues found that patients on a low-fat diet plus 50 grams of soy protein had a 12 percent lower cholesterol level than patients on a low-fat diet and similar amount of non-fat milk protein.

WHAT WE LEARNED FROM THESE CLINICAL STUDIES

These clinical studies have taught us that there are a number of components in foods that offer significant benefits for both risk reduction and treatment of coronary artery disease. These components are present primarily in whole plant foods including vegetables, fruits, legumes, nuts, seeds and whole grains. Soluble fiber, phytochemicals and soy protein are all found exclusively in plant foods – animal foods do not contain these substances. We are also beginning to recognize that the relationship between dietary fat and coronary artery disease is far more complex than we previously realized. While polyunsaturated fats and monounsaturated fats offer some advantage for blood cholesterol levels, the quality of these fats is of great importance (see Chapter 6). In addition, a healthful balance of omega-6 and omega-3 fatty acids can improve coronary artery disease risk.

STUDIES SHOWING REVERSAL OF CORONARY ARTERY DISEASE

Although scientists had proof of the beneficial effects of diet changes on blood cholesterol levels, they did not know if it was possible to produce a regression or reversal of atherosclerosis (the build-up of cholesterol and other fatty substances in the walls of the blood vessels). Exciting research from the late 1980s and early 1990s has demonstrated that when the reduction in blood cholesterol levels is profound, a regression of atherosclerosis can be achieved.

Dr. David Blankenhorn and his colleagues at USC Medical Center divided 162 patients into a study group and a control group. The study group used a combination of a low-fat, low-cholesterol diet (less than 22 percent of calories from fat, less than 125 mg cholesterol per day), regular exercise (20–30 minutes at 80 percent of maximum heart rate at least three times per week) and cholesterol-lowering drugs. The control group received a less rigid diet and a placebo. The study group experienced an average 43 percent reduction in LDL cholesterol and a 37 percent rise in HDL (protective) cholesterol. The control group showed improvements of no more than 5 percent in blood cholesterol levels. About 16 percent of the study group actually experienced regression of atherosclerosis.

Dr. Dean Ornish produced a more profound regression of atherosclerosis using a very low-fat vegetarian diet of 75 percent complex carbohydrate, 15 percent protein, 10 percent fat, less than 5 mg cholesterol per day, skim milk, no caffeine and minimal egg white. The experimental group also performed relaxation techniques and did 20–30 minutes of exercise every day. A control group followed a "heart-healthy" diet containing no more than 30 percent of calories from fat. Overall, 82 percent of the experimental group experienced significant regression or reversal of atherosclerosis, while 53 percent of the control group experienced a progression or worsening of their disease.

The message regarding coronary artery disease is crystal clear. Studies show if you center your diet on high-fat, fiber-free animal foods such as meat and milk, your chances of dying of this disease are very good. On the other hand, if you center your diet on a variety of minimally processed plant foods, your odds of dying of coronary artery disease are significantly lower. If you would like any more specific information on the studies which support these findings, please contact us through our publisher, Book Publishing Company.

The implications for the prevention and treatment of coronary artery disease are enormous. A diet containing an abundance of antioxidant-rich vegetables and fruits; plenty of legumes, whole grains and other foods rich in soluble fiber; an appropriate balance of omega-6 to omega-3 fatty acids; and minimal amounts of trans-fatty acids, saturated fats and cholesterol can offer considerable protection against coronary artery disease. Such a diet has one major advantage over drugs – the side effects are pleasant. You can anticipate some weight loss, more energy and quite possibly some improvement in other conditions like arthritis. It sure beats stomach aches, diarrhea, flushing, nausea, liver damage, cataracts and gallstones, which many people experience on cholesterol-lowering drugs.

CANCER

One in four individuals in North America can expect to die of cancer. It is estimated that of these cancers, some 30–40 percent are diet-related in men, and as many as 60 percent are diet-related in women. The cancers that are most often associated with diet are cancer of the mouth, pharynx, larynx, esophagus, stomach, colon, liver, pancreas, lung, breast, uterus and prostate. Although we are beginning to understand the links between diet and certain forms of cancer, there are many questions yet unanswered. The one thing that we do know is that, unlike coronary artery disease, mortality rates from cancer show no signs of abating.

Vegetarians experience a lower death rate from all forms of cancer than do non-vegetarians. Studies comparing vegetarian Seventh-Day Adventists with similar non-vegetarian Seventh-Day Adventists have reported 50 percent less cancer in the vegetarian group. In comparison to the general population, Seventh-Day Adventist vegetarians suffer 59 percent less cancer of all kinds, and 97 percent less colon cancer. Other studies have reported similar benefits from vegetarian diets.

Throughout the world, people in developed countries experience significantly higher cancer rates than those of people in developing countries. The World Health Organization's executive summary on the relationship between diet and chronic disease attempts to explain this difference:

> Diets high in plant foods, especially green and yellow vegetables and citrus fruits, are associated with a lower occurrence of cancers of the lung, colon, esophagus and stomach. Although the mechanisms underlying these effects are not fully understood, such diets are usually low in saturated fat and high in starches and fiber as well as in some vitamins and minerals, including beta-carotene and vitamin A.

Although it is not entirely clear why people consuming plant-based diets are at a reduced risk for cancer, there are many interesting clues in the scientific literature.

Food Components that May Protect Against Cancer

DIETARY FIBER
Considerable evidence exists for the protective effects of dietary fiber, particularly with reference to insoluble fiber and colon cancer (see Chapter 7 for specific mechanisms involved). Numerous epidemiological studies have assessed the relationship between dietary fiber and colon cancer. Many have found that an inverse association exists. Some researchers have suggested that it may be other components in fiber-rich foods that offer protection rather than the fiber itself.

Cancer of the colon is significantly lower in vegetarians than in non-vegetarians, and the difference is even more pronounced in vegans. The reasons for the reduced incidence of in vegetarian populations is believed to be owing, at least in part, to the high fiber content of the diet.

VITAMINS AND MINERALS

Vitamin A and carotenoids
Studies indicate a beneficial effect of vitamin A, and specifically carotenoids, on reducing cancer risk, particularly cancers of the lung, colon, skin and esophagus. Carotenoids include over 500 compounds found primarily in dark green, orange and deep yellow vegetables as well as tomatoes and other fruits. About 10 percent of carotenoids can be converted to vitamin A in the body,

and of these, beta-carotene converts to vitamin A the most readily. The question facing scientists was whether the protective effect of vitamin A is mainly from the pre-formed vitamin (found in animal foods such as milk and liver), from specific carotenoids such as beta-carotene or from other carotenoids with less or no vitamin A activity. The bulk of the evidence to date strongly suggests that carotenoids, including beta-carotenes, exert the greatest influence on cancer incidence in humans. Researchers remain uncertain whether these effects are due solely to the carotenoids or other substances found in vegetables and fruits that are high in carotenoids. For this reason, experts recommend that we eat our vegetables instead of relying on supplements.

Vitamin C

Vitamin C is an antioxidant and thus may have a positive effect in reducing the formation of carcinogens (cancer-causing compounds). Diets low in vitamin C may be associated with a greater incidence of cancer of the stomach, esophagus and mouth.

Nevertheless, there is insufficient evidence to suggest that megadoses (supplements containing nutrients at a level of at least 10 times the RDA of vitamin C) either prevent or cure cancer. In the *Nurse's Health Study* (Willet, 1992) researchers found no relationship between vitamin C megadoses and breast cancer incidence even when the large doses were taken over periods of ten years or more.

Other vitamins and minerals

Several studies are underway to clarify the role of vitamins in cancer prevention, including vitamin D, vitamin E and folic acid, and minerals including selenium, calcium, iron, zinc, copper, molybenum and iodine. Each of these nutrients has shown promise as a potential protective agent. In some cases, it appears that a lack of the nutrient is the critical factor in promoting cancer, rather than large quantities reducing cancer activity.

At this point, there is little justification for taking megadoses of any of these nutrients in an attempt to reduce cancer risk. In some cases, megadoses may do just the opposite.

PHYTOCHEMICALS IN PLANTS

Phytochemicals include a broad range of chemicals naturally present in plants. They protect plants from stresses such as harsh climates, infections and destruction by animals and insects. Many phytochemicals have some potential for protecting people against cancer, but the jury is still out as to the significance of this effect for cancer prevention and treatment. Among the most widely recognized are the "phytoestrogens," including isoflavones such as genestein (in soyfoods), and lignans (in flaxseed). Researchers have suggested that the anti-estrogen activity of these substances may help to explain why Japanese women who consume two or more ounces of soyfoods (tofu and miso) per day have a far lower risk of breast cancer than North American women. Table 2.2 lists a few of the important phytochemicals which have been studied. These anticarcinogens can be classified according to their primary mode of action as follows:

1. *Blocking agents*: inhibit tumor formation (shown in Table 2.2 as "Block").
   - Induce enzyme systems involved in detoxifying and excreting harmful chemicals from the body.
2. *Suppressing agents*: slow cancer cell growth (shown in Table 2.2 as "Suppress").
   - Prevent oxidative damage involved in creation and growth of carcinogens.
   - Diminish production of free radicals.
3. *Combined blocking and suppressing agents*: inhibitors with blocking and suppressing activity (shown in Table 2.2 as "Block/Suppress").
   - For example, many "phytoestrogens" are strong antioxidants (suppressors) and can block the potentially carcinogenic effects of the more potent human estrogen (blockers).

Food Substances that May Increase Cancer Risk

FAT

A high-fat diet has been implicated in cancer of the colon, breast and prostate. Evidence from population studies suggests that the greatest link is for total fat, and in some cases, for saturated fat.

The strongest evidence regarding the connection between fat and cancer is for colon cancer. Numerous studies have demonstrated a positive association between total fat consumption and the incidence of colon cancer. Although most studies have not differentiated between total fat, animal fat and other specific types of fat, two large epidemiological studies have shown a strong positive relationship between animal fat and colon cancer. It is generally believed that dietary fat acts as a promoter of colon cancer rather than as an initiator of the disease.

Table 2.2 Phytochemicals in Food

Anticarcinogenic Plant Constituent	Activity of this Chemical	Common Sources
Glucosinates • isocyanates	Block	cruciferous vegetables (cabbage, brussels sprouts, broccoli and cauliflower)
Indoles	Block	cruciferous vegetables
Organosulfuric compounds • allium	Block	allium vegetables (garlic, onions and chives)
Coumarins	Block	umbelliferous vegetables (carrots, parsley, parsnips and celery), citrus fruits
Flavonoids	Block/Suppress	umbelliferous vegetables, citrus fruits and green tea
Diphenolics • isoflavones	Block/Suppress	soy products (tofu, soymilk, etc.), licorice root
• lignans		flaxseeds, lentils, whole grains, legumes
Terpenes • d–carvone	Suppress	essential oils of citrus fruits, caraway, dill, green coffee beans and spearmint
• d–limonene		grapefruit and other citrus fruits
• triterpenoids		licorice root, legumes
Phenolics • curcumin	Block/Suppress	curry spice
• ellagic		grapes, strawberries and nuts
• caffeic		fruits, vegetables, coffee, tea, soy beans and cereals

TOTAL ENERGY

Excessive energy (calorie) intake leading to obesity may be related to cancer of the breast, prostate, colon, rectum and female reproductive organs. Numerous studies have confirmed that a low energy intake decreases both the initiation and promotion of tumors, although in human populations it is difficult to know whether these effects are owing to low calorie intake or low fat intake.

Not all cancers seem to be negatively affected by too many calories, and certain cancers, including those of the stomach, lung and bladder, may actually increase with lower body weight. (One suspects that these statistics could be slanted by thin smokers who are at greater risk for these types of cancers.) The consensus, though, is that a relatively low energy intake and low body weight reduces overall cancer risk. This effect is not as significant as when total dietary fat is reduced.

NATURALLY OCCURRING CARCINOGENS

Some food molds produce carcinogenic toxins called *mycotoxins*. One of the more widely recognized is *aflatoxin* which has been linked to liver cancer in some populations. Aflatoxins are produced by molds that grow in moist, warm environments on nuts (especially peanuts), seeds and grains. These toxins are of little concern in countries that have good harvesting, handling, storage, distribution and transportation practices. To minimize exposure to toxins produced from molds, always choose fresh looking foods and store them in a cool, dry place or in the refrigerator.

Other chemicals in foods have been found to be carcinogenic. Examples include piperine, safrole and terpenes in black pepper, solanine in the green skin and sprouts of potatoes, and safrole in some spices. The message here is that we must remember to be moderate in our intake of all foods and to select wholesome and fresh-looking products.

CARCINOGENS ADDED IN GROWING OR PROCESSING FOODS

Pesticides
The impact of pesticides on our risk for cancer is a matter of tremendous debate. Pesticides vary considerably in their potential for causing cancer. Those that have been found to pose the greatest threat, including DDT and other chlorinated hydrocarbons, are no longer used in most developed countries, although they remain in use in many developing nations. The question is whether or not human exposure to pesticides is sufficient to make this a real issue in terms of cancer risk.

When we consider pesticide residues with respect to food, we often think of fruits, vegetables and other plant foods, but in fact many pesticide residues are present in even higher amounts in animal foods. Grains grown for animals are often heavily treated with pesticides. The animals consume the grains, and the fat-soluble pesticide residues become concentrated in the fat of the animals. As fat is marbled throughout the meat (although it may be hard to see at times), it is impossible to consume the meat without eating some fat.

At present, we do not have enough information to quantify the risk of cancer caused by pesticides. We do know that the risk is disproportionately higher for children, who have smaller bodies and therefore a reduced capacity to handle toxic substances. The Environmental Working Group of the Agricultural Pollution Prevention Project, a non-profit environmental research organization based in Washington, D.C., published a report in 1993 titled "Pesticides in Children's Food." One of the key findings reads: "Millions of children in the United States receive up to 35 percent of their entire lifetime dose [maximum safe amount] of some carcinogenic pesticides by age 5. This pattern is most evident for pesticides used on foods heavily consumed in the first year of life, such as the fungicides captan (35% of lifetime risk by age 5) and benomyl (29%) and the insecticide dicofol (32%)."

Considering what we do know, it makes sense to reduce our exposure to pesticide residues in foods. We can begin by selecting foods that are lower on the food chain, washing fruits and vegetables well before eating them, buying produce that has been grown organically (without the use of pesticides) when possible and growing our own.

Food additives
The public has long been under the impression that food additives are the most potent of food carcinogens, although their relative importance to overall cancer risk is probably far less than is generally perceived.

Preservatives commonly used in the industrialized world include antioxidants such as BHT and BHA, mold inhibitors such as sodium benzoate and calcium or sodium propionate, sulfites and nitrites. To date, the only one of these substances to be linked with cancer promotion is nitrites. Indeed, scientists have found that some chemical preservatives, particularly the antioxidants may play a favorable role in cancer prevention.

Nitrites can interact with substances in the stomach to form nitrosamines, which have been associated with cancer of the stomach and esophagus. Dietary nitrites come mainly from cured meats (nitrites have proven to be the safest, most acceptable way of preserving these foods). Vitamin C is now commonly used in meat curing to help minimize the conversion of these nitrites to nitrosamines.

Another chemical called *nitrate* can be converted to nitrite in our gastrointestinal system. Our exposure to nitrates comes mainly from our own saliva, in some drinking water and in vegetables. The vitamin C naturally present in vegetables helps minimize the conversion of nitrates to nitrites.

Many other food additives, including artificial sweeteners, artificial fats, colors and flavors are used on a regular basis in our food supply. In the past, some of these substances, consumed at very high doses, have been linked to cancer in laboratory animals and have subsequently been restricted or removed from the food supply. Regardless, it is wise to select whole foods whenever possible rather than heavily processed foods which contain food additives. The whole foods are not only free of additives, but they are generally higher in nutrients and fiber.

Chemical changes that occur in food preparation

A number of cooking and food preparation methods can increase the formation of cancer-causing substances. Smoking, barbecuing, charcoal broiling and frying can increase the formation of *mutagens* (substances that cause changes in the genetic material of cells) and the deposition of carcinogens, such as benzopyrene, on foods. The higher the fat content of the food and the greater the temperature reached in cooking, the more these carcinogens are produced. Select methods of cooking that avoid direct contact with flames or smoke: baking, roasting, poaching, stewing and oven-broiling.

Based on our present state of knowledge, there is considerable potential for cancer prevention and treatment through diet. The prescription looks somewhat similar to that for coronary artery disease. Include a wide variety of minimally processed plant foods such as fresh vegetables and fruits, legumes and whole grains in the diet. Limit fat and avoid burning or smoking foods.

THE LINK BETWEEN DIET AND DISEASE: A CALL FOR ACTION

The debate about whether or not diet plays a role in chronic degenerative disease is over. There presently exists enough information to make recommendations that could vastly improve the health of our population. National governments are recognizing the value of this information and are making changes in federal nutrition policies which more accurately reflect the current state of knowledge.

Actions such as new food guides and revised nutrition recommendations have been central to the disease reduction that we have seen, particularly with reference to coronary artery disease. However, the priority given to these kinds of efforts is rarely sufficient to produce the level of disease reduction that one would hope for. The World Health Organization Study Group on diet and the prevention of chronic diseases provides the following commentary:

> When food policies are acknowledged to have an impact on the consumer's choice of food, it becomes extremely important to consider whether these

policies are encouraging consumers to choose foods conducive to good health. With diet now linked to the major chronic diseases, such considerations take on special urgency. As the health component of most food policies remains rigidly aligned with the dietary requirements set out 50 years ago to prevent deficiency diseases, adaptation to protect populations from dietary excesses will not be easy. Efforts to prevent chronic diseases through dietary intervention have not been given high priority by any government. Most governments have yet to realize that policies aligned with current medical views on diet and health can bring economic advantages. A very large proportion of international trade in cereals is for animal feed. If policies viewed high fat content in meat carcasses as a hazard rather than a standard for defining high quality and price, farmers would no longer have to follow the intensive feeding practices needed to produce fatty meat carcasses. Farming policies that do not require intensive animal production systems would reduce the world demand for cereals. Use of land could be reappraised, since cereal production for direct consumption by the population is much more efficient and cheaper than dedicating large areas to growing feed for meat production and dairying.

We can see these kinds of issues coming into play as we consider the shifts that have occurred in the nutrition recommendations of our own government. National nutrition recommendations and food guides have clearly shifted toward an emphasis on grains, vegetables and fruits. We might assume that, in making this shift, the new guides would encourage a reduction in our consumption of animal foods and the use of the appropriate plant foods in their place. Interestingly, the emphasis has been on choosing leaner meats and lower-fat dairy products rather than on reducing the quantity of such foods used.

The challenge that faces national governments is to make healthy choices the easy choices. In so doing, they need not concern themselves with establishing distinct sets of recommendations for each degenerative disease. The reality is that the same dietary factors are implicated in most of these diseases.

Nutrition Recommendations for the Prevention of Chronic Diseases *

1. Center your diet on a wide variety of plant foods.
Plant foods should be the foundation of your diet. Animal foods, if used, should be accompaniments to meals rather than the central theme.

To obtain the maximum benefit, include a wide variety of grains, legumes, vegetables and fruits, in addition to small amounts of nuts and seeds.

* These recommendations are appropriate for people over 2 years of age.

Plant foods supply abundant nutrients, fiber and phytochemicals without the cholesterol and excessive fat found in many animal foods. Follow the vegetarian food guide (see Chapter 8) to be sure to obtain adequate quantities of these foods.

2. Limit your use of fats, especially trans-fatty acids and saturated fats.
Over-consumption of fat is risky business. Limit all fats, particularly trans-fatty acids and saturated fats. Trans-fatty acids are found mainly in margarine, shortening and hydrogenated or partially hydrogenated oils. Saturated fats are present in animal foods, tropical oils, and hydrogenated vegetable fats (to a lesser extent).

It is quite possible for a person consuming a plant-centered diet to eat too much fat, especially if full-fat dairy products, eggs, fried foods and sweet baked goods such as pies and cakes are regularly consumed.

Your total fat intake should not exceed 15 to 30 percent of calories for healthy adults and 10–20 percent of calories for those with elevated blood cholesterol levels. For children, fat should range from 25 to 35 percent of calories.

3. Include a source of omega-3 fatty acids in the diet.
Omega-3 fatty acids are important in helping to maintain health and prevent disease. Plant foods that are rich in omega-3 fatty acids include flax oil, flaxseeds, canola oil, soy products, walnuts, leafy greens and wheat germ.

Be sure that these foods are fresh when purchased, and store, in the refrigerator or freezer.

4. Choose whole grain rather than refined products.
Whole grain foods offer fiber in addition to many valuable vitamins and minerals. The soluble and insoluble fiber found in these foods provides protection against disease.

5. Achieve and maintain a healthy body weight.
Both overweight and underweight can increase the risk of degenerative disease. The safest way to maintain a healthy body weight is to eat a varied, balanced diet and to exercise regularly.

6. Use sugars and salty foods in moderation.
Too much sugar can dilute the nutritional quality of your diet and contribute to tooth decay. The best sweets come packaged by nature as fruits. Excessive consumption of salty foods may contribute to hypertension and some forms of cancer. Heavily salted foods include salty snack foods, many commercially pre-

pared foods (such as soups, canned pasta products, frozen entrées, packaged pasta and rice mixes), pickles and condiments.

7.   Limit your use of smoked, charred and cured foods.
These methods of food preparation and preservation can increase our exposure to carcinogens, and therefore should be minimized.

8.   Use plant foods grown without the use of pesticides whenever possible.
Some pesticide residues on foods can contribute to cancer and can be particularly hazardous for children. Try to select foods that have been grown without pesticides or with minimal use of pesticides.

9.   Alcohol, if consumed, should be used in moderation.
Excessive consumption of alcohol displaces valuable nutrients and can contribute to degenerative disease.

The Diet of Choice: Mainly Plants

The evidence points directly to a vegetarian or near-vegetarian diet as the diet of choice in the prevention of chronic degenerative disease. Considering the track record of such diseases, vegetarianism can be a real health advantage. This advantage has not gone unnoticed.

The American Dietetic Association, in their position paper on vegetarian diets, concludes:

> A considerable body of scientific data suggests positive relationships between vegetarian lifestyles and risk reduction for several chronic diseases, such as obesity, coronary artery disease, hypertension, diabetes mellitus, colon cancer and others.

The evidence regarding the potential for vegetarian diets in preventing, and perhaps even in treating, chronic degenerative disease is strong. Regardless of these benefits, many people are skeptical when they hear reports of vegan infants who are suffering from malnutrition or adults who have developed vitamin B_{12} deficiency. The big question that arises is: do concerns regarding the adequacy of vegetarian diets outweigh their potential benefits?

THE ADEQUACY OF THE VEGETARIAN DIET

To assess the nutritional adequacy of a vegetarian diet, we will look at the evidence that has been provided by groups who have been living on a plant food diet for generations and by some of the new vegetarians who have been experimenting with different patterns of eating.

GENERATIONS OF VEGETARIANS

Many cultures have existed for generations on vegetarian or near-vegetarian diets. These people enjoy the advantage of knowing what works and what doesn't work. From such groups come many important lessons.

The Sherpas, living in the eastern Himalayas, have long been admired for their incredible endurance on mountain expeditions. Their diet consists largely of grains (rice, millet, barley and wheat) and lentils, accompanied by greens, potatoes and yak's milk cheese. Meat is eaten only on occasion, and the stricter Buddhists of the group avoid it completely.

Numerous developing countries can attest to the adequacy of a varied, plant-based diet. In many areas of the world meat is scarce, and the average family cannot afford to include it, except on rare occasions. When the native diet is varied and abundant, these groups are generally well nourished. Problems arise when there is insufficient food or the dietary mainstay is a starchy food of relatively low nutritional value (i.e., corn or oat gruel). When legumes, fruits and vegetables are added, these problems are generally resolved.

In North America, the group of vegetarians that has been most extensively studied is the vegetarian Seventh-Day Adventists. In the early 1950s, Drs. Hardinge and Stare from Harvard University did the first extensive study on the nutritional status of this group. About half of the study participants were high-risk individuals such as pregnant women and teens. This study provided the evidence necessary to establish that the adequacy of a well-planned vegetarian diet is beyond dispute. Since this time, numerous studies have further examined the health status of Seventh-Day Adventist vegetarians. These studies have consistently demonstrated that lacto-ovo vegetarian children can grow normally and maintain excellent health throughout adult life. Indeed, the average vegetarian Adventist lives four to five years longer than otherwise similar non-vegetarian Adventists.

All of these groups, and many more, have succeeded in creating wonderfully healthful vegetarian diets. The key is in variety. When a wide range of wholesome plant foods are used and energy needs are met, necessary nutrients are amply provided.

THE NEW VEGETARIANS: A CAUSE FOR CONCERN?

The new vegetarians include a diverse group of people who have, for a variety of reasons, become disenchanted with our present way of eating. Not only are they choosing to cut down on, or completely cut out, foods of animal origin, but they often also reduce or eliminate other foods, such as processed products, concentrated fats and sugar. These people are in some ways pioneers, testing new ways of making vegetarian nutrition work. Some put together patterns that work very well, while others run into problems along the way and must try a variety of options before arriving at a suitable plan. In general, the more restrictive the pattern, the more difficult it is to achieve a healthful balance.

It is reassuring to know scientific studies have confirmed the adequacy of balanced vegetarian diets for people of all ages. These studies assess the nutritional status of participants in one or more of three ways: anthropometric assessment (age, height and weight), biochemical assessment (blood values of nutrients) and dietary assessment (analysis of foods eaten).

In 1989, a French study by Millet assessed the vitamin status of 37 vegetarians using both biochemical and dietary assessment. Results were compared to non-vegetarian controls. The vegetarians had higher intakes of thiamin, riboflavin, and vitamins C, A and E. The two nutrients which were found to be lower in the diets of the vegetarians were vitamin B_{12} and vitamin D. Low blood levels of vitamin D were found in 38 percent of the vegetarians, as compared to 27 percent of the non-vegetarians. Vitamin B_{12} was low in 6 percent of the male vegetarians and 17 percent of the female vegetarians. Numerous similar works have been carried out, with comparable results. Most experts agree that a lacto-ovo vegetarian diet can provide completely adequate nutrition. Some health professionals are somewhat less comfortable with vegan diets, even though the American Dietetic Association acknowledges their adequacy. The reason for their discomfort is largely that such eating patterns are unfamiliar and require a framework that may be outside our cultural norm.

SCIENTIFIC STUDIES ASSESSING
THE ADEQUACY OF VEGAN DIETS

Among the first research to address the nutritional adequacy of all-plant diets was Hardinge and Stare's classic U.S. study in 1954 of the diets of 27 vegans. These diets were generally well-balanced, with only a few subjects having less protein, calcium and riboflavin than the recommended allowances. These vegan diets were rich in iron, thiamin and vitamins A and C.

In 1962, Guggenheim, Weiss and Fostick studied the diets of 119 vegans from Jerusalem. Detailed dietary assessments were carried out, and the only nutrient which was present in inadequate amounts in the diets was riboflavin. Even without milk, the calcium content of the diet averaged 825 mg per person per day.

Dr. Ellis and colleagues carried out a number of investigations looking at the nutritional adequacy of vegan diets between 1966 and 1978. The studies

examined the health of small groups of British vegans (less than forty participants per study). The subjects were from professional and middle classes, and
were well-informed regarding the vegan diet. Most of the study participants
used a vitamin B_{12} supplement. Detailed medical examinations were carried
out, including both physical assessments and blood work. Ellis's work showed
that vegans were lighter in weight than omnivores, had lower blood cholesterol
levels and lower serum vitamin B_{12} levels, although signs of B_{12} deficiency were
rare. Although Ellis did include some children in these studies, the numbers
were not large enough to draw any significant conclusions.

In 1981, a small Swedish study examined the nutritive value of vegan diets
using a technique that determined the nutritional value of foods by chemical
analysis rather than using food composition tables. In addition, each subject was
evaluated for clinical (blood pressure, height, weight and visual assessment) and
biochemical (blood tests) parameters. Although the diets were low in protein
(these vegans deliberately limited their intake of protein-rich foods), iodine,
zinc and vitamin B_{12}, the clinical and biochemical data showed no signs of nutritional deficiencies. All other nutrients were well within recommended levels.

Overall, the studies assessing the nutritional status of vegan adults have
provided reassurance that a well-planned vegan diet can supply adequate nutrition, provided that a source of vitamin B_{12} is present in the diet. The real acid
test regarding the nutritional quality of a vegan diet comes when it is fed to
the most vulnerable of our species – infants and children.

In 1988, T.A.B. Sanders reported on a longitudinal study of British vegan
children. In this study, the majority of children grew and developed normally,
although they tended to be slightly smaller than children in the general population. Intakes for calcium, vitamin D and energy were generally below the
recommended intakes. Most of the children were given vitamin B_{12} supplements. Overall, the health of these children was good, and the author concludes that, provided sufficient care is taken, a vegan diet can support normal
growth and development in infants and young children.

The largest study on vegan children was done in 1989 on The Farm in
Summertown, Tennessee. In this classic work, 404 vegan children between the
ages of 4 months and 10 years were compared to U.S. reference patterns for
age, weight and height. By the age of 10 years, children from The Farm were
similar in height (¼" less) and weight (2.4 lb leaner) to the average U.S. child.
This study concluded that a vegan diet can support normal growth in infants
and young children.

Other studies have revealed less reassuring pictures. Overly restrictive
vegan diets have produced gross malnutrition in vegan infants and children. In
1982, Shinwell and Gorodischer published a report of 72 infants from a com-

munity of Americans living in Israel. These children suffered from multiple nutritional deficiencies, including protein-calorie malnutrition, iron-deficiency anemia, vitamin B_{12} deficiency, rickets, zinc deficiency and growth retardation. P. C. Dagnalie published 15 studies between 1988 and 1992 looking at the nutritional status of infants and children in macrobiotic communities in the Netherlands. Protein-energy malnutrition, growth retardation, and several nutrient deficiencies were reported in a significant proportion of the children assessed. The common denominator for these sad tales is that the chosen patterns were restricted in more than just animal foods. In some cases fat, protein and energy were limited as well. Parents often used unfortified home-prepared soy or nut "milks" as the main dietary constituent for these children. Fortified and other commercial products were denied and nutritional supplements often avoided.

Although these kinds of reports are rather disturbing, we must recognize that they are the result of very restrictive, poorly planned diets and are *not* the inevitable result of a vegan diet. Indeed, vegan diets for infants and children can be completely adequate. Health professionals and parents alike need to become aware of the unique nutritional needs of infants and children and how best to meet these needs without animal products.

THE BOTTOM LINE

Both vegetarian and vegan diets can provide completely adequate nutrition and foster good health. There is nothing inherently wrong with either one. If you choose to eliminate only meat from your diet, you must find suitable plant replacements for some nutrients. If you choose to eliminate dairy products as well, you need to consider a few more nutrients. When you eliminate all foods of animal origin, there is still one more nutrient that deserves special attention. The next chapters will guide you through the science of vegetarian nutrition and help you to translate that science into a healthful, practical and enjoyable way of eating.

Without Meat –
Exploding the Myths

The typical North American diet is often referred to as a "meat-based diet," reflecting deeply held beliefs that animal foods outrank plant foods in value. To the question, "What's for supper tonight?" the answer is rarely "broccoli" or "potatoes." It's usually "hamburgers" or "fried chicken." For many people, it's hard to imagine Thanksgiving dinner without the turkey. This focus on animal foods extends to the very heart of our relationship with food.

Three powerful myths have led many of us to believe that a plant-based diet is nutritionally inferior to a meat-centered diet:

Myth 1: A diet without meat cannot easily provide enough protein for good health.

Myth 2: The quality of plant protein is inadequate to meet our needs.

Myth 3: Iron deficiency anemia is a likely outcome of the switch to a vegetarian diet.

None of these statements is true; each is based on research and thinking from a bygone era. In fact, *no nutrients essential to human life are found in meat that are not also found in a diet composed entirely of plant foods.* As we look down the food chain, we see that all of the nutrients that are used to build animal and human bodies come from plants and microorganisms. Protein and iron required for the muscles and blood of even such large herbivores as elephants are derived from grains, legumes and vegetables. The bones and the milk of cows contain much calcium, which comes from the plant food they eat.

Even vitamin B_{12}, sometimes thought of as the nutrient we must get from animal foods, actually originates from the bacteria and other microorganisms that grow in animals and on plants. Changes in methods of agriculture and food production have altered the availability of vitamin B_{12} on plant foods. To be certain of their intake of this essential nutrient, vegans must rely on fortified foods or nutritional supplements.

In this chapter we will examine the truth about our needs for protein, iron and zinc, and look at plant sources for these nutrients. In later chapters we will explore sources of calcium, vitamin B_{12} and other important nutrients in diets without dairy products and other foods of animal origin.

Whether you are beginning to cut down on the amount of meat in your diet or have made a complete shift from meat, fish, poultry and other animal foods, you need to pay special attention to three nutrients: protein, iron and zinc. We begin with protein, that essential part of all plant and animal cells, and a myth about the need for animal protein.

PROTEIN

Myth 1: A diet without meat cannot easily provide enough protein for good health.

Vegetarians are often asked, "How will you get enough protein?" For a variety of reasons this concern has been overemphasized. During the first half of the twentieth century, there was considerable emphasis on the elimination of deficiency diseases, including protein-energy malnutrition. In North America, meat was seen as the saving grace, and governments began to encourage a growth in animal agriculture by subsidizing farmers. Animal foods became widely available, resulting in substantial increases in our protein intake. While people in developing countries consume, on average, 60 grams of protein daily, in developed countries the average has risen to over 100 grams per day. This means that for many in the West, over 15 percent of our calories comes from protein. The result of excessive protein consumption is not simply bigger muscles, as we might like to believe. According to the World Health Organization (WHO) Technical Report 797: "There are no known advantages from increasing the proportion of energy derived from protein (above 15 percent of total calories) and high intakes may have harmful effects in promoting excessive losses of body calcium and perhaps in accelerating age-related decline in renal function."

It appears that the somewhat lower protein contents found in vegetarian diets may turn out to be a health advantage.

Protein is present in most foods, with the notable exceptions of sugar, fats and oils. In fact, diets which provide enough calories and are based on an assortment of plant foods will easily meet and exceed protein requirements. Evidence has supported the adequacy of protein intake from plant-based diets since the classic study by Hardinge and Stare in the 1950s. Figure 3.1 shows the comparison of intakes of protein (plant and animal) of male and female lacto-ovo vegetarians, vegans and omnivores. On this chart, the protein intakes are expressed as percentage of recommended intake, which is set at 100 percent. *For all groups, the average protein intake was more than one-third higher than the recommended intake.*

In the diets of the omnivores shown here, approximately two-thirds of the protein was of animal origin and one-third of the protein was from plant sources; this ratio reflects a pattern similar to the overall protein intake of people in North America and Europe.

Recommended Protein Intakes

How much protein do you really need for good health?

The exact amount of protein you require depends on your age, body size and to some extent on the composition of your diet. Protein needs are greater than average for some athletes (for example, while building muscle mass) and for people recovering from certain illnesses. Scientists have established recommended intakes which include a minimum requirement and a margin of safety (because people differ metabolically and proteins differ in composition and digestibility). For most individuals, they represent an intake well in excess of real needs.

The recommended intakes of protein assume that people are getting enough total calories. If they are not (for reasons of economics, illness, extreme weight loss diets, anorexia nervosa or *unusually* high levels of energy output), protein will be used to meet energy needs rather than being spared for its roles in building body proteins and regulating the manner in which cells function. During pregnancy and other stages of growth, protein needs are increased and thus recommended intakes are higher (see Chapter 9 and Appendix 2).

RECOMMENDED PROTEIN INTAKE
ON THE BASIS OF BODY WEIGHT

The recommended intakes for most nutrients vary between countries, depending on the interpretation of data by scientific committees and on other factors, such as the food sources that are commonly used in each country. In the

Figure 3.1 Protein Intake on Various Diets

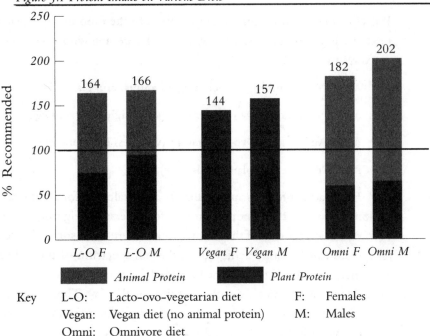

Key   L-O: Lacto-ovo-vegetarian diet   F: Females
          Vegan: Vegan diet (no animal protein)   M: Males
          Omni: Omnivore diet

United States, the amount of protein recommended for healthy adults is 0.36 grams (g) protein per pound (lb) of body weight (0.8 g/kg). Thus, the recommended intake for an adult man or woman weighing 135 lb is 0.36 x 135 = 49 g protein. This includes a margin of safety, and can be expected to be above the actual needs of almost all 135 lb individuals. The recommended intake for an adult weighing 180 pounds is 0.36 x 180 = 65 grams protein. To calculate your recommended protein intake, simply multiply your weight in kilograms by 0.8.

RECOMMENDED PROTEIN INTAKE
AS A PERCENTAGE OF TOTAL CALORIES

Another way of looking at protein recommendations is to consider the percent of total calories coming from the three nutrients: protein, carbohydrate and fat. Carbohydrate and protein provide approximately 4 calories per gram, whereas fat, a concentrated form of energy, provides 9 calories per gram. The current recommendation by the WHO Study Group for dividing the caloric intake of adults among these three nutrients is given in Table 3.1.

Table 3.1 Recommended Distribution of Calories

Protein	Fat	Carbohydrate
10% to 15%	15% to 30%*	55% to 75%

★ The Dietary Guidelines for Americans suggest 30% as an upper limit; the WHO Study Group states that further benefits would be expected by reducing fat intake toward 15% of total energy.

Protein in Various Menus

But what does all this mean when it comes to the food on your plate? On the next few pages are typical one-day menus for people who have chosen different ways to eat:

Menu No. 1 Omnivore (including all animal and plant foods)

Menu No. 2 Lacto-Ovo-Vegetarian (with high dairy and egg)

Menu No. 3 Lacto-Ovo-Vegetarian (with less dairy and egg)

Menu No. 4 Vegan (plant foods only)

Each menu provides approximately 2200 calories (for a moderately active person) and more than enough protein for a person weighing 135 pounds. It becomes clear that even if the calorie intake were to be somewhat lower, protein needs can be easily achieved on the full spectrum of these diets. Below each menu are foods that might be added for a 180 pound person, to give a total caloric intake of 2800–2900 calories for the day. These four menus will be referred to throughout the book to illustrate the sources of different minerals and vitamins in animal- and plant-based diets.

MENU NO. 1: OMNIVORE

Our omnivore has made some efforts in the direction of healthy eating. He or she:

- uses lean meats and avoids the skin on chicken;
- chooses low-fat yogurt and 2% milk;
- chooses a variety of foods from each group in the Food Pyramid.

Table 3.2 Menu No. 1: Omnivore

		Protein (grams)	
Breakfast	Orange juice, ¾ cup	1.4	
	Cornflakes, 1 cup	2.1	
	Milk, 2%, 1 cup	8.6	
	Toast, whole wheat, 1 slice	2.6	
	Butter, 1 pat	0	
	Non-caloric beverage	0	
	Breakfast total	14.7	(433 calories)
Lunch	Roast beef sandwich:		
	Bread, white, 2 slices	4.9	
	Beef, round lean, 2 oz	20.3	
	Margarine, 2 pats	0.1	
	Mayonnaise, 1 tsp	0.1	
	Lettuce, 1 leaf	0.2	

	Carrot sticks, 1 carrot	0.7	
	Low-fat fruit yogurt, ¾ cup	7.1	
	Apple, 1	0.3	
	Non-caloric beverage	0	
	Lunch total	33.7	(663 calories)
Supper	Chicken, roasted 3.5 oz	24.8	
	Potato, scalloped, ½ cup	3.7	
	Green peas, ½ cup	4.5	
	Dinner roll, white, 1	3.2	
	Butter, 1 pat	0	
	Non-caloric beverage	0	
	Supper total	36.2	(491 calories)
Snacks and	Cheesecake, ⅒ pie	9.6	
Desserts	Strawberries, 4 large	0.4	
	Apple juice, ¾ cup	0.2	
	Snacks total	10.2	(623 calories)
	Total Protein	94.8 g	(2210 calories)

Recommended protein for a 135 lb adult is 49 grams.

Menu No. 1: Nutritional Summary

	% Calories			Intake in milligrams (mg)	
	Recommended	Menu No. 1			
Protein	10%–15%	17%	Iron	15.6 mg	
Fat	15%–30%	32%	Zinc	10.8 mg	
Carbohydrate	55%–75%	51%	Calcium	907 mg	
			Cholesterol	386 mg	

For a 180 pound person, we *add* the following foods to the preceding menu, bringing the caloric intake up to 2810 calories:

		Intake in milligrams (mg)	
Breakfast	Toast and butter, 1 slice		
Lunch	Sandwich, ½	Iron	20.2 mg
Supper	Chicken, 2 oz	Zinc	13.6 mg
Snacks	Muffins, 2	Calcium	1030 mg
		Cholesterol	527 mg

This brings the day's intake for the 180 pound omnivore to 130 grams protein.

The recommended protein intake for someone of this weight is 65 grams.

COMMENTS ON THE OMNIVORE'S DIET

Protein

Although animal foods are often looked upon as the essential protein foods while plant foods are considered to be insignificant sources, in this menu, plant foods contributed 40 percent of the recommended intake of protein. With the addition of the animal foods, which are concentrated protein sources, the final total is approximately *twice* the recommended intake for protein.

Fat

You may think that a fat intake of 32 percent of total calories is high. In fact, the fat intake in this menu is significantly *lower* than the average North American intake of 37–38 percent calories from fat. A lower intake of fat would be possible with non-fat dairy products and low-fat fish, but the proportion of protein would still be high. To better fit the recommended pattern, it would be beneficial to shift some of the calories from protein and fat to carbohydrate.

MENU NO. 2: LACTO-OVO VEGETARIAN

The second menu is for a vegetarian who is essentially replacing the meat, fish and poultry with eggs and dairy products.

Table 3.3 Menu No. 2: Lacto-Ovo Vegetarian (Dairy & Egg Emphasis)

		Protein (grams)	
Breakfast	Orange juice, ¾ cup	1.4	
	Oatmeal, 1 cup	6.4	
	Milk, 2%, 1 cup	8.6	
	Whole wheat toast, 1 slice	2.6	
	Butter, 1 pat	0	
	Non-caloric beverage	0	
	Breakfast total	19.0	(467 calories)
Lunch	Egg salad sandwich:		
	Whole wheat bread, 2 slices	5.2	
	Hard-boiled eggs, 2 small	10.1	
	Margarine, 2 pats	0.1	
	Mayonnaise, 1 tsp	0.1	
	Lettuce, 1 leaf	0.2	
	Carrot sticks, 1 carrot	0.7	
	Apple, 1	0.3	
	Chocolate chip cookies, 2 small	1.2	
	Non-caloric beverage	0	
	Lunch total	17.9	(565 calories)

Supper	Cheese and tofu lasagne	32.0	
	Garlic bread:		
	French bread, 1 small slice	1.3	
	Butter, 1 tsp	0	
	Green salad, 1 cup	1.8	
	Italian dressing, 1 Tbsp	0	
	Non-caloric beverage	0	
	Supper total	35.1	(700 calories)
Snacks and	Cherry pie, ⅛ pie	3.0	
Desserts	Banana, 1 medium	1.2	
	Apple juice, ½ cup	0.1	
	Snacks total	4.3	(475 calories)

Total protein: 76.3 grams (2207 calories)

Recommended protein for a 135 lb adult is 49 grams.

Menu No. 2: Nutritional Summary

	% Calories			Intake in milligrams (mg)	
	Recommended	*In Menu No. 2*		Iron	16.6 mg
Protein	10%–15%	13%		Zinc	8.9 mg
Fat	15%–30%	34%		Calcium	1170 mg
Carbohydrate	55%–75%	53%		Cholesterol	455 mg

For a 180 pound person, we add the following foods to the preceding menu, bringing the caloric intake up to 2800 calories:

Breakfast: Toast, butter and jam, 1
Lunch: Cookie, 1
Supper: Lasagne, ½ cup
Snack: Blueberry muffins

Intake in milligrams (mg)	
Iron	20.6 mg
Zinc	9.8 mg
Calcium	1440 mg
Cholesterol	524 mg

This brings the day's intake for the 180 pound lacto-ovo vegetarian
to 100 grams protein.

The recommended protein intake for someone of this weight is 65 grams.

COMMENTS ON THE LACTO-OVO VEGETARIAN MENU NO. 2

Protein

Without any meat, poultry or fish, the protein in this menu is 1½ times the recommended intake; as a percentage of calories, it is within the recommended range of 10–15 percent of calories from protein. Although there is no emphasis on concentrated plant protein sources such as legumes or tofu in the menu, half of the protein comes from plant foods.

Fat

Even though this menu is vegetarian, it is high in total fat, saturated fat and cholesterol.

MENU NO. 3: LACTO-OVO VEGETARIAN
WITH LESS DAIRY AND EGG

Next we look at a vegetarian menu with a greater emphasis on plant foods, although milk is used on cereal, and baked goods have egg as an ingredient. In this menu, the plant foods alone provide enough protein to exceed the recommended intake. A few of the protein sources may be new to you. For example, almond butter (a spread similar to peanut butter) replaces butter on the toast, providing the minerals calcium, iron and zinc as well as protein.

Table 3.4 Menu No. 3: Lacto-Ovo-Vegetarian (Lower in Egg and Dairy)

		Protein (grams)	
Breakfast	Orange juice, ¾ cup	1.4	
	Vitamin B$_{12}$-fortified cereal, 1 cup	3.7	
	Milk, 2%, 1 cup	8.6	
	Whole wheat toast, 1 slice	2.6	
	Almond butter, 1 Tbsp	2.4	
	Non-caloric beverage	0	
	Breakfast total:	18.7	(464 calories)
Lunch	Hummus (low-oil recipe), ½ cup	9.6	
	Pita bread, 1 pocket	4.0	
	Cherry tomatoes, 4	0.5	
	Carrot sticks, 1 carrot	0.7	
	Apple, 1	0.3	
	Oatmeal raisin cookie, 1	1.4	
	Non-caloric beverage	0	
	Lunch total	16.5	(534 calories)
Supper	Spaghetti, whole wheat, 1½ cups	11.4	
	Tomato-lentil sauce (pg 230), 1¼ cups	13.9	
	Parmesan cheese, 2 Tbsp	4.2	
	Green salad, 1 cup	1.8	
	Flaxseed oil dressing, 1 Tbsp	0.0	
	Non-caloric beverage	0.0	
	Supper total	31.3	(620 calories)
Snacks and	Apple brown Betty, ¾ cup	2.7	
Desserts	Banana, 1 medium	1.2	
	Cashews, ¼ cup	5.3	
	Snacks total	9.2	(562 calories)
	Total Protein	75.7 grams (2180)	

The recommended protein intake for the 135 pound adult is 49 grams.

Menu No. 3: Nutritional Summary

	% Calories	
	Recommended	In Menu No. 3
Protein	10%–15%	13%
Fat	15%–30%	25%
Carbohydrate	55%–75%	62%

Intake in milligrams (mg)	
Iron	24.1 mg
Zinc	11.9 mg
Calcium	968 mg
Cholesterol	47 mg

For a 180 pound person, we add the following foods to the preceding menu, bringing the caloric intake up to 2800 calories:

			Intake in milligrams (mg)	
Breakfast:	Toast with almond butter, 1 slice			
	Cereal, ½ cup		Iron	30.0 mg
Lunch:	Cookie, 1 large		Zinc	15.2 mg
Supper:	Roll, 1		Calcium	1150 mg
Snack:	Muffins, 2		Cholesterol	118 mg

This brings the day's intake for the 180 pound vegetarian to 93.6 grams protein.

The recommended protein intake for someone of this weight is 65 grams.

COMMENTS ON LACTO-OVO VEGETARIAN DIET, WITH LESS DAIRY AND EGG

Protein
In this menu, the protein provided is more than adequate.

Fat
The percentage of calories from fat is within the range of recommended intake and is low in cholesterol.

MENU NO. 4: VEGAN
The vegan menu includes a number of less commonly used but highly nutritious foods. For example, tahini (a spread made from ground sesame seeds) and blackstrap molasses on toast are rich sources of minerals.

Table 3.5 Menu No. 4: Vegan

		Protein (grams)	
Breakfast	Orange juice (calcium-fortified), 1 cup	1.4	
	Multigrain cereal, 1 cup	7.0	
	Wheat germ, 2 Tbsp	3.4	
	Non-fat soymilk, calcium-fortified, 1 cup	3.0	
	Whole wheat toast, 1 slice	2.6	
	Tahini, 2 tsp	1.8	
	Blackstrap molasses, 1 tsp	0	
	Non-caloric beverage	0	
	Breakfast total	19.2	(495 calories)
Lunch	Eggless "egg" salad sandwich (with nutritional yeast and low-fat tofu, recipe pg 216-17)	13.2	
	Carrot sticks, 1 carrot	0.7	
	Apple, 1 medium	0.3	
	Muffin (recipe pg 246-47), 1	6.0	
	Non-caloric beverage	0	
	Lunch total	20.2	(508 calories)
Supper	Spiced lentils: Lentils, 1 cup	17.8	
	Onions, ¼ cup	0.4	
	Brown rice, 1½ cups	6.8	
	Kale and romaine salad, 2 cups	3.4	
	Salad dressing, tahini, 1 Tbsp	1.3	
	Non-caloric beverage	0	
	Supper total	29.7	(701 calories)
Snacks and	3 Tbsp walnuts, 3 figs	4.4	
Dessert	Carrot cake, small slice	4.4	
	Total snacks	8.8	(437 calories)
	Total protein	77.9 grams (2141 calories)	

The recommended protein intake for the 135 pound adult is 49 grams.

Menu No. 4: Nutritional Summary

	% Calories				Intake in milligrams (mg)	
	Recommended	In Menu No. 4			Iron	26.9 mg
Protein	10%–15%	14%			Zinc	15.5 mg
Fat	15%–30%	18%			Calcium	1105 mg
Carbohydrate	55%–75%	68%			Cholesterol	0 mg

For the 180 pound vegan, the following foods are added, bringing the total calories up to 2800:

Breakfast:	Toast, tahini and	*Lunch:*	Sandwich, ½
	molasses, 1 slice	*Supper:*	Rice, ½ cup
	Cereal, ½ cup	*Snacks:*	Banana and 1 cup apple juice

This brings the day's intake for the 180 pound vegan to 95.2 grams protein.

The recommended protein intake for someone of this weight is 65 grams.

Intake in milligrams (mg)	
Iron	33.2 mg
Zinc	16.2 mg
Calcium	1235 mg
Cholesterol	0.0 mg

COMMENTS ON MENU NO. 4 FOR VEGAN

Protein

Although there are no animal foods in this menu, plant foods provided one and a half times the recommended protein intake.

Fats

The fat content is well below 30 percent, with the use of low-fat tofu and non-fat soymilk. Higher-fat versions of these products might be substituted, increasing the fat to 20–25 percent of total calories. The fats and oils present in nuts, seeds and tofu contribute valuable essential fatty acids – but no cholesterol.

PROTEIN, FAT AND CARBOHYDRATE IN FOODS

Many of us are unaware of the substantial amounts of protein contributed by the plant foods in our diets. Although we generally think of meat and other animal foods as concentrated sources of protein, in fact a plant-based diet can easily meet our protein needs.

Table 3.6 on the next page shows the percentage of calories from protein, fat and carbohydrate in some common plant and animal foods. When we compare these with the recommended distribution for our total diet, it becomes clear that a heavy reliance on animal foods can easily lead to excessive protein and fat.

Which Plant Foods Give Us Protein?

GRAINS

Grains such as wheat, oats, millet and rice, which are not often thought of by Westerners as significant protein foods, provide almost half the world's protein. Certain grains, such as South American amaranth and quinoa, have amino acid patterns comparable to those found in foods of animal origin. It is interesting to note that in grains, the percentage of calories provided by pro-

tein is in the neighborhood of 10 to 15 percent, the precise quantity recommended by health experts as a desired goal for our overall diet. As a bonus,
grains are low in fat and provide iron, zinc, B vitamins and fiber.

Table 3.6 Distribution of Calories from Protein, Fat and Carbohydrate in Foods

Percent Calories From:*	Protein	Fat	Carbohydrate
Animal Foods			
Cod	92%	8%	0%
Salmon, sockeye	52%	48%	0%
Beef, lean ground	37%	63%	0%
Beef, regular ground	33%	67%	0%
Eggs	32%	65%	3%
Cow's milk, 2%	27%	35%	38%
Cheddar cheese, medium	25%	74%	1%
Plant Foods			
Legumes and their products			
Tofu, firm	40%	49%	11%
Lentils	30%	3%	67%
Kidney beans	28%	1%	71%
Garbanzo beans (chickpeas)	21%	14%	65%
Vegetables			
Spinach	40%	11%	49%
Broccoli	32%	11%	57%
Carrots	8%	3%	89%
Nuts, seeds and their products			
Almonds	14%	74%	12%
Sesame butter (tahini)	11%	76%	13%
Grains			
Oatmeal	17%	16%	67%
Wheat	15%	5%	80%
Quinoa	13%	15%	72%
Millet	11%	7%	82%
Rice	9%	5%	86%
Fruits			
Orange	8%	1%	91%
Apples	1%	5%	94%
Recommended Distribution in Diet:	10%–15%	15%–30%	55%–75%

* Percentages were derived using the values 4 calories per gram for protein and
carbohydrate and 9 calories per gram for fats.

LEGUMES

Legumes – plants which have seeds in pods – are the protein powerhouses of the plant kingdom, with approximately twice the protein content of cereal grains. There are more than 13,000 kinds of legumes, but many North Americans would have trouble naming five. Familiar legumes include peas, lentils, peanuts, soybeans and chickpeas. Like meat, legumes are good sources of iron and zinc. Legumes provide four distinct advantages over meat: they contain no cholesterol, very little fat (and the fat which is present is primarily unsaturated), abundant fiber and significant amounts of calcium. Legumes fit right into today's nutritional recommendations, and frequent consumption of legumes has been shown to reduce high blood-cholesterol levels and improve blood sugar control in diabetics.

Soybeans are valuable because they contain relatively high amounts of polyunsaturated oil and have a protein quality comparable to animal foods. Tofu, a traditional product of soybeans, has been called "the cow of China"; it provides protein and iron, as does meat, and when made with calcium it is a good source of this mineral as well. Tofu will take up the flavor of other ingredients in a dish, making it an extremely versatile food (see Chapter 12 for recipe ideas).

North American farmers are major producers of about 20 types of legumes or beans, and we can truly support our agricultural economy when we use these foods. Adding legumes to one's diet has elements of taking a world food tour – think of all the tasty dishes from home and around the globe. We may have a favorite family recipe for pea or lentil soup, enjoy chili at a Mexican restaurant or have acquired a taste for Middle Eastern or East Indian dishes while traveling. Preparing ethnic foods at home is a wonderful way to begin incorporating more legumes into our diets.

NUTS AND SEEDS

Nuts and seeds are high in fat (about 75 percent of total calories), however they can be tasty sources of protein and other nutrients in the vegetarian diet. When we eliminate meat, and perhaps dairy products as well, our intake of fats (especially in the forms of saturated fats and cholesterol) drops substantially. Nuts and seeds provide valuable oils. For example, walnuts will contribute essential fatty acids to vegetarian diets. For growing children and for other vegetarians with high-energy needs, these high-calorie foods balance the low-fat levels of most other plant foods, and thus are important additions. Nuts and seeds also provide vitamins and minerals, including iron and zinc. Tahini (sesame seed butter) or almond butter make a calcium-rich replacement for butter or margarine on morning toast or on breads. Seed butters form a flavorful base for salad dressings, replacing all or part of the oil to provide a highly nutritious addition to salads (see Chapter 12).

VEGETABLES

For many North Americans, the total contribution of protein from vegetables is minimal. Consider the small portions of vegetables on many dinner plates. However, as the diet becomes more plant-centered, their presence becomes more significant. Recall that some vegetables derive 30–40 percent of their calories from protein (Table 3.6).

CONVENIENCE FOODS

In addition to simple grains, legumes and nuts, many new "fast" foods developed from these plant sources are available in the freezer, refrigerator and produce sections of supermarkets and health food stores. There is a wide variety of veggie burgers, tofu dogs and other meat "analogs." These products resemble meat in taste and texture and have its nutritional benefits without the saturated fat and cholesterol.

MEETING OUR TOTAL PROTEIN NEEDS

Proteins are composed of long chains of smaller units called amino acids. There are 20 amino acids commonly found in nature which are built by plants from the air, soil and water. With a supply of amino acids, plants can then build proteins.

In humans, the protein-building process is somewhat different. To meet the needs of this process, we have three requirements:

1. We must have enough total protein in the diet.

2. The protein must be digestible. In other words, it must be easy for our digestive systems to break down the protein into its component building blocks, the amino acids, and to absorb these.

3. When digested, the total protein in our diet must yield adequate amounts of each of nine "essential amino acids." These are called essential because they *must* be supplied in the diet. Unlike plants, we cannot make these nine amino acids. Our dietary protein also includes an assortment of other (nonessential) amino acids; our bodies are capable of building these by remodeling other amino acids.

The first point above refers to *protein quantity*, points 2 and 3 to *protein quality*.

Earlier in this chapter, we debunked the first myth, that plant foods could not provide an adequate quantity of protein. Now let's look at the second great protein myth.

Myth #2: The quality of plant protein is inadequate to meet our needs.

Until the last decade, there has been a widely held misconception that plant protein is "second rate" when compared with animal protein and that plant protein is "lacking something" or missing essential amino acids. These misconceptions have had the unfortunate effect of leading many people to undervalue plant protein. In fact, plant protein can easily meet anyone's and everyone's needs for protein and can provide adequate amounts of every one of the amino acids we require.

Early assessments of protein quality were centered on the growth response of young rats to various proteins. The limitations of this method are discussed on page 54. The new and improved method combines our knowledge of protein digestibility with an assessment of the amino acids present in the protein. We'll look first at protein digestibility in vegetarian diets.

PROTEIN DIGESTIBILITY

During the process of digestion, dietary protein is broken down to form a common pool of amino acids. Different proteins vary in their digestibility. Plant protein, in its raw form, is generally less easily digested than animal protein. Various cooking methods, such as the boiling and simmering used with grains and legumes, tend to increase digestibility. Processing techniques can also dramatically improve protein digestibility. For example, in the Orient for over 3,000 years people have processed soybeans to make tofu. In doing this, they created a plant food with protein digestibility similar to that found in animal products.

For a lacto-ovo vegetarian diet, with its mixture of plant and animal protein, the practical significance of differences in digestibility between plant and animal foods is slight, and we do not need to adjust our recommended total protein intakes.

Some experts recommend that when a vegan diet is composed of many raw foods, coarse grains and other high-fiber foods, the recommended protein intake may be increased by about 10 percent. Put into perspective, this has little practical significance for most North American vegans as actual protein intakes tend to be well in excess of recommendations. In planning diets for growing children, it is important to take into account that they require more protein per pound of body weight than adults, yet they have small stomachs and limited food capacity. For these reasons, it is desirable to include foods which have been cooked or processed in ways to maximize digestibility in the diets of infants and children. Breast milk provides protein which is easily digestible. Infant formula, tofu, tempeh, textured soy protein and cooked plant foods are valuable additions to the diets of children, and an excessive emphasis on raw foods should be avoided. Adequate caloric intakes ensure that the protein in the diet will be utilized for growth rather than being used to meet energy needs. For further recommendations for children, see Chapter 9.

ESSENTIAL AMINO ACIDS

Figure 3.2* on page 53 shows estimated requirements of the nine essential amino acids for humans past infancy. ** For infants, the reference pattern is based on the amino acid composition of breast milk.) The requirements are stated in milligrams of amino acid per gram of protein in the diet. In practical terms, if a person ate *just* the recommended intake of protein described on pages 38-39, each gram of that protein would need to provide him or her with amounts of each of the essential amino acids shown in the pattern. The names of the nine essential amino acids are shown in the key at the bottom of page 52.

We can use the pattern shown in Figure 3.2 as a gauge against which to measure the amino acids in specific foods and in our overall diets. Figure 3.3 shows the essential amino acids patterns in tofu, eggs, pinto beans, quinoa (a South American grain) and wheat. As you can see, the patterns of amino acids in the first three of these foods meet and exceed the pattern in Figure 3.2. The pattern in eggs is typical of the highest quality animal protein; those provided of tofu and pinto beans are similar in that they contain more than adequate amounts of all essential amino acids per gram of protein.

THE CONCEPT OF "THE LIMITING AMINO ACID"

As illustrated in Figure 3.3, the patterns of essential amino acids differ from food to food. When we compare the pattern for a single food to the requirements shown in Figure 3.2, one amino acid may be present in relatively small amounts. For example, quinoa and wheat are short in lysine. In this situation, lysine is called the limiting amino acid. This is of great importance when the total quantity of protein in the diet is barely adequate, as is true for some children in developing countries. It would also be of great importance if one of these grains were the only food available.

---

*This figure has been revised since the initial printing of the second edition of *Becoming Vegetarian* to reflect recent research.
**From Protein Quality Evaluation: Report of Joint FAO/WHO Expert Consultation, Food and Nutrition Paper 51. Rome, 1991

Key for Figures 3.2 and 3.3 – Essential Amino Acids

Tryp	Tryptophan	Lys	Lysine
Thre	Threonine	Met+	Methionine (plus Cystine)
Iso	Isoleucine	Phe+	Phenylalanine (plus Tyrosine)
Val	Valine	Leu	Leucine
Hist	Histidine		

3.2 Suggested Pattern of Essential Amino Acids Requirements

milligrams per gram of protein

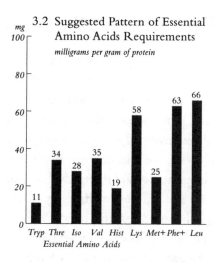

3.3 Essential Amino Acids in Tofu

milligrams per gram of protein

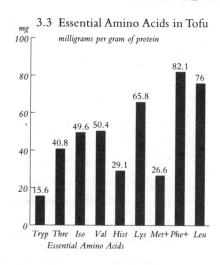

3.3 Essential Amino Acids in Egg

milligrams per gram of protein

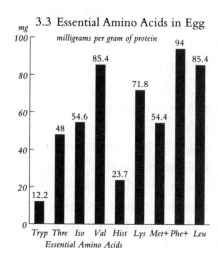

3.3 Essential Amino Acids in Pinto Beans

milligrams per gram of protein

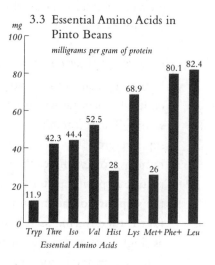

3.3 Essential Amino Acids in Quinoa

milligrams per gram of protein

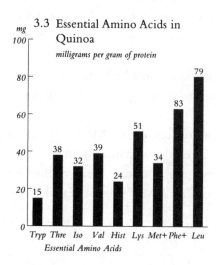

3.3 Essential Amino Acids in Wheat

milligrams per gram of protein

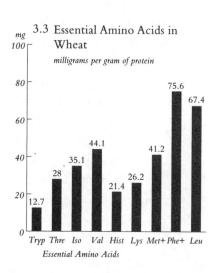

MEETING ALL AMINO ACID REQUIREMENTS WITH PLANT FOODS

Where people have access to an abundance and variety of plant foods, such limitations can be easily compensated in two ways. First, each food has strengths and weaknesses in its amino acid pattern when compared with human requirements. For example, soybeans, pinto beans, other legumes and many other foods in vegetarian diets provide relatively large amounts of lysine. When we eat a diverse selection of plant foods, we end up with the entire range of amino acids necessary to meet our protein-building needs. Second, in a hypothetical situation where all dietary protein comes from any single plant food, intake of that food could simply be increased, to provide higher-than-recommended amounts of protein and, in the process, enough lysine.

Note that although the same pattern (Figure 3.2) is used for all ages above infancy, in fact, adult needs for amino acids are somewhat lower than those of growing children. Thus, this process actually underestimates the actual value of plant proteins for adults.

EARLY RESEARCH ON AMINO ACID REQUIREMENTS

In the first half of this century, when protein quality was originally studied in controlled laboratory situations, single foods were used as the sole protein source. The research focused on how well a single animal or plant food would support growth, often in rats. Young rats grow very quickly, compared to humans; for example, they double their birth weights in six days. Rats also require a specific pattern of essential amino acids, including large amounts of the sulphur-containing amino acids such as cystine, needed to build proteins for the fur covering their bodies. When animal and plant foods were compared as single protein sources, it was found that animal proteins, being more con-centrated in total protein and in sulphur-containing amino acids, were better suited to the needs of rats. The scientists who conducted the animal studies designated the proteins from plants as "incomplete proteins" because, when used as sole protein sources, the plant foods did not sustain the *very* fast growth in baby rats.

These conclusions from animal studies have limited relevance because:

1. the protein and amino acid needs of growing rats are far different from those of humans at any age;

2. single foods were used as protein sources, rather than the combina-tions that would be freely chosen by either animals or humans.

When the findings from laboratory animal studies were applied to humans, the value of the plant protein in our diets was underestimated.

PROTEIN COMPLEMENTATION UPDATED

In the early 1970s, the concept of protein complementation became widely accepted as a basic requirement in the planning of vegetarian eating patterns. This concept stressed the need for complementing specific quantities of grains and legumes at the same meal. Some people were left with the impression that one needed to spend hours with scales and calculator in hand before getting dinner ready. In the 1990s, the complementation of plant proteins at the same meal is no longer regarded an essential part of vegetarian meal planning for four reasons:

1. All plant foods are complete in that they contain each and every one of the essential amino acids.

2. Commonly eaten plant food combinations, and some plant foods alone, easily provide sufficient amounts of all essential acids per gram of protein.

3. The total protein intakes of most North American vegetarians are substantially greater than their requirements.

4. Foods eaten throughout the day form an amino acid pool in muscle and other body tissues and can be drawn on over the course of the day.

Because children require more concentrated sources of essential amino acids than do adults, a somewhat more cautious approach is recommended. In planning meals and snacks for vegan and other vegetarian children, it makes sense to focus on protein-rich plant foods: breast milk, soy-based formula, tofu, legumes, nuts and seeds (or their butters for young children) and grains. Milk and eggs are included in the protein-rich foods for lacto-ovo vegetarian children. Beyond providing a variety of foods each day as described in the vegetarian food guide for children (see Chapter 9), planned complementation of plant foods is not necessary.

To quote the WHO Study Group, in tracing our evolving understanding of protein needs: "Progressively, it was realized that even in totally vegetarian diets containing a diversity of foods, plant sources tended to complement each other in amino acid supply. If the energy needs of the child or adult are met by these diets – then so are the protein needs."

The concept that all plant foods are "lacking" certain essential amino acids is outdated and inaccurate. Updated concepts of protein complementation mean that you do not have to carefully calculate combinations of grains with legumes when planning menus. A simple approach, resulting in meeting your needs for all minerals and vitamins as well as the essential amino acids, is to follow the vegetarian food guide in Chapter 8 (pages 137 to 139). For children at each stage of development, follow the recommendations in Chapter 9. Plant foods that form the basis of delicious, flavorful meals around the world provide a complete range of the necessary amino acids in more than adequate quantities. As we will see in the next sections, these legumes, whole grains and certain other plant foods also provide the valuable trace minerals iron and zinc.

IRON IN VEGETARIAN DIETS

We may think of iron as the mineral from red meat, an association strengthened by educational materials and advertising originating from the meat industry. Athletes, in particular, have been conditioned to link their performance with diets featuring steaks and burgers. In this section we will examine facts about the iron in our bodies and in our food supply. In doing this, we will shed light on another myth.

> *Myth 3:* Iron deficiency anemia is a likely outcome of the switch to a vegetarian diet.

IRON DEFICIENCY ANEMIA

Although we have eliminated many deficiency diseases in the developed world, iron deficiency is one that remains for a small but significant number of people in specific age groups. The effects of iron deficiency include fatigue, a weakened immune system and reduced ability to concentrate. The groups most likely to encounter difficulty in meeting their needs for iron are children, women in the child-bearing years and the elderly. Iron deficiency anemia occurs in a small percentage of vegetarians and non-vegetarians alike. However, many studies looking at the nutritional status of vegetarians in North America and Western Europe show that long term vegetarians *do not* have a greater incidence of iron deficiency anemia than does the population at large.

When people stop eating meat, they often replace it with familiar dairy-based dishes, such as pizza, macaroni and cheese, grilled cheese sandwiches, cream soups and cheese lasagne. Unfortunately, dairy foods are not only poor sources of iron, they actually inhibit iron absorption. For these reasons, if dairy foods are used, it is a good idea to stay close to the number of servings recommended in the food guide, rather than consuming excessive amounts. Replace meat with plant foods that are good iron sources (see Table 3.8 in this section). It is also important to understand some of the workings of iron in our foods and in our bodies.

Types of Iron in the Diet

When we eliminate meat, fish and poultry from our diets, we are eliminating those foods made of blood and muscle. We do not need blood-containing foods to form our own hemoglobin, the iron-containing protein in our red blood cells. All the ingredients necessary for the formation of healthy blood, including iron, protein, vitamin C and folic acid, are present in plant foods. After absorption, when iron reaches our cells and is used to manufacture hemoglobin for the blood, it is equally well utilized whether its origins were broccoli or a steak. The key difference between the iron from a hamburger and the iron from a veggie burger is in the way the iron is absorbed.

HEME AND NONHEME IRON

There are two forms of iron present in foods: heme iron and nonheme iron. Forty percent of the iron in meat, and a lesser amount in fish and poultry, is called "heme iron." Heme iron is present in animal flesh in the form of muscle myoglobin and blood hemoglobin. People usually absorb 15 to 35 percent of the heme iron from foods. The remainder of the iron in meat and all of the iron in plant foods and eggs is called "nonheme iron."

Nonheme iron is absorbed differently from the heme portion of the iron found in meats. Understanding this difference can help everyone to make the most of their dietary iron, since more than 85 percent of the iron in non-vegetarian Western diets and all of the iron in vegetarian diets is in the nonheme form. The proportion of nonheme iron that is absorbed varies from 2 to 20 percent or more, depending in part on other foods eaten at the same time. Other components of the diet can have a significant effect in either increasing (foods rich in vitamin C) or decreasing (black tea or dairy products) the absorption of nonheme iron. (See pages 61–62.) These accompanying foods do not affect the absorption of heme iron in the same way.

The Roles of Iron in the Body

Iron is best known for its role in transporting oxygen from the lungs to cells throughout the body via hemoglobin. Iron is also present in muscle tissue, where it helps to store oxygen for future use. Small amounts of iron help us regulate cell metabolism and resist infection. Our bodies efficiently recycle iron, but we need to replace the small amounts lost – less than 1.5 milligrams per day. Because we don't absorb all of the iron present in food, the recommended iron intakes for adults are in the range of 8 to 15 milligrams per day. Women need more iron than men, because iron is lost in blood each month during menstruation. Increased amounts of iron are also needed during pregnancy, childbirth and lactation, during the growth spurts of childhood and adolescence and for endurance athletes.

The walls of our intestines are highly selective about how much iron they will allow to pass from our food supply into the bloodstream. The proportion absorbed from the overall diet varies, depending on a wide range of factors.

For example, when our iron reserves are low, iron absorption from a meal may double.

Lab Tests and Supplements

Lab tests can give a complete picture of a person's iron status. As with protein, we are finding that more iron is not necessarily better. There are health risks linked to high intakes of iron and the overconsumption of iron supplements. For a small proportion of people who have a hereditary disorder, iron overload is a problem because of super-efficient iron absorption. If you're at all concerned about the adequacy of your iron intake, it is a good idea to have blood tests done reflecting red blood cell status (hematocrit and hemoglobin) and iron stores (ferritin, transferrin saturation and red cell protoporphyin).

In many cases, iron deficiency anemia is indicative of overall poor diet, including low intakes of vitamin C-rich fruits and vegetables. Since many nutrients are involved in the process of building healthy red blood cells, an overall improvement in diet, including vegetables, fruits and iron-rich foods, could prove effective in the long run.

Recommended Intakes of Iron

The recommended intake of dietary iron for premenopausal women, aged 19 to 49 years, is 15 mg per day. The recommended intake for other adults is 10 mg per day. These figures are based on average requirements with an additional safety factor, are expressed on a daily basis and should be regarded as the average recommended intake over a period of time, such as a week.

Iron in the Menus in this Chapter

The total iron in the menus on pages 40–47 is shown in Table 3.7.

Table 3.7 Iron Provided in Menu Nos. 1 to 4

	For 135-pound person	For 180-pound person
1. Omnivore Menu	15.6 mg	20.2 mg
2. Lacto-Ovo Vegetarian Menu	16.6 mg	20.6 mg
3. Lacto Ovo Vegetarian Menu	24.1 mg	30.0 mg
4. Vegan Menu	26.9 mg	33.2 mg

Comparison with Recommended Intakes

All menus met and exceeded the recommended adult intakes of 8 to 15 milligrams for a day. The dietary iron of vegetarians can vary considerably, with lower intakes in dairy-centered diets. With increased grains and legumes, vegetarian diets tend to be high in iron. This can offset the lower absorbability of nonheme iron. Dietary factors that increase or decrease nonheme iron absorption are also significant.

MENU NO. 1
Over 75 percent of the iron in this menu comes from plant sources. In this, as in the next two meal patterns, the orange juice at breakfast (with 65 to 95 mg vitamin C) increases the absorption of the iron from the accompanying cereal and toast. Fresh-squeezed juice gives more vitamin C than does canned or frozen. Total vitamin C: 156 mg.

MENU NO. 2
Ninety percent of the iron comes from plant sources in this menu and ten percent from eggs. At supper, the 40 mg of vitamin C provided by tomato sauce, onions and salad helps iron absorption from tofu in the lasagne and from pasta and bread. Total vitamin C: 146 mg.

MENU NO. 3
The iron in this and the next menu was from plant sources. At lunch, the lemon used in the hummus recipe and the cherry tomatoes taste good together; they also increase the absorption of iron from garbanzo beans. At supper, 80 mg of vitamin C provided by green salads, tomato sauce and onions assists with the iron absorption from from lentils and pasta. Total vitamin C: 230 mg.

MENU NO. 4
Almost one-third of the iron comes from tofu and lentils; additional iron comes in small amounts from *every* food eaten. A hearty salad and onions bring the vitamin C intake at supper to over 100 mg, enhancing iron absorption from all of the foods eaten. Total vitamin C: 205 mg.

Iron Intakes and Status of Vegetarians

Many studies in developed countries comparing the intakes of dietary iron of vegetarians with those of omnivores of the same age show the iron intakes of the vegetarians, including vegans, to be higher. Overall, the reported incidence of iron deficiency anemia is not greater than with omnivores. Vegetarians, including vegans, have been shown to consume more fruits and vegetables, and to have substantially greater intakes of vitamin C-rich foods, enhancing the iron absorption from plant foods. As with omnivores, some studies have shown that children and elderly women are at greater risk for iron deficiency. Although nonheme iron tends to be less well absorbed than heme iron, this appears to be offset by the combination of higher total iron intake and optimal absorption in the diets of many vegetarians.

Sources of Iron in Vegetarian Diets

Table 3.8 shows the iron contents of a range of foods.

Table 3.8 Iron in Foods

	Volume	Weight (g)	Iron Content (mg)
Legumes and Foods Made from Legumes			
Tofu, firm	½ cup	124	2★
Tofu, regular	½ cup	124	1.5–5★
Lentils, cooked	½ cup	100	3.3
Beans (kidney, garbanzo, pinto, white, black-eye), cooked	½ cup	85	2.2–2.6
Beans (adzuki), cooked	½ cup	115	2.3
Hummus	½ cup	123	1.9
Soymilk (see label for iron content)	1 cup	240	0.3–1.5★
Split peas	½ cup	98	1.3
Nuts and seeds			
Tahini	2 Tbsp	30	2.7
Almond butter	2 Tbsp	32	1.2
Grains and cereal foods			
Cream of wheat (fortified), cooked	¾ cup	179	9–11
Fortified dry cereals	1 serving		4.0–18.0
Quinoa, uncooked	¼ cup	42	3.9
Wheat germ	2 Tbsp	14	1.3
Whole wheat bread	1 slice	25	0.9
Oatmeal, cooked	½ cup	130	0.8
Vegetables			
Wax beans, canned or cooked	½ cup	119	3.1
Potato, with skin	1	202	2.8
Peas, raw, boiled or split, cooked	½ cup	80	1.2
Broccoli or bok choy, cooked	½ cup	80	0.9
Kale, cooked	½ cup	65	0.6
Tomato, whole	1	123	0.6
Seaweeds			
Hijiki, dry	¼ cup	10	6.4
Nori, 1 sheet, dry		3	0.4
Fruits			
Prunes, dried	10	84	2.1
Apricot halves, dried	10	35	1.7
Prune juice	½ cup	128	1.5
Other foods			
Blackstrap molasses	1 Tbsp	20	3.2
Egg	1 large	50	1.0
For purposes of comparison:			
Beef hamburger, lean, cooked	2 oz	58g	1.2

★A 90 g serving of these products provides 6%–36% of the DV (Dietary Value = 18 mg iron). Check labels.

There are other breakfast cereals and grain products, not shown in Table 3.8, which are enriched with iron, often providing 4 milligrams of iron per serving. Iron-fortified infant cereals can be added to hot cereal, pancakes and muffins for older children and for adults. Meat analogs, tofu burgers and similar products provide iron; for details, read package labels.

Dietary Factors that Increase Iron Absorption

VITAMIN C
Foods rich in vitamin C work wonders with the iron from plants. Breakfast can be a great time to boost your iron intake. For example, studies have shown the amount of absorbed iron from cereal or toast to be doubled or tripled when eaten with a large orange or a glass of juice providing 75 to 100 mg of vitamin C. In one study, papaya accompanying a grain meal increased iron absorption up to six times. Fruits and vegetables with smaller amounts of vitamin C also enhance the absorption of nonheme iron, but to a lesser extent. Note that this contradicts popular ideas of "food combining" which dictate that fruits be eaten separately from other foods. If you want to do your hemoglobin a favor, along with iron-rich foods, include a vegetable or fruit high in vitamin C (see page 137). Fruits and vegetables provide the maximum amount of vitamin C when they are raw, although cooked foods (for example, onion or tomatoes in a soup or casserole) can also be effective.

CAST IRON COOKWARE
Another sure way to increase iron intake is to cook with cast iron utensils. In one study of Brazilian infants, when cast iron utensils were used to prepare food, dietary iron was increased six times or more. Cast iron cookware and steel woks have been shown to significantly increase the amounts of bioavailable iron in foods. This effect is particularly evident with acidic foods such as tomato sauce or sweet and sour sauce.

Dietary Factors that Decrease Iron Absorption

While some factors help to increase iron absorption from foods, several factors decrease it. To get the most iron from the plant foods in your diet, it helps to eat and drink fewer of the things that block iron absorption at mealtime.

TANNIN-CONTAINING BEVERAGES
The primary culprit is tea, the second most widely consumed beverage in the world (next to water). Both black tea and oriental green tea, from the same plant,

contain tannin. Tannin combines with iron to form an insoluble compound. For example, black tea with breakfast has been shown to cut the iron absorption in half. Coffee, containing similar compounds, seems to have a lesser effect. Most herbal teas do not contain tannin.

MILK AND CHEESE

A glass of milk (or a piece of cheese) has been shown to decrease iron availability by as much as 50% from accompanying foods. Dairy foods consumed two hours before or after food sources of iron do not affect absorption.

OXALATES

Sorry Popeye, but spinach isn't really the best source of iron, after all. Although his example was widely used to inspire children to eat their greens, the iron in spinach is bound with oxalates, making it largely unavailable. Oxalates are acids also found in rhubarb, Swiss chard and chocolate. On the other hand, broccoli, kale and oriental greens such as bok choy provide abundant *available* iron.

PHYTATES

Phytates are the storage form of phosphorus in seeds and are associated with the fiber in raw whole grains, legumes, nuts and seeds. (For further discussion on phytates, fiber and minerals see Chapter 7.) Phytates, particularly in raw foods such as wheat bran, have been a concern because they can bind a portion of the iron, zinc and calcium in foods, making the minerals unavailable for absorption. However, during specific food preparation processes such as soaking in water (as with legumes, oats and bulgur), the yeast raising of bread doughs, and the sprouting of seeds and legumes, these phytates are destroyed by enzymes called phytases. The roasting of nuts also decreases phytate levels. Thus, food preparation methods developed over the centuries don't have the sole benefit of making the foods more tasty; these methods increase the mineral availability as well.

SOY PRODUCTS

Soybeans are high in iron, but contain two inhibitors of iron absorption: phytates and a protein component. Traditional methods used to produce fermented soyfoods (such as tempeh, miso and soy sauce) and to process tofu and silken tofu greatly increase the availability of the iron by breaking down these inhibitors. Thus, soyfoods can be important contributors of dietary iron. Eating vitamin C-rich vegetables or fruit at the same time as tofu or tempeh further enhances iron absorption.

Challenges to Iron Out: Common Errors and Solutions

The following situations illustrate pitfalls which could lead to low iron intakes for those shifting toward plant-based diets:

- A vegetarian teen eats just the non-meat portion of family meals and snacks on fries, milk shakes and granola bars.
- A busy parent may find that cheese is a convenient source of protein and calcium and rely on it for many quick meals.
- An expectant mother eating many refined foods may try to relieve constipation with special wheat bran supplements.
- A business executive eats many meals at restaurants, often ordering many pasta and cheese-laden entrées, with black tea as the beverage.

In these situations, the amount of iron eaten and absorbed could be low, and after a prolonged period of time, the person's energy level may drop. Each might think that a vegetarian diet is inadequate to meet his or her nutritional needs and that it is necessary to reintroduce meat. Simple changes in the diet could solve these problems:

- The teen needs to explore the wonderful world of vegetarian convenience foods; burgers, luncheon slices, instant bean soups and frozen entrées all make meals more interesting *and higher* in iron. Youngsters can easily learn to make hummus themselves and keep it at the front of the fridge for a quick after-school snack. Families who have members with different dietary patterns can enjoy tacos together, with optional vegetarian chili (cooked in a cast iron pot) or meat filling.
- The busy parent may prepare a delicious tofu dish in minutes after work and use the leftovers for next day's sandwich (see the very easy-to-make Tofu Fingers on page 233–34). Tofu made with calcium also provides iron, zinc and protein. She or he can pick up a bean salad from a delicatessen and stock the freezer with quick vegetarian entrées based on beans, tofu and grains. Almond butter or a thin layer of tahini and molasses makes a mineral-rich spread for toast in the morning.
- The pregnant woman using refined foods can include instead more whole grains, vegetables and fruits. In doing this, she increases her iron intake and gets more fiber from whole foods rather than from fiber supplements (see Chapter 7).
- The restaurant eater may order oriental tofu dishes, a lentil or split pea soup, a bean curry or bean burritos with a salad; the accompanying vegetables will increase iron absorption. If traveling out of town, he or she could check through the Yellow Pages for vegetarian or ethnic restaurants. It is also a wise idea to drink tannin-containing teas between meals (rather than with your iron sources). With meals, drink juice, water

or tannin-free herbal teas.

Iron-Clad Rules

Getting enough iron in your plant-based diet is not really so difficult.

1. Eat iron-rich foods every day (see Table 3.8). Following the food guide in Chapter 8, you can obtain iron from every one of the food groups. Don't waste calories on junk foods (high in fat, high in sugar, lacking in iron).

2. Help your body absorb the iron you do take in. Eat vitamin C-rich fruits and vegetables at meals. Avoid consuming black tea, other tannin-containing beverages and raw wheat bran with your iron sources. Use foods that are yeasted (such as bread), sprouted, (such as bean sprouts), roasted (such as nuts) and fermented (such as tempeh).

3. Use cast iron cookware.

4. Have your iron status checked to see how you're doing while you get used to a new "plant food" way of eating.

ZINC

Whereas much concern has been focused on protein and iron, relatively little attention has been paid to zinc. In fact, whether you are omnivorous or vegetarian, it is not difficult to put together a diet which provides adequate protein and iron. By contrast, consuming the recommended levels of zinc seems to be more of a challenge for both omnivores *and* vegetarians. At this time, there are many unanswered questions regarding the role played by zinc in health maintenance, the adequacy of zinc in our overall food supply, the suitability of recommended allowances and the zinc status of North Americans. For these reasons, our discussion here will primarily focus on the positive aspects of achieving adequate zinc intake with vegetarian foods.

Zinc in the Body

Zinc has a central role in metabolism, and ensuring an adequate intake is important throughout the life cycle. Zinc plays a part in more enzyme systems than the rest of the trace elements combined and affects many fundamental processes of life. It is essential for reproduction, growth, sexual maturation, wound healing and for our immune systems. In cells, zinc is a protector against the destructive action of free radicals, which are discussed on pages 108–9. Zinc has a role in our ability to taste; some seniors who have lost the sense of taste are actually zinc deficient. Infants and children who are not getting enough zinc will have slower physical growth and poor appetites. Zinc deficiency resulting from the inadequate food intake in anorexia nervosa could act as a sustaining factor in the disease by promoting a true loss of appetite.

Lab Tests

There is not a single, specific and sensitive way to assess zinc status; instead a combination of tests is used. Thus, testing is expensive and is not done on a routine basis, with the result that we have limited feedback about the zinc status of North Americans. In *Principles of Nutritional Assessment* by Dr. Rosalind Gibson, a taste test is described which can be used along with laboratory tests.

Recommended Zinc Intakes

The recommended intakes for zinc are 12 mg for women and 15 mg for men. These recommendations are based on average requirements, with an additional safety factor. In the case of zinc, the safety factor is particularly large, because there seems to be a wide range in people's requirements for this mineral. One reason men need more zinc is that they loose an estimated 0.6 mg zinc with each seminal emission. Ardent vegetarians might be well advised to keep a bowl of cashews on the bedside table (an ounce of these nuts provides 1.5 mg of zinc)!

Zinc in the Sample Menus in this Chapter

The zinc provided in the menus on pages 40–47 is shown in Table 3.9.

Table 3.9 Zinc Provided in Menu Nos.1 to 4

	For 135-pound person	For 180-pound person
1. Omnivore Menu	10.8 mg	13.6 mg
2. Lacto-Ovo Vegetarian Menu	8.9 mg	9.8 mg
3. Lacto-Ovo Vegetarian Menu	11.9 mg	15.2 mg
4. Vegan Menu	15.5 mg	16.2 mg

MENU NO. 1

In this menu, the zinc was provided primarily by the beef, chicken, dairy products and peas. The refined flour in the bread has lost ⅔ of its zinc.

MENU NO. 2

The majority of the zinc in this menu comes from the cheese and tofu in the lasagne at supper and the oatmeal, milk and toast at breakfast. The egg sandwich provides a little more zinc. The other foods – vegetables, fruits, spreads, salad dressing, cookies and pie – don't make significant contributions. Zinc falls slightly below recommended levels and could be increased by adding wheat germ to the oatmeal, snacking on nuts or including other foods from Table 3.10 below.

MENU NO. 3

This lacto-ovo vegetarian menu meets approximately the recommended intakes for zinc. Whole wheat pasta and small quantities of lentils and cheese eaten at supper provided the largest amount of zinc. At breakfast, oatmeal, milk, toast and almond butter all contain zinc. Hummus, pita bread and cashews are additional zinc sources.

MENU NO. 4

In this vegan menu zinc comes from foods eaten throughout the day. At breakfast, cereal with wheat germ and sesame tahini (in place of butter) on toast provide zinc. The tofu salad sandwich at lunch is a good source of zinc. Tahini, used in place of salad oil, adds zinc (as well as calcium). Walnuts, given here as a snack, provide zinc and omega-3 fatty acids. Vegans also tend to use a wide assortment of grains such as brown rice, quinoa and millet; all of these make a contribution to the day's total zinc intake.

Zinc Content of Vegetarian Foods

The zinc content of a variety of foods is given in Table 3.10.

Table 3.10 Zinc in Foods

	Volume	Weight (g)	Zinc Content (mg)
Legumes and Foods Made from Legumes			
Adzuki beans	½ cup	115	2.0
Tofu, firm	½ cup	126	2.0
Tofu, regular	½ cup	124	1.0
Baked beans	½ cup	127	1.8
Tempeh	½ cup	83	1.5
Garbanzo beans, cooked, or hummus	½ cup	120	1.3
Lentils	½ cup	100	1.2
Miso	2 Tbsp	34	1.2
Assorted legumes (black, kidney, lima, mung, pinto beans or split peas), cooked	½ cup	90	1.0
Peanut butter	2 Tbsp	32	0.9

Nuts and seeds (dried) and butters			
Pumpkin or flax seeds	¼ cup	34	2.62
Tahini, unroasted	2 Tbsp	30	1.4–2.9
Cashews or sunflower seeds	¼ cup	36	1.8
Cashew butter	2 Tbsp	32	1.6
Pecans	¼ cup	27	1.5
Almonds	¼ cup	36	1.1
Almond butter	2 Tbsp	32	1.0
Walnuts	¼ cup	27	0.8
Grains and Cereal Foods			
Wheat germ	2 Tbsp	15	2.1
Quinoa, uncooked	¼ cup	42	1.4
Millet, uncooked	¼ cup	50	0.8
Brown rice, cooked	½ cup	98	0.6
Oatmeal, cooked	½ cup	130	0.6
Whole wheat bread	1 slice	25	0.4–0.6
White bread	1 slice	24	0.2
Vegetables			
Peas, raw or cooked	½ cup	80	1.0
Potato, with skin	1	202	0.6
Fruits			
Avocado	1	173	0.7
Milk and Milk Products			
Milk	½ cup	122	0.5
Cheddar cheese	½ oz	14	0.4
Other Foods			
Nutritional yeast powder	1 Tbsp	6.7	1.0
Egg	1 large	50	0.7
For purposes of comparison:			
Beef hamburger, lean, broiled	2 oz	56	3.0
Chicken, roasted light meat	2 oz	56	0.7
Cod	2 oz	56	0.2

In vegetarian diets which have been shown to support good zinc status, we see a reliance on nuts, legumes, a variety of whole grains and processed soy products such as tofu, tempeh and soy-based meat analogs. Zinc is also found in eggs and dairy products. The way foods are prepared or processed is important, as it will effect the availability of zinc from plant foods. Rates of absorption can vary from 15 to 40 percent. To avoid problems with insufficient zinc in the vegetarian diet, include a variety of zinc-rich foods every day and choose preparation methods and food combinations that will maximize its availability.

Substances that Inhibit Zinc Availability

PHYTATES AND WHEAT BRAN SUPPLEMENTS

As we saw in the iron section of this chapter, the phytates that are associated with fiber in some cereals, legumes and nuts can reduce the availability of minerals. While a certain amount of dietary phytate appears to be beneficial overall, excessively high ratios of phytate to zinc can reduce zinc absorption. This can occur when unleavened bread is a mainstay of the diet or when substantial amounts of raw wheat bran are added as a supplement. The addition of raw wheat bran to a plant-based diet is neither necessary nor advisable. (See also the section on phytates in Chapter 7).

CALCIUM-PHYTATE-ZINC COMBINATIONS

In these combinations (or when calcium supplements are taken along with foods high in phytates), a calcium-phytate-zinc complex is formed in which the zinc is tightly bound and not available for absorption. To maximize zinc absorption, avoid taking calcium supplements at the same time as phytate-containing, zinc-rich foods such as wheat bran and other grains, legumes and nuts. For the same reason, it may be inadvisable to consume large amounts of calcium in dairy products along with phytate-rich foods such as wheat bran.

Processes that Enhance Zinc Availability

Preparation methods such as the soaking and cooking of legumes, the yeasting of bread and the sprouting of seeds all increase the availability of zinc from plant foods. Zinc availability is further increased when acid foods or ingredients are consumed along with zinc sources. For example, when chickpeas are soaked (or sprouted) before being cooked and made into hummus, enzymes break down the phytates and release zinc so that it can be easily absorbed. The lemon in the hummus assists with absorption as well. Similarly, when acid foods such as onions or other vegetables are added to a tofu stir-fry, they help to increase your intake of zinc from the meal. When bread is rising at the bakery or on your kitchen counter, again, zinc is being made available. Roasted nuts contain substantially less phytate than raw nuts. Scientists are just beginning to understand some of the food preparation methods that long-term vegetarians have been using for years to ensure good nutrition. Fortunately for the people with busy lifestyles, the places we can shop are also becoming more health oriented, so we can purchase these foods ready-made.

Single Mineral Supplements

Don't rush out and buy zinc pills. Zinc, iron, copper and calcium all interact with one another, and large intakes of one of these can interfere with your utilization of another mineral. Unless medically indicated, avoid taking a single mineral supplement. If you wish to use supplements, a multivitamin-mineral complex containing quantities at recommended levels (rather than higher) will be more supportive of good health. Check that the supplement you use contains zinc; many do not.

Guidelines for Maximizing Zinc Intake

For optimum zinc intake from your diet follow these guidelines.

1. Consume a variety of zinc-rich foods. Eat zinc sources throughout the day, including whole grains, wheat germ, tofu, tempeh, miso, legumes, nuts and seeds. Lacto-ovo vegetarians can add eggs and dairy products.

2. Make the most of the zinc in your diet. Use legumes (which have been soaked), yeasted breads, roasted nuts and sprouts.

3. Eat whole foods rather than refined foods. Products such as white flour have lost much of the zinc in the refining process.

4. Large amounts of wheat bran added to a diet high in whole grains and legumes are not only unnecessary, but can interfere with mineral absorption.

It is clear that meats can be safely removed from the diet, giving all the advantages of lower intakes of saturated fat and cholesterol while at the same time meeting the needs for protein, iron and zinc. Generally, these nutrients are not as concentrated in plant foods as they are in animal foods, but we don't need such concentrated sources. In fact, as we'll see in the next chapter, eating these *less*-concentrated sources of protein may help our calcium balance.

For some people, removing meat from the diet is just the first step in their journey towards a plant-based diet. The second step is reducing or eliminating dairy foods as well. This decision is one that is often met with some concern from those around us. After all, our food guide offers alternatives to meat. But are there alternatives to dairy products?

WITHOUT DAIRY PRODUCTS

It used to be so simple. But, these days, consumers are receiving many messages about the use of dairy products.

On the one hand, our culture teaches us that milk and its products are an essential food group; government publications tell us that we *must* eat foods from each group to be healthy. Children learn that if they don't drink their milk, they won't grow strong bones. Adults get the impression that the best way to prevent, or even cure, osteoporosis is to drink more milk.

On the other hand, we hear reports of cow's milk causing allergies, congestion and diabetes. In fact, there are even recommendations *against* using milk by some physicians.

So, what is the truth? Is milk nature's most perfect food, or is it poison?

In reality, cow's milk is neither nature's perfect food (except for a baby calf), nor poison. The Food Guide Pyramid recommends that we consume in the range of 2–3 cups of milk daily or comparable amounts of cheese or yogurt. Many North Americans and Europeans rely on milk and its products as major sources of calcium, vitamin D and riboflavin. With American styles of eating, it can be a challenge to get these nutrients without milk. But this doesn't make cow's milk an essential food. People in many parts of Africa and the Orient don't include milk in their diets and yet have bone health as good or better than that found in regions that rely on dairy. These people get all the minerals and vitamins found in milk from other sources.

The Food Guide Pyramid provides little guidance about the foods which could be relied on as "Milk Alternatives." Thus many people are under the impression that if dairy products are not used, calcium supplements are essential. It would be a great help to have listed, right there on the Pyramid, exactly which plant foods could be relied on to provide abundant and available calcium. Not only would it be of great assistance to those who don't use dairy at all, it would also help dairy users who don't meet recommended intake levels to extend their calcium intake.

REASONS WHY PEOPLE LIMIT OR ELIMINATE DAIRY PRODUCTS

When asked why they use little or no dairy products, the reasons that people give generally fall into three categories: common cultural practices, human health and compassion for animals.

Cultural Usage

For the First Nations people, and for many immigrants who are a part of the ethnic melting pot of America, milk is not a traditional food. There are cultures throughout the world that have not kept dairy cattle and yet developed balanced and nutritious eating patterns. They found other sources of the nutrients in milk. It is worth noting that some of these cultures show rates of osteoporosis *far* lower than the rates for the United States, Canada and Sweden, countries with high dairy consumption.

Health Reasons

Dairy products, as it turns out, are not "nature's perfect food" for a lot of people. Health reasons for not using milk include:

LACTOSE INTOLERANCE

After about four years of age, when nature probably intended our weaning from human milk to be complete, many people stop synthesizing the digestive enzyme lactase. They develop an intolerance to lactose, the sugar in milk; in 2% milk, one-third of the calories are from lactose. It is estimated that 60–90 percent of non-Caucasians and 5–15 percent of Caucasians show some degree of lactose intolerance. Sometimes a limited use of milk and cultured products such as yogurt or hard cheese is acceptable for these people.

ALLERGY AND SENSITIVITY TO MILK PROTEINS

Dairy products are a leading cause of food allergy and food sensitivity. Four proteins in milk can cause a wide variety of allergic responses in people of all ages, but primarily in infants and young children.

FAT CONTENT

Whole cow's milk is a high-fat fluid, designed by nature to turn a 60–70 pound calf into a 300–600 pound cow in one year. Many milk products such as cheese and butter, even in some of the reduced-fat versions, are still higher in total fat, saturated fat and cholesterol than many consumers realize. As we saw in Table 3.6, (page 48), 2% milk, which has become much more popular than whole milk, still derives a third of its total calories from fat.

OTHER REASONS

There is evidence that for some children who are prone to diabetes the ingestion of protein from cow's milk or powdered cow's milk formula during infancy may have initiated Type 1 diabetes.

Other reasons cited for not using dairy products are a concern about the use of hormones and antibiotics in today's large dairy operations.

Reasons of Compassion for Animals

DAIRY COWS

Our agricultural industry clearly tries very hard to feed healthy food to a growing population. However, in meeting the demand for high quality dairy products at low prices, factory farming has moved a long way from the story book picture of contented cows, grazing in green fields with a calf frolicking nearby. While in some places this picture is still true, increasing numbers of the more than ten million dairy cows in North America live in factory farm conditions. Many dairy cows are separated from their calves immediately after delivery, to prevent the development of bonding between cow and calf. Instead of her natural life of 12–15 years, the life span of a dairy cow is 6 years, the typical age when her productivity drops and she is "culled" from the herd to become meat.

When we look at the issues of hormone use with dairy cattle, we start to get a glimpse of the changing face of agriculture in North America. The treatment of cows with a synthesized hormone, BST (bovine somatotropin), also known as rBST or BGH (bovine growth hormone), leads to an increase of 10 percent or more in milk production. The milk produced appears to be safe for human consumption, and prior use of the hormone cannot be detected in the milk. The use of BST has been approved by the Food and Drug Administration in the United States. At the same time, a moratorium has been put on its use in many countries. Dairy farmers and members of the public have voiced concerns for the BST-treated cow, who produces more milk than usual, sometimes at the expense of her own body weight, and who may suffer increased reproductive problems and vulnerability to infection (mastitis).

For some consumers, the origins of the white beverage that we grew up on seem to be changing a little too much for comfort.

VEAL CALVES

As repeated pregnancies are necessary for the continued yield of milk by the dairy cow, during her three to four years of milk production, she is "freshened" (impregnated) once a year. A female calf may join the army of milk producers. A male calf is likely to become tender veal, after being raised for about 14 to 24 weeks in confined conditions which prevent normal muscle development. The stomachs of calves may be used to provide the rennet needed in cheese production.

People often choose not to eat meat because of an unwillingness to consume animal flesh. As vegetarians become more knowledgeable about the origins of their food, it becomes apparent that the production of dairy products is closely connected with the meat industry. As a result, a decreased use of dairy products often follows the elimination of meat.

The Need for Alternatives to Dairy Products on Food Guides

One or more of these cultural, health or animal-related reasons can be sufficiently compelling to convince some people not to use dairy products or to use only small amounts. In developed countries, declines in the consumption of fluid milk can be attributed to the pursuit of more healthful diets (lower in fat and cholesterol) and to increased numbers of immigrants from countries where milk is not a staple food.

When people don't use meat, fish and poultry, they will generally replace these foods with legumes, tofu and nuts. The use of these alternatives is supported by the presence of beans and nuts on the Food Pyramid alongside the meat, giving an official stamp of approval to the plant foods which provide iron, protein and zinc. On the other hand, there is inadequate recognition of alternative sources of the nutrients found in dairy products. Thus, people who use little or no dairy products are often unaware of the replacement foods which need to be included in their diets.

The Food Pyramid adequately addresses the needs of many Americans. However, its value is limited for those who, for a variety of reasons, use little or no dairy. To increase its usefulness and appeal, calcium-rich dairy alternatives should be listed side by side with dairy products.

The Vegetarian Food Guide, given in Chapter 8 of this book, includes a "Milk and Milk Alternates" food group. Here we lay the foundation for this food group and for meeting one's needs for calcium, vitamin D and riboflavin with a plant-based diet. We begin with the mineral that is most abundant in our bodies.

CALCIUM

Calcium is the mineral of the decade. It is featured on billboards, radio and TV advertisements; it fills the supplement shelves of pharmacies and health food stores. It is found in milk – and in plants. In this chapter, we address one myth that is prevalent in our society:

> *Myth:* It is virtually impossible for your diet to meet your calcium needs without milk and milk products.

It is a commonly held belief that without milk, we must either take supplements or face certain osteoporosis. This myth is based on three misconceptions: first, that our calcium status is dependent on very high intakes of calcium, rather than on calcium balance (more about this later); second, that there are few, if any, calcium-rich alternatives to milk products; and third, that the calcium from plants is less available. In this next section, we will look at the truth behind these misconceptions. Before we tackle the myth, it's important to have some understanding of the role of calcium in the body.

Calcium in the Body

Over 99 percent of the calcium in the body is found in bones and teeth. The calcium in bones is in a state of constant turnover and bone is being remodeled throughout our lives. Even though only 1 percent of the calcium in our bodies is found in blood and in other tissues, its function here is vital. Calcium is a part of all cell membranes and is involved with muscle contraction and relaxation, blood clotting, the transmission of nerve impulses, and the absorption of vitamin B_{12}.

Calcium Balance

The body maintains its levels of calcium in blood and bones with a complex system of checks and balances. Even as you read this, your body is adjusting the amount of calcium in your blood, keeping it at an exact level. To maintain this level, your body has some capacity to change the proportion absorbed from foods and to alter the quantity of calcium lost in urine. You can also draw on the calcium stored in bone, if necessary. The relationship between calcium intake and calcium losses from the body is known as calcium balance.

THE NEED FOR POSITIVE CALCIUM BALANCE EARLY IN LIFE

Throughout the growing years, we need to maintain a positive calcium balance by taking in more calcium than we lose. It is of prime importance that a good foundation of calcium be laid in bones during the first quarter century of life and that we attain "peak bone mass" during this time (for specific guidelines, see Chapter 9). Generally, people who are most in need of calcium absorb the highest percentage from the diet, so that absorption is greatest during pregnancy, lactation and the growing years. Thus, children may absorb up to 75 percent of dietary calcium, as compared with rates of 20–40 percent observed in young adults.

CALCIUM LOSSES AND BONE MAINTENANCE LATER IN LIFE

Beyond the mid-30s, natural bone loss begins in men and women. For this period of our lives, we can expect to have a slight negative calcium balance. Calcium loss accelerates around the time of menopause in women, then slows down again. Your diet and lifestyle choices throughout these years can help keep your bones strong by maximizing calcium absorption and minimizing calcium loss. Thus, although you don't need excessive calcium supplements, adequate calcium intake is certainly important.

FACTORS CONTRIBUTING TO POSITIVE CALCIUM BALANCE

Your calcium status, and the amount of calcium in your bones, depends on more than just the amount of calcium in your diet. Calcium intake is just one part of the rather complex equation of calcium balance. A great many nutrients interact with calcium and can affect its absorption from foods and our losses in urine. Vitamin D has a key role in helping calcium absorption. Boron, a mineral found in vegetables, fruits, nuts, legumes and flax seeds may have a role in preventing calcium loss.

The balance of body hormones also plays a part. For example, estrogen helps to maintain the framework of our bones and by acting as a "calcium conserver." In North America, estrogen replacement therapy is a solution chosen by many women to prevent calcium losses in later life. New areas of research have focused with interest on plant estrogens found, for example, in tofu and other soy products. It is thought that these may have a protective effect on the bone health of Chinese and Japanese women.

Apart from diet, exercise is of the utmost importance. Weight-bearing exercise such as walking, running or cycling, done at least three times a week, is a significant factor in helping us retain the calcium we have.

FACTORS CONTRIBUTING TO NEGATIVE CALCIUM BALANCE

"Calcium thieves" such as excess protein or salt can cause substantial calcium losses. Other factors such as alcohol intake, smoking, heavy intakes of caffeinated beverages (coffee, tea and some soft drinks) and prolonged periods of inactivity can also tip the scales in a negative direction.

Of particular interest to vegetarians and near-vegetarians are studies which have shown that the amount of calcium lost in urine is increased with high intakes of protein. When we take in more protein than we need, the breakdown and excretion of the excess sulphur-containing amino acids causes the urine to become more acidic. As the urine becomes more acidic, it carries out calcium with it. Meat, poultry, fish and eggs are concentrated sources of protein and of sulfur amino acids. Plant foods also contain these sulfur amino acids, which are essential for building body protein. However, plant foods are less concentrated sources of total protein and of these amino acids, so excesses are less likely. While calcium losses are counteracted, at least in part, by the high phosphorus levels in foods such as meats, increasingly our high protein intake is being targeted as a significant factor contributing to our high incidence of osteoporosis. As we saw in the last chapter, North Americans tend to consume, *on average*, about 100 grams of protein daily, far in excess of the recommended 50 to 70 grams. Two-thirds of this protein is of animal origin.

Vegetarians tend to have total protein intakes closer to recommended levels; this turns out to be an advantage when it comes to calcium balance.

ASSESSMENT OF CALCIUM STATUS

The calcium status of an individual cannot be assessed by routine blood tests. This is because we generally keep our blood calcium level constant, drawing from the calcium in bone when necessary. More complex bone density tests (called "dual photon densitometry") can be used to estimate calcium stored in bone, but bone tests reflect more than just calcium status. Many nutrients are involved in the building of bone. Some aspects of diet, such as excessively high protein intakes, can lead to calcium losses and decreased bone strength. Furthermore, lifestyle factors such as exercise, smoking, stress and hormonal levels affect calcium balance. Thus lifelong bone health is a reflection of the interplay of all of these, not just of calcium intake.

Recommended Calcium Intakes

How much calcium does an adult need each day? To put things into perspective, a variety of recommendations from different parts of the globe is shown in Table 4.1

Table 4.1 Adult Calcium Recommendations from Expert Groups Around the World

Group or Country Making Recommendation	Intended Population Group*	Recommended Calcium Intake (mg)
U.S. Recommended Dietary Allowances (RDA)	Age 11 to 24 years	1200
	Above Age 24 years	800
U.S. National Institute of Health (N.I.H.) Consensus Development Conference, June 1994	Age 11 to 24 years	1200–1500
	Men 25 to 50	800
	Women 25 to 50, and over 50 with estrogen replacement	1000
	Women at menopause without estrogen replacement	1500
	Both sexes over 50	Increase toward 1500
Canada, 1990	Women 19 to 49	700
	Men over 19 and women over 49	800
United Kingdom, 1991	Age 19 and over	700
Japan, 1992	Age 19 and over	600
World Health Organization	Adults	400–500**

*Specific recommendations for pregnant and lactating women are not included in this chart. See Chapter 9. **The WHO figure is a "Suitable Group Mean Intake" and has been unchanged for the past 30 years. As it is considered that the current state of knowledge concerning assessment of calcium status and optimal intake is inadequate, no "Recommended Intake" has been set. The 1989 WHO Technical Report 779 on "Health of the Elderly" suggests figures more in line with those listed above for the NIH (1994) figures listed above.

Why is there such a great range in the opinions of people who have spent their lives studying calcium status and bone health? Exactly *what level of calcium intake can be considered adequate* is clearly a matter of considerable debate. This is because:

1. there is no easy, routine way to assess calcium status;

2. the body has the capacity to adapt to a wide range of calcium intakes;

3. eating patterns and other habits differ from country to country in many ways that affect calcium balance.

In setting the recommendations shown above, experts have taken into account the lifestyle factors which exist for their respective population groups.

To quote the World Health Organization Technical Report #797 (1990):

Populations in developing countries appear to be at less risk from fractures than those in developed countries, despite their lower body weights and calcium intakes, possibly because they smoke less, drink less alcohol, do more physical work (which promotes bone formation) and consume less protein and salt (both of which increase obligatory calcium loss from the body).

Certainly we do need adequate calcium intake, and this is especially important during the growing, bone-building years. But other factors in the equation of calcium balance must be changed in the lifestyles of those people in developed countries who wish to avoid the tragedies of osteoporosis in the later years. Pushing the recommended intakes for calcium ever upward, without changing these other factors, is like trying to fill the bathtub by pouring in more and more water – but never putting in the plug.

The factors which can help us to build strong bones in the early years and to retain calcium in later life include adequate dietary calcium intake as *well as:*

• an emphasis on physical fitness, with regular weight bearing exercise;

• hormonal balance which supports bone maintenance;

• adequate vitamin D, for example by spending a few minutes in the sun each day;

• an avoidance of excess dietary protein, and in particular animal protein which is high in the sulphur-containing amino acids;

• avoidance of smoking;

• moderation in use of alcohol, caffeine and salt.

For those vegetarians whose *lifestyle* choices support calcium retention, it seems likely that calcium intakes lower than those recommended for Americans in Table 4.1 will support lifelong bone health. There are many questions yet to be answered. In designing eating patterns for vegetarians, including those who consume little or no dairy, we have used the same recommended calcium intakes given for other North Americans as a goal. But can we really get that much calcium *without milk?*

We have come to think of dairy products as the sole source of calcium in our diets. People are often unaware that other dietary sources exist. As we will see, there are plenty of excellent plant sources, with abundant available calcium. First, let's look at the four menus from the last chapter, see how much calcium they provided and which foods provided it.

Table 4.2 Calcium Provided in Menu No. 1 to No. 4 (pages 40 to 47)

	For 135 Pound Person	*For 180 Pound Person*
1. Omnivore Menu #1	907 mg	1030 mg
2. Lacto-Ovo Vegetarian Menu #2 (Dairy and egg emphasis)	1170 mg	1440 mg
3. Lacto-Ovo Vegetarian Menu #3 (Less dairy and egg)	968 mg	1150 mg
4. Vegan Menu #4	1105 mg	1235 mg

The calcium in all of these menus meets and exceeds the RDAs for people over the age of 24. To help meet the recommendations for young adults (1200 mg), calcium-fortified orange juice, soy beverages, tortillas and other products could be used as well.

It is important to note that in all three of the vegetarian menus, calcium is supplied in small amounts by plant foods in meals and snacks throughout the day. Research has shown that calcium is absorbed far more efficiently when it is consumed in many small doses. When the same amount of calcium is given in a few concentrated portions, it is less well absorbed.

OMNIVORE MENU
Typically in American diets, 55 to 75 percent of the calcium is provided by dairy products. In the omnivore's menu, dairy foods provide 70 percent of the calcium.

LACTO-OVO VEGETARIAN MENUS
In Menus 2 and 3, approximately 45 to 50 percent of the calcium is from dairy products. About half of the calcium is supplied by plant foods.

VEGAN MENU
In the vegan menu, almost every plant food eaten contributes to the total, over 1000 mg of calcium. Two calcium-fortified products were used: orange juice and soymilk. If tofu made with calcium were to be used for the tofu salad sandwich, the calcium provided by this menu would be higher still.

Plant Foods as Calcium Sources

Certain plant leaves and flowers (otherwise known as green vegetables) are some of the best calcium sources around. North Americans are notorious for not eating their vegetables, so it is no wonder many people have low calcium intakes, especially if they aren't fond of milk.

These calcium-rich plant foods are regularly used in other parts of the world – and they're used well. Greens can be seasoned deliciously and presented attractively. Seeds are often ground and provide a creamy texture to some dishes. If you are going to put together meals high in calcium without dairy products you will probably be in for a few taste adventures. The recipes in Chapter 12 will help you get started. Table 4.3 gives the calcium contents of a range of foods that contain calcium, some common, others perhaps unfamiliar.

In the production of tofu, either a calcium or a magnesium salt is used as part of the process. Check the label to see if the tofu you are buying has added calcium; for the non-packaged variety you'll have to ask the supplier. A variety of calcium-fortified foods, from tortillas to soymilks, are also available.

Some of the foods listed in Table 4.3 are high in calories, while others are low. Sesame tahini and tofu are at the higher end of the range and can be helpful for increasing the caloric intakes of children and underweight adults. The vegetables and seaweeds are extremely low in fat and calories. All of these foods provide other minerals in addition to calcium. Native people living in coastal areas of North America traditionally used local seaweeds, including kelp and dulse, and have obtained some of their calcium from these.

Seaweeds are actually vegetables from the sea and have a long history of use in Japan. Some Japanese dishes use seaweed as a main ingredient. When Westerners start out, they often prefer smaller amounts providing saltiness and seasoning, or in Western food variations such as the type of sushi known as California roll. In the recipe section (Chapter 12) we include the exceptionally high-calcium hijiki seaweed as an option in the delicious "Green Sea Soup" and the stir-fry. Miso soup made with seaweed is a delicious appetizer; in Japan it is also a regular breakfast food.

Calcium Availability from Foods

Overall we absorb 30 to 50 percent of the calcium in the North American diet. Recent studies by Dr. Connie Weaver of Purdue University have shown that the absorption of calcium from some vegetables is much higher than was formerly believed, although it is important to remember that they are also less concentrated sources of calcium than dairy products.

Table 4.4 shows the calcium absorption from foods when portions containing comparable amounts of calcium were given. When we combine the information from Table 4.3 and Table 4.4, we find that some plant foods can be real calcium powerhouses in our diets. So, although greens are less concentrated

Table 4.3 Calcium in Foods

Legumes and Foods Made from Legumes	Volume	Weight (g)	Calcium Content (mg)
Tofu, various types (check labels)	½ cup	124	100–320★
Fortified non-dairy beverages	½ cup	125	125–250★
Unfortified non-dairy beverages	½ cup	125	5-95
Hummus	½ cup	122	81
Tempeh (a fermented soy product)	½ cup	83	77
Black turtle, navy, pinto, white beans	½ cup	93	41–81
Seeds and Nuts			
Whole sesame seeds	2 Tbsp	56	176
Tahini (sesame butter)	2 Tbsp	56	128
Almond butter	3 Tbsp	48	129
Almonds, dry roasted	⅓ cup	42	120–176
Vegetables			
Broccoli, cooked	1 cup	156	178
Okra, frozen, cooked	1 cup	184	176
Chinese cabbage, cooked	1 cup	170	158
Collard greens	1 cup	190	148
Mustard greens, cooked	1 cup	140	104
Kale, cooked	1 cup	130	94
Rutabaga, cooked	1 cup	170	72
Fruits			
Figs, dried	5 medium	94	135
Orange	1 medium	140	56
Calcium-fortified orange juice	½ cup	125	up to 150 mg★
Seaweeds (Sea Vegetables)			
Hijiki, dry	¼ cup	10	162
Wakame, dry	¼ cup	10	104
Milk Products			
Milk, whole, 2% or skim	½ cup	122	144–151
Yogurt, various types	½ cup	122	135–225
Natural cheeses	¼ cup	28	50–200
Other Foods			
Blackstrap molasses	1 Tbsp	20	137
Calcium-fortified tortillas	1 serving		20–150

★ Check labels; the Dietary Value (DV) for calcium is 1000 mg.

sources of calcium than milk, they can make substantial contributions to daily calcium intake. In fact, this is the case in many parts of the world where dairy products are not regularly consumed.

Preparation techniques which make food appetizing at the same time often increase the availability of calcium from plant foods; soaking (beans), sprouting (seeds and legumes), yeasting and fermentation (bread, miso) and

Table 4.4 Percentage of Calcium Absorbed from Foods

	Percentage Absorbed
Vegetables, cooked (broccoli, brussels sprouts, chinese and green cabbage, cauliflower, kale, kohlrabi, mustard greens, rutabaga, turnip greens, watercress)	50–70%
Milk	32%
Tofu	31%
Almonds, sesame seeds	21%
Beans, cooked (pinto, small red, white)	17%
Spinach, cooked	5%

roasting (nuts) release calcium so that we can absorb it. See Chapter 7 for a further discussion on mineral availability.

There are a few plant foods which, although they contain plenty of calcium, are *not* good sources of this mineral, due to their high oxalate contents. These include spinach, beet greens, swiss chard, rhubarb and the grain amaranth. As you can see in Table 4.4, little of the calcium in spinach is available for absorption.

American Dietary Intakes of Calcium

OVERALL POPULATION

American studies dating back to the 1950s have shown that calcium is one of the three nutrients most often consumed below recommended levels. In particular, intakes of calcium in the diets of women show a wide range, with many falling short of desired levels. Many women do not consume the amounts of dairy products suggested in food guides, so including non-dairy alternatives would make it easier to meet recommended intakes of calcium.

VEGETARIANS

Vegetarians were shown in the 1977/1978 National Food Consumption Survey (USDA, 1984) to have calcium intakes that were higher than those of the general population at all ages. Calcium intakes of the vegetarians ranged from 7 to 54 percent higher for comparable age groups. Particularly interesting were findings for young women from 9 to 34 years of age. In these years of bone mineralization, calcium intakes of vegetarians were 17 to 39 percent higher than the intakes of omnivores. This survey grouped lacto-ovo vegetarians and vegans together.

VEGANS

The few studies that have been done on adult vegans show intakes in the range of 500 to 1000 mg calcium, although some individuals had lower intakes. A study of 40 vegans in Israel showed their average calcium intake to be 825 mg per day. In this study, nuts and seeds provided one third of the calcium. People also ate seaweeds, as well as more common plant sources of calcium. Vegans use greens, soy products, nuts and seeds as calcium sources. Some studies of vegan children have shown low calcium intakes; this is certainly a cause for concern, because bone mineralization occurs in the growing years. Our Vegetarian Food Guide, as well as guidelines in Chapter 9, will help people of all ages achieve adequate intakes of calcium.

Incidence of Osteoporosis

A number of studies have been done comparing the long-term effects on bone density of lacto-vegetarian diets and of omnivorous diets. Marsh studied 1600 lacto-ovo vegetarians in Michigan and found that, whereas female omnivores had lost 35 percent of bone mass by 80 years of age, female vegetarians had lost only 18 percent. No differences were reported for men. She suggested that the lacto-ovo vegetarian lifestyle of the women studied, including their lower intakes of animal protein, appeared to be a protective factor in postmenopausal bone loss.

From the limited research that has been done, the elderly vegans studied did not appear to show lower bone density than omnivores.

Calcium Supplements

There is a role for calcium supplements, but as with other supplements, they should not be assumed to be adequate replacements for real food. When we depend on nutritious foods, we end up with a balance of *many* of the nutrients we need for building bone and for other body functions. Nature provides all of these together, in greens, beans, nuts and seeds. Supplemental calcium may not be as well absorbed as small amounts in food throughout the day.

If calcium intake from foods is inadequate, supplements can be useful, but for people in good health, there appears to be no advantage in higher-than-recommended intakes. In fact, excesses of calcium can bind zinc, especially in the presence of high-fiber, high-phytate foods, making it unavailable. People who are predisposed to the formation of kidney stones should avoid high intakes of calcium.

It is certainly possible to meet recommended levels of calcium intake at any age without the use of dairy products. Those vegans and near-vegans who consume a variety of calcium-rich plant foods throughout the day will obtain sufficient calcium. Others, who are not using these foods, would be well advised to begin incorporating them into their diets. Plant sources of calcium include green vegetables, tofu made with calcium, nuts, seeds and blackstrap molasses. Other plant foods contribute small amounts of calcium. If necessary, calcium-fortified foods can be used to bring intakes up to recommended levels.

Overall guidelines are given on pages 87–88 under: "Seven Simple Steps for Strong Bones (For the Non-Dairy Set)." Now let's look at a vitamin that forms a strong partnership with calcium.

VITAMIN D: THE SUN WORSHIPPER'S VITAMIN

When we expose our skin to sunlight, even for just a few minutes, vitamin D is formed. Vitamin D is also commonly added to milk. These two very different sources — sunlight and fortified foods — are the main ways we get vitamin D.

The importance of sunlight to the sturdiness of the skeleton was referred to even in ancient times. More recently, folk wisdom suggested that recovery from some diseases would be speeded by time spent in the sun. In the twentieth century, we found that certain ultraviolet rays in sunlight would help our bodies create vitamin D. It was also discovered that vitamin D could be taken orally, in foods or supplements, and that both routes were equally effective treatments for a once common disease called rickets.

The Role of Vitamin D in the Body

Vitamin D is essential for the proper formation of the skeleton. If we have too little vitamin D, the skeleton will be inadequately mineralized, leading to a condition called rickets in children and osteomalacia in adults. One of the best known roles of vitamin D is to maintain blood calcium at exactly the right level. It does this by regulating the movements of calcium in three places: absorption in the intestine, losses through the urine and storage in the bones.

Origins of Food Fortification with Vitamin D

From the 17th to the 19th century, rickets plagued children who played in the narrow, dark streets of industrial cities (or worked indoors). In 1900, over 85 percent of the children in some smoggy urban areas of North America and Europe had this crippling disease. Subsequently, the roles of vitamin D and sunlight in curing rickets were identified. In the United States, cow's milk was chosen as a vehicle to distribute vitamin D to the population as a whole and to children in particular. As a result, rickets has become rare here.

Natural Food Sources of Vitamin D

There is little doubt that before the era of vitamin supplementation and food fortification, sunlight was the major provider of vitamin D for most of the world's population. Vitamin D is naturally present in fish liver and a few other foods. The exposure of certain plant foods to ultraviolet light has also been demonstrated to produce a form of vitamin D (vitamin D_2). For example, certain seaweeds, dried in the sun, have shown vitamin D_2 activity.

Our Current Sources of Vitamin D

Americans generally get vitamin D from fortified foods, sunlight and supplements. Vitamin D comes in several usable forms; you can get it in fortified foods or supplements as either Vitamin D_2 or D_3.

FORTIFIED FOOD SOURCES

Foods that are often fortified with vitamin D include non-dairy milks, cereals, vegan and regular margarines, butter, milk and infant formula.

SUNLIGHT AS A VITAMIN D SOURCE

People who are regularly exposed to adequate amounts of sunlight have no requirement for vitamin D from foods. When our skin is exposed to the ultraviolet light in sunshine, we can make vitamin D out of a cholesterol compound naturally present in the skin. This ultraviolet light doesn't pass through glass, so we can't get the beneficial effects of sunlight through a window. To determine whether an individual is getting enough sunlight for adequate vitamin D production, a number of factors must be taken into consideration.

Age

The capacity of the skin to produce vitamin D in the elderly is 25 to 50 percent that of younger people. Infants and children need more vitamin D to help absorb calcium for quickly growing bones; nature has cleverly arranged that they also have a greater capacity to produce the vitamin.

Skin color

People with dark skin require substantially more exposure to sunlight for vitamin D production. Whereas light-skinned people need 10–15 minutes of sunlight a day, people with increasingly darker skin need from 30 minutes to 3 hours daily (on face and hands). The melanin pigment in dark skin absorbs some of the ultraviolet radiation. This appears to be a protective adaptation, developed by people in sunny climates. It has been suggested that over the evolution of mankind, as people moved to northern latitudes, skin pigmentation decreased to allow for adequate production of vitamin D. If you've ever wondered about those blond, light-skinned Scandinavians in the north and the darker-skinned people close to the equator – these differences probably developed partly because of our need for vitamin D!

Use of sunscreen

Sunscreen protection factors (SPF) of 8 and above will prevent vitamin D synthesis. Our need for vitamin D must be balanced with the obvious need for protection from overexposure to the sun, especially in the hot hours of the day. For vitamin D synthesis, midmorning sun is fine.

Type of clothing worn

Vitamin D production varies with the amount of clothing worn over the surface area of skin exposed. For example, the attire of some Middle Eastern women covers the head and face, preventing vitamin D production.

Sunlamps

Sunlamps can be used to produce vitamin D in the skin. As with overexposure to sunlight, they may cause skin damage, so use caution or controlled ultraviolet light chambers.

Time of year and geographical location

Vitamin D production in skin differs seasonally and according to the latitude at which we live, as these factors affect the amount of ultraviolet radiation. On a cloudy summer day, even the "skyshine" will stimulate some vitamin D production. We have the ability to store vitamin D, so it's all right to get more sun in the summer and less in the winter, although our serum levels of the vitamin do drop. It has been estimated that the amount of ultraviolet radiation received even on sunny days in winter, is 16 times less than in summer. The "vitamin D winter," during which little or no vitamin D production occurs in skin, is longer at northern latitudes. It may be too long for the limited vitamin D reserves of infants and children, so they will need a supplement or fortified food source in Alaska and northern states. Table 4.5 shows months without vitamin D production at specific latitudes and locations.

Table 4.5 Months Without Vitamin D Production at Specific Locations and Latitudes

Latitudes and location	Months without vitamin D production
61° N (Bergen, Norway)	October to March
52° N (Edmonton, Canada)	November to February
42° N (Boston)	December to January
34° N (Los Angeles)	none

You can roughly estimate your vitamin D winter by using the closest latitude. Shorter periods of time in the sun would be appropriate in the southern parts of the United States; as one moves north, longer exposures are needed for an equivalent amount of vitamin D production. Overexposure to the sun does *not* result in the production of harmful excesses of vitamin D, although it can, of course, lead to skin problems. Moderate sun exposure seems the wisest course.

As you might have guessed, making a recommendation for the minimum sunlight exposure necessary for vitamin D production can be complicated by all of the above factors. However, the following guidelines will help you meet your vitamin D needs. You can choose sunlight, fortified foods, supplements or a combination.

GUIDELINE FOR GETTING ENOUGH
VITAMIN D FROM SUN EXPOSURE

A general guideline for Americans (south of Alaska) is an average of 10 to 15 minutes of sun daily, midmorning to late afternoon, on the face and hands, for light-skinned people. Darker-skinned people need more (30 minutes to three hours daily, depending on skin color).

GUIDELINES FOR GETTING ENOUGH
VITAMIN D FROM FOODS AND SUPPLEMENTS

For those who derive their vitamin D from fortified foods or supplements, the recommended adult intakes are 10 μg (400 IU) for ages 19 to 24, and 5 μg (200 IU) for persons 25 years and over. Recent recommendations from the National Institutes of Health emphasize the importance of vitamin D for seniors, whose exposure to sunlight may be minimal and whose ability to make vitamin D decreases with age – 10 μg won't hurt and might help! The Daily Value (DV) for vitamin D on the labels of fortified foods is 10 μg.

EXCESS VITAMIN D

Care must be taken, especially with infants and children, not to consume more than recommended amounts of vitamin D. Three to five times the recommended intake of vitamin D over an extended period of time can cause "hypercalcemia" (too much calcium in the blood) which is a serious condition. This can occur with high dosage supplements or a combination of milk, other vitamin D fortified foods and supplements.

Seven Simple Steps for Strong Bones (For the Non-Dairy Set)

1. Follow the recommendations in the Milk and Milk Alternates section of the

Vegetarian Food Guide.

• Eat dark green vegetables *daily*; include broccoli, kale, collards, bok choy and Chinese cabbage on your regular shopping list. Find an Oriental grocery store; grow greens in your garden or on your balcony (kale grows even in cold weather). Learn some delicious ways to prepare greens (see Chapter 12 for ideas). Minerals are lost in the cooking water, so steam vegetables or use the mineral-rich cooking water in soups or in grain preparation.

• Use tofu made with calcium. For those people who aren't sure they like tofu, realize that, like flour, it is an ingredient. You wouldn't want to eat a bowl of flour, though you may love many baked goods. Tofu is unusually versatile; it can be made into everything from soup to dessert, so it can be used often without your menus becoming repetitious (see Chapter 12).

• Make sesame seeds and nuts a part of your meals and snacks. Find delicious ways to use sesame tahini. On toast or bread, perhaps with blackstrap molasses, it provides calcium, iron and zinc all at once! Tahini is also an excellent base for salad dressings.

• Try Oriental favorites, such as sushi, made with the seaweed nori. Use other sea vegetables such as hijiki in stir-fries and soups.

2. Emphasize the foods mentioned above, along with a balanced, varied diet, during the growing years. Infants need breast milk or fortified soy formula, and as children get older they can add fortified soymilk.

3. Take advantage of some of the calcium-fortified foods, if necessary, to bring your total calcium intake up to recommended levels.

4. Don't keep company with the calcium thieves; avoid high intakes of salt, alcohol and caffeine, excessive amounts of animal protein and a sedentary lifestyle.

5. When you go out for dinner, frequent Japanese, Chinese, Middle Eastern and vegetarian restaurants. These will cater to your "non-dairy calcium" needs.

6. Take the opportunity to stretch your legs and walk around the block on your lunch break. You'll not only feel good, but 10 minutes (for Caucasians) to 30 minutes (for dark-skinned people) of sunlight will help you make vitamin D for the day.

7. Exercise is a prime bone strengthener; walking, jogging and other weight-bearing exercise is essential for lifelong bone health.

RIBOFLAVIN

We'll turn our attention to one other vitamin commonly found in dairy products, but also available from many plant foods. Riboflavin is involved with energy metabolism and is active in every cell in the body. It also helps to maintain body tissues, including skin, and mucous membranes such as those in the mouth and eyes. Riboflavin deficiencies, although rare, show up as cracks at the corner of the mouth and changes in the tongue and mucous membranes of the mouth.

Recommended Intakes of Riboflavin

Since our need for riboflavin is tied to our use of energy, the recommended dietary allowances (RDAs) are stated in terms of the calories we burn. The recommended intake is 0.6 mg for each 1000 calories you take in each day, with a minimum recommendation of 1.2 mg total.

Each of the four menus in Chapter 3 provides more than one and a half times the recommended intake of riboflavin. The vegan menu contains the greatest amount of riboflavin – 225 percent of the recommended intake.

Riboflavin in Diets With and Without Dairy Products

A third of North Americans' dietary riboflavin comes from dairy products and another third comes from meat, poultry, fish and eggs. Thus, there is sometimes concern that vegetarian diets without dairy products will be low in riboflavin. It is true that in a few studies, vegetarians have shown low intakes of riboflavin. This is both surprising and unnecessary because riboflavin is plentiful in many plant foods.

When people use little or no dairy products it is important that they choose other sources for the riboflavin found in milk and milk products. In a vegan diet, one-third of the riboflavin may come from vegetables and fruits, a quarter from legumes, nuts and seeds and the rest from grains. Vegans often include good sources of riboflavin not familiar to many omnivores, such as nutritional yeast, yeast extracts, wheat germ and sprouts.

In fact, it is not difficult to obtain sufficient riboflavin in a diet without dairy products. Whole grains (rice, rye, millet, wheat) and enriched flours provide riboflavin in amounts very similar to the 0.6 mg per 1000 calories suggested in the RDA's recommended intakes. Including riboflavin-rich foods can also inspire you to try out some new vegetables. You're likely to get small amounts – about 10 percent of your recommended riboflavin intake – from each serving of a great many foods throughout the day: grains, vegetables, legumes, soymilk, dried fruit, nuts and seeds. Table 4.6 lists a few of the food sources of riboflavin in vegetarian diets; there are many others not on this list.

Riboflavin is found in many of the same plant sources as calcium, and it also turns up in some unexpected foods like peas, avocados and raspberries.

You'll easily meet recommended riboflavin intakes by regularly including a variety of riboflavin-rich foods and by following the Vegetarian Food Guide given in Chapter 8.

Table 4.6 Riboflavin in Foods

	Volume	Weight (grams)	Riboflavin (milligrams)
Yeast			
Nutritional yeast, Red Star T6635+ flakes	1 Tbsp	4	2.4
Legumes and Legume Products			
Beans (assorted varieties), cooked	1 cup	190–200	.08–.16
Tofu, tempeh	½ cup	125	.09–.13
Soymilk	1 cup	250	.4–.5*
Nuts and Seeds			
Almonds	3 Tbsp	48	.30
Sesame tahini	2 Tbsp	30	.14
Grains			
Wheat germ	2 Tbsp	14	.12
Whole wheat bread	1 slice	24	.08
Enriched white bread	1 slice	24	.07
Enriched/fortified cereals (see labels)	1 serving		.40–1.68*
Vegetables			
Broccoli, cooked	1 cup	156	.32
Mushrooms, raw	1 cup	70	.32
Peas, boiled	1 cup	160	.24
Avocado, California	1 medium	173	.21
Lotus root	10 slices	81	.18
Sweet potato	1	114	.15
Sprouts (alfalfa, mung, soy)	1 cup	105	.13–.21
Asparagus	6 spears	90	.11
Fruits			
Raspberries, strawberries	1 cup	123	.11
Figs, dried	5	94	.09
Dairy Products and Eggs			
Milk, whole, 2%, skim	½ cup	122	.17–.21
Yogurt	½ cup	114	.16
Egg	1	50	.14

* The Daily Value for riboflavin is 1.7 mg.

Summing It Up

An overview of the scientific literature shows us that modern vegetarians tend to be a segment of the population that is particularly interested in and knowledgeable about nutrition. In fact, a number of studies from North America and Europe have noted that although vegetarians had lower caloric intakes than omnivores, the intake of vitamins and minerals was generally higher because nutritious foods were selected.

It seems likely that there is more awareness of "meat alternatives" than "milk alternatives," because the latter are not yet an established part of national food guides. Whatever your reasons for leaving out dairy – from health to animal rights – your objectives will be best achieved by making appropriate choices to replace the nutrients found in milk. Here are three practical points to remember when making those choices:

1. *Make meals and snacks count.*

Throughout the day, beginning with the almond butter on your morning toast, the greens and tahini dressing for salad, the calcium-fortified tofu in your dinner through to the late night snack of figs, remember that calcium comes in *moderate* amounts from a wide assortment of plant foods. The vast majority of your choices can contribute. Although we refer specifically to calcium here, the same principle certainly applies to intake of other vitamins and minerals.

2. *Lifelong bone health reflects many aspects of your diet and lifestyle – not just the intake of milk or calcium.*

Take note of the "Seven Steps for Strong Bones" on page 87–88.

3. *Choose a variety of nourishing plant foods.*

A look at the food sources of riboflavin (Table 4.6) shows us that foods not particularly well-known as nutritional powerhouses may still be good sources of an essential ingredient. The next chapter delves more deeply into the value of a varied diet.

THE VEGAN OPTION: MORE FOOD FOR THOUGHT

For many people who have started to move away from animal foods, a pure vegetarian or vegan diet could be the ultimate goal. Wherever you are on the continuum between omnivorous and vegan diets, you will probably find it reassuring to know that a diet totally free of animal products *can* keep you in excellent health.

At one time, vegan diets were considered to be risky by scientific experts, but by 1975, Dr. W. Crosby and a committee representing the American National Academy of Sciences had concluded that a vegan diet is a safe dietary option: "individual pure vegetarians from many populations of the world have maintained seemingly excellent health." They advocated that vegans take particular care in certain areas: first, to supplement their diets with vitamin B_{12}, and second, to eat a wide variety of foods. The need for care in planning the diets of children was emphasized by the committee. It is now clear that vegan diets can be adequate throughout the growing years as long as there is a focus on foods high in calories and other nutrients (for specific recommendations, see Chapter 9).

In Chapter 3 we presented plant sources of protein, iron and zinc for people who don't include meat, poultry or fish in their diets. Chapter 4 covered sources of calcium, vitamin D and riboflavin for those who don't use dairy products. In this chapter, we address the two additional points for vegans made by the American National Academy of Sciences: ensuring reliable sources of vitamin B_{12} and the need for a varied diet. The material in this chapter is also important for the many near-vegans who use *few* dairy products, eggs, or other foods of animal origin.

VITAMIN B12

Vitamin B_{12} was the last vitamin to be discovered, finally isolated in 1947. It is a complex, beautifully symmetrical molecule, similar in many respects to hemoglobin. Whereas hemoglobin has an atom of iron in a central position, the mineral cobalt is at the center in vitamin B_{12}.

Vitamin B12 in the Body

ROLE AND DEFICIENCY SYMPTOMS

Vitamin B_{12} is involved in the metabolism of certain amino acids and fatty acids. It plays a role in cell division, the maturation of red blood cells, brain and spinal cord function and helps to maintain the protective sheaths surrounding nerve fibers.

Most cases of vitamin B_{12} deficiency occur not among vegetarians but in the general population. One deficiency symptom is a type of anemia (megaloblastic anemia), in which red blood cells do not mature properly. Deficiency of vitamin B_{12} can also lead to damage to the nerves and spinal cord. Symptoms of deficiency are weakness and fatigue, difficulty with balance when walking and numbness and tingling in fingers and toes, like a "pins and needles" sensation. Other symptoms are confusion, inability to concentrate and changes in the color and surface of the tongue. Nerve damage from prolonged vitamin B_{12} deficiency can be severe and irreversible, but it rarely occurs because deficiencies are generally diagnosed before this point.

Because vitamin B_{12} plays a role in cell division, it is especially necessary during times of growth. Thus an adequate intake of vitamin B_{12} is particularly important for pregnant and lactating women, infants and children. Babies are vulnerable to B_{12} deficiency, because they do not have stores of the vitamin to draw on. Although reports of dietary vitamin B_{12} deficiency are very rare, the consequences of deficiency are serious and such tragedies can easily be prevented by supplementation.

ABSORPTION

Over 95 percent of all B_{12} deficiencies reported in the United States occur not because of inadequate B_{12} in the diet, but because of a diminished ability to absorb the vitamin as people age. Vitamin B_{12} is absorbed in the small intestine. Its absorption depends on the presence of three different substances: gastric acid (the acid in our stomachs), digestive enzymes and a substance called intrinsic factor. As people age, gastric acidity decreases, so that by 60 years of age, 1 percent of people have lost the ability to absorb the vitamin. It is estimated that by the time we reached 127, we would all have lost this ability. (This is difficult to prove, though!) Some senior citizens who are admitted to nursing homes with a diagnosis of confusion are, in fact, suffering from a loss of ability to absorb vitamin B_{12}. Where this is true, in many cases it can be reversed quickly by injections of the vitamin.

Because the dietary sources of this vitamin are almost exclusively animal foods, the central issue for vegans is generally not absorption, but ensuring that they have adequate and reliable sources of B_{12}.

STORAGE IN THE BODY

Excess vitamin B_{12} can be stored in the liver and other tissues. In fact, most people have a supply that will last three years or more. Because we can efficiently recycle the vitamin in our systems, the stores of some people last as long as 20 years.

Laboratory Testing for Vitamin B_{12}

Deficiency can be detected in the early stages by blood tests and is easily treated and prevented. The following people should get laboratory testing for vitamin B_{12} status:

- anyone who has been vegan for more than 3 years and who has not had a regular, reliable source of this vitamin through fortified foods or supplements
- any vegan or near-vegan experiencing symptoms of B_{12} deficiency such as numbness and tingling in the fingers and toes
- anyone who has doubts about his or her vitamin B_{12} status

It would be wise for vegans to have B_{12} status checked early in pregnancy. Note that infants, who have not built up B_{12} stores, cannot communicate about deficiency symptoms, so make sure they have a reliable intake of this vitamin.

Dr. Michael Klaper, a physician whose medical practice focuses on vegan health issues, gives the following sound recommendations: "If total serum B_{12} is below 130 picograms per ml, B_{12}-fortified plant foods or supplements should be added to the diet. (If the test is available, measurement of the B_{12}-carrier protein, holotranscobalamin II, should also be done, as it provides a more sensitive indicator of early B_{12} deficiency.)"

Recommended Intakes for Vitamin B_{12}

We need only very minute amounts of vitamin B_{12}. This is because the vitamin is so effectively conserved by the body; amounts that are released into the intestine (in bile) are almost totally reabsorbed. The RDA for adults is 2 µg, 2.2 µg for pregnant women and 2.6 µg for lactating women (2 micrograms = 2/1000 of a gram). Since we can store this vitamin, a larger dose supplement can be taken several times a week if this is preferred to daily intake, although during pregnancy, daily intake is advised.

Our Sources of Vitamin B_{12}

The *actual* sources of vitamin B_{12} are some very helpful microorganisms capable of building the intricate vitamin B_{12} molecule. Higher forms of life, such as animals and humans, do not have this capability. We rely on bacteria and microorganisms for our supply of B_{12}. The bacteria thrive in the *lower* intestines of animals and humans and can make all of the vitamin B_{12} we need. Unfortunately, we can't absorb the vitamin B_{12} from these bacteria because absorption takes place *higher* up in the intestine. Therefore, reliable food sources or supplements of B_{12} are essential.

VITAMIN B_{12} IN ANIMAL FOODS

For most North Americans, the primary sources of vitamin B_{12} are the animal foods in their diets. Vitamin B_{12} (derived from microorganisms) is widely distributed in animal tissues and therefore can be found in meat, fish, poultry, eggs, milk and milk products.

VITAMIN B_{12} IN PLANT FOODS

Vitamin B_{12} is not present *in* plant foods themselves in significant amounts. It can be found *on* plant foods, in minute amounts of dirt or bacterial contamination. When plant foods are scrupulously cleaned, the bacteria and B_{12} are removed. Unfortified plant foods should not be relied on as B_{12} sources.

The amounts of true vitamin B_{12} available from plant foods are negligible or uncertain for the following three reasons:

1) Modern methods of agriculture have altered the amounts of B_{12} in soil and on crops.

Different agricultural practices can result in wide variations in B_{12} levels. For example, cobalt-rich soils containing organic waste from the intestinal production of beetles and burrowing or grazing animals will contain plenty of B_{12}. In turn, there can be substantial amounts of vitamin B_{12} on plants grown on these soils. Modern farming methods can result in decreased B_{12} availability. Studies have shown increased risk of B_{12} deficiency when vegans moved from countries with less hygienic supplies of food and water to developed countries. The progress that humanity has made in hygiene is laudable and has certainly cut down on infectious disease. At the same time, however, modern methods of agriculture and food production have had the effect of removing some natural dietary sources of B_{12}.

2) Hygienic food processing methods can also mean less vitamin B_{12}.

Fermented foods such as tempeh and miso have the reputation of containing vitamin B_{12} – a reputation based on production methods which were used in the past. In traditional methods, more bacteria were present – and more vitamin B_{12}. Modern practices include sanitary controls which eliminate many of the B_{12}-producing bacteria. As a result, these foods can no longer be counted on as reliable sources of the vitamin. Similarly, the amount of B_{12} on seaweeds depends both on the type of seaweed and on the bacteria present in the water in which it grew.

3) Instead of true B_{12}, compounds called analogs may be present in some foods.

Vitamin B_{12} analogs (non-cobalamin corrinoids) are substances that are similar, but not identical, to true vitamin B_{12}, so they don't function the same way in the body. Analog B_{12} molecules can occupy the same locations on the cell surfaces that B_{12} uses to bind, thereby crowding out the true B_{12} molecules from their rightful receptor sites. By thus preventing the vitamin from performing its usual roles, analog molecules could theoretically create a functional deficiency of vitamin B_{12}. In this way, a substance containing substantial amounts of analogs won't help you meet your need for vitamin B_{12} – it could even make the situation worse. Scientific reports have indicated that substances such as spirulina and other types of algae are likely to have analogs present and are ineffective at meeting our needs for true B_{12}.

UNRELIABLE SOURCES OF VITAMIN B_{12}

The following should *not* be counted on as B_{12} sources:
- Fermented foods such as miso, tempeh, tamari, sauerkraut, umeboshi plums
- Seaweeds, spirulina, algae

B_{12} DESTROYERS

Vitamin C, in doses of 500 mg or more, taken within an hour of B_{12} sources, may destroy or decrease the availability of vitamin B_{12}. The anaesthetic nitrous oxide (laughing gas) can destroy vitamin B_{12} and should be avoided by those with borderline vitamin B_{12} status.

RELIABLE SOURCES OF VITAMIN B_{12}

To be certain of adequate intake, vegans are advised to regularly consume a vitamin B_{12} supplement or foods which are fortified with vitamin B_{12}. With fortified foods, look for the words "cobalamin" or "cyanocobalamin," referring to true B_{12}, on the ingredient list. To determine the amount of true B_{12} in a particular substance, a letter can be written to the technical department of the company producing the substance, requesting a laboratory report to verify the presence of cobalamin (vitamin B_{12}) and the absence of non–cobalamin corrinoids (vitamin B_{12} analogs).

Table 5.1 Vitamin B_{12} in Foods Used by Vegetarians

	Volume	Vitamin B_{12} Content (µg)	Daily Value*
Vegan foods			
Nutritional Yeast (Red Star T-6635+):**			
flakes	1 Tbsp	2.0	33%
Fortified textured soy protein	½ cup wet	1.0	16%
Kellogg's Nutri-Grain, Post Grape Nuts	½ cup	1.5	25%
Ralston Muesli	1 serving	2.0	33%
Ralston Graham Chex	1 serving	2.7	45%
Healthy Choice, Just Right Cereals	1 serving	6.0	100%
Eden Soy Extra Soy Beverage, Original	1 cup	3.0	50%
Fortified infant formula	(see product label)		
Lacto-ovo vegetarian foods			
Egg, cooked	1	0.4–0.6	
Milk, whole, 2% or skim	1 cup	0.9	
Yogurt	6 oz	0.2–1.2	
Cheese	1 oz	0.2	

*Food label readers, note that the daily value (DV) for vitamin B_{12} is 6 µg – three times the RDA for adults, which is 2 µg. As an example, 1.5 µg = 25% DV = 75% RDA.
**Newly marketed as Red Star Vegetarian Support Formula

One reliable (fortified) food source of vitamin B_{12} which is acceptable to vegans is a particular brand of nutritional yeast, Red Star T-6635+. During its production, this yeast is mixed with true vitamin B_{12} and then re-analyzed for cyanocobalamin content. Red Star T-6635+ nutritional yeast can be found in the bulk food section of many health food stores and is available in powder and flakes. Other brands of nutritional yeast may not be reliable B_{12} sources. To be certain of getting the correct brand, it may be necessary to ask the store manager or order it from The Mail Order Catalog, P.O. Box 180, Summertown, Tenn, 38483, phone (800) 695–2241, fax (615) 964–3518. This yeast can be sprinkled on salads, grains or casseroles, adding a cheese-like flavor. In the recipe section of this book, it is used in scrambled tofu, two sandwich fillings, Red Star tofu fingers, millet patties, gravy, gluten cutlets and savory roast. Limit your daily intake of nutritional yeast flakes to 3 Tbsp per day (for adults); in rare instances a greater intake than that may cause damage to kidneys over time.

True vitamin B_{12} (cyanocobalamin) is added to a variety of other fortified foods. The amounts of true vitamin B_{12} in some foods used by vegans and lacto-ovo vegetarians are listed in Table 5.1 Ensure optimal health for yourself and your family – especially at critical stages of growth – with these sources, other vitamin B_{12}-fortified foods or a vitamin B_{12} supplement.

IMPORTANCE OF A VARIED DIET

The second key to successful vegan eating is variety. There is a whole world of plant foods to explore; this can be the beginning of a food tour around the globe. People sometimes have the impression that meals without meat and dairy are going to be pretty monotonous events. Instead, vegans generally find that their food horizons expand tremendously, and they begin to use many plant foods with which they were previously unfamiliar. This is definitely the way to go. Ingenious alternatives to many dishes have been developed: delicious gravies without meat fat, creamy pies without dairy products and baked goods without eggs or milk (see recipes in Chapter 12). Learning how grains and legumes are prepared in other parts of the world can also serve as an introduction to new seasonings and cooking methods. Those who don't cook can explore restaurants and ethnic delis as well as the vegan options at health food restaurants.

Such variety offers *more* than flavor and interest. Each type of legume, grain, vegetable or nut has distinct nutritional advantages: soy has abundant protein, greens provide calcium, walnuts contain omega-3 fatty acids and so on. A varied diet helps us to balance our nutritional needs for more than 50 nutrients daily. New research offers amazing insight into benefits beyond vitamins and minerals, offered by the world of plants. As you see in Table 2.2 on page 25, "extranutritional" components in many plants have the potential for protecting people from cancer. Garlic has more than 70 active ingredients; some of these can lower blood pressure or play protective roles in relation to coronary artery disease. The substance which gives turmeric and curries their characteristic color also acts as an antioxidant. Beta carotene contributes a strong yellow pigment to the beautiful orange, red, green and yellow vegetables and fruits you see in every produce stand. In your body, this same beta carotene acts as a scavenger of free radicals.

In the most successful transitions to plant-based diets, highly nutritious ingredients replace items much lower in nutritional value. For example, tahini can replace fat or oil in salad dressing or as a spread. Whole wheat flour, dried fruits and blackstrap molasses can take the place of highly refined flour and sweeteners in muffins and other baking. Some foods not commonly thought of as nutrient contributors, such as herbal teas, can provide small amounts of zinc and iron. The amounts in a cup may seem small, but over the course of a day, they certainly prove more nutritious than soda pop!

New vegan convenience foods are available through supermarkets, from the freezer section to the bulk food bins. You'll find, after an initial orientation period, the new way of eating becomes just as easy as the old.

DIFFERENT STAGES, DIFFERENT NEEDS

For many fat-conscious or overweight Americans, a plant-based diet, high in raw foods and fiber can be a direct route to better health. For children, vegetarian diets should emphasize some plant foods that are higher in fat and calories and lower in fiber. At the end of Chapter 2 we covered some of the difficulties that have arisen in vegan communities when children were given diets that are too low in calories, protein, zinc, vitamin B_{12} and other nutrients. Chapter 9 outlines the specific foods that should be emphasized during the growing years.

Nutrition is currently a field drawing enormous interest. Health-promoting diets have flooded the market. With a natural inclination to find the best, we may experiment with eating patterns from far and near. Some turn out to be adequate while others may lead to nutritional difficulties. For example, some overly restrictive patterns limit intakes of beans, fruit, processed foods such as tofu and fortified foods in the diets of children. This can limit growth and intake of necessary nutrients. It is important that vegan diets not be overly restrictive, especially for children. Instead, use the vegetarian food guide (pages 137 to 139) and the guidelines in Chapter 9 as a foundation. These guidelines have a sound scientific basis and will ensure intake of necessary nutrients at all ages and support optimal growth in children. People who wish to explore dietary alternatives can use the food guide as a basis upon which to add other ideas about eating practices and combinations.

FORTIFIED FOODS

Legislation regarding the fortification of foods was developed in order to reduce the incidence of specific deficiency diseases occurring in the general population. Food fortification has proven to be an effective means of preventing these deficiencies. Specific foods, such as cow's milk and table salt, were chosen to be the means by which a particular nutrient reached a target population because they are widely consumed. Policies were designed on the basis of food consumption patterns of the majority of the U.S. population. They were not tailored to suit the needs of those adopting alternative diets. An awareness of fortification policies can be helpful to those who are not using these foods. For example, vitamin D, when added to milk, has prevented rickets in a great many children. Vegans themselves must take the responsibility of ensuring that they and their children receive adequate sunlight or use fortified foods or supplements. Iodine deficiency is regarded as the greatest single cause of preventable brain damage and mental retardation in the world. In the United States this deficiency has been eliminated due to the fortification of table salt with iodine; for the little salt you use, choose iodized brands. About ⅓ tsp of iodized salt will meet your daily iodine requirement. Iodized sea salt is also available in many health food stores. Fortunately due to increases in food fortification throughout the world, iodine deficiency (along with the goiter and cretinism that go with it), will be virtually eliminated by the year 2000!

Other fortified foods which vegetarians may find useful are infant formulas, such as soy formula which is fortified with vitamins B_{12} and D, calcium and many other nutrients. These could even be used in food preparation for children and adults. For vegans, calcium-fortified beverages and foods fortified with vitamin B_{12} can be of great value.

Just because a diet is vegan doesn't mean that it will be restrictive. Food manufacturers interested in keeping ahead of the consumer interest in health are making it easier to be vegan than ever before in history.

HEALTH ADVANTAGES OF VEGAN DIETS

There is room for many options within the framework of vegan eating: high-energy, gourmet, low-fat and heart-healthy. Overall, studies comparing the caloric distribution of protein, carbohydrate and fat of vegans with those of omnivores show vegan patterns to be much closer to national recommendations. It is clear that there are many health advantages to be gained by following a vegan or near-vegan diet in the prevention of chronic disease. All nutrient needs can be met. Well-designed vegan diets offer the possibility of excellent health, and in fact can be nutritionally superior.

FATS AND OILS:
A BALANCING ACT

During the past couple of decades, fat has received some unflattering press from both the popular media and the scientific world. Consumers have been made painfully aware that an excessive consumption of fat can contribute to coronary artery disease, and research suggests that it may play a significant role in the development of other chronic diseases such as cancer and diabetes. Many of the benefits of a vegetarian diet have been attributed to the fact that it is generally lower in fat than an omnivorous diet. Although this emphasis on reducing total fat in the diet is well-justified, it is only one part of the equation. The connection between dietary fat and health goes far beyond the issue of quantity. One must also consider the source of fat, the degree to which it has been processed and the delicate balance between two fatty acids that are essential to human life. These are matters of *quality*, and experts are now recognizing that the quality of the fat we consume also has tremendous impact on health and disease. Achieving an optimal intake of fats and oils requires much more than taking meat off your menu; it means making well-informed choices that support human health – indeed a fine balancing act.

BACK TO BASICS: THE STRUCTURE OF FAT

Fats and oils are known as lipids in the scientific world, although we often refer to them simply as fats. The major distinguishing feature between fats and oils is that at room temperature fats are solid, while oils are liquid. Fats are generally found in animal foods such as meat, poultry and dairy products, while oils are commonly derived from plant seeds like olive, rape seed, corn and sunflower.

Fats and oils are made up of basic units called fatty acids. Fatty acids do not generally roam free in the body; most of them travel in threesomes as a part of larger molecules called triglycerides. Most of the fatty acids that we need for survival can be produced in the body, but there are two that we cannot make and must obtain from food: the essential fatty acids.

Fatty Acid Categories

Fatty acids are classified as being saturated, monounsaturated and polyunsaturated. Fats and oils are made up of a mixture of fatty acids from each of these three categories, although we often think of different fats and oils as being purely one type of fatty acid. For example, corn oil, which contains about 62 percent polyunsaturates, 25 percent monounsaturates and 13 percent saturates, is referred to as a polyunsaturated oil. The breakdown of these fatty acids in a variety of fats and oils is shown in Figure 6.1.

SATURATED FATTY ACIDS

Fatty acid molecules are made up of chains of carbon atoms with hydrogen and oxygen atoms attached. When a fatty acid molecule is completely packed or "saturated" with hydrogen atoms along its carbon chains, it is called a saturated fat. Foods rich in saturated fats are generally solid at room temperature. The main sources of saturated fat are:

- animal fat (from beef, pork, lamb, other meats and poultry);
- dairy fat (milk, butter, cheese, cream and other dairy products);
- tropical "oils" (thick oils such as coconut, palm and palm kernel);
- cocoa butter;
- hydrogenated fats (such as shortening and hard margarines).

Although these foods are high in saturated fat, they also contain monounsaturated and polyunsaturated fats. Saturated fats are often considered "bad" because they are the biggest dietary contributor to high blood cholesterol levels. Their effects on health are at least in part dependent upon the length of their carbon chains; some have far greater cholesterol-raising potential than others.

MONOUNSATURATED FATTY ACIDS

When a fatty acid molecule has a single point that is not saturated with hydrogen atoms, it is called a monounsaturated fatty acid. Foods rich in monounsaturated fats are generally liquid at room temperature and semi-solid when refrigerated, as with olive oil. The principle dietary sources of monounsaturated fatty acids (greater than 60% of the fat is monounsaturated) are:

Figure 6.1 Comparison of Dietary Fats

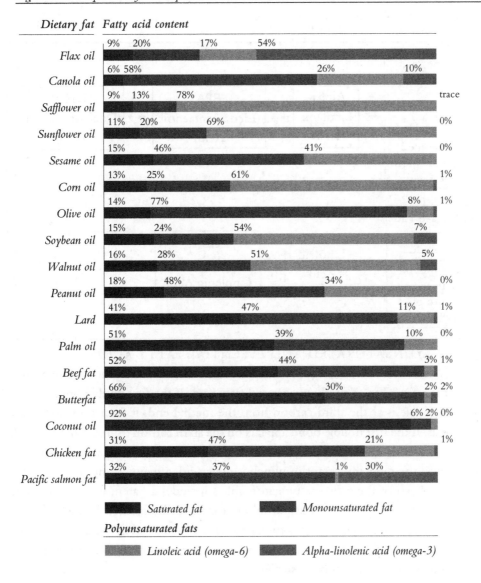

Dietary fat	Fatty acid content
Flax oil	9% 20% 17% 54%
Canola oil	6% 58% 26% 10%
Safflower oil	9% 13% 78% trace
Sunflower oil	11% 20% 69% 0%
Sesame oil	15% 46% 41% 0%
Corn oil	13% 25% 61% 1%
Olive oil	14% 77% 8% 1%
Soybean oil	15% 24% 54% 7%
Walnut oil	16% 28% 51% 5%
Peanut oil	18% 48% 34% 0%
Lard	41% 47% 11% 1%
Palm oil	51% 39% 10% 0%
Beef fat	52% 44% 3% 1%
Butterfat	66% 30% 2% 2%
Coconut oil	92% 6% 2% 0%
Chicken fat	31% 47% 21% 1%
Pacific salmon fat	32% 37% 1% 30%

■ Saturated fat   ■ Monounsaturated fat

Polyunsaturated fats

■ Linoleic acid (omega-6)   ■ Alpha-linolenic acid (omega-3)

- olive oil, canola oil and hazelnut oil;
- avocados and olives;
- hazelnuts, pistachios, almonds, macadamia nuts and pecans.

Up until the mid-1980s it was believed that monounsaturated fats had a neutral effect on blood cholesterol levels. It is now known that replacing saturated fats with monounsaturated fats can be as effective, and perhaps more effective, in lowering LDL cholesterol levels than replacing them with polyunsaturates.

Figure 6.2 Essential Fatty Acid Families

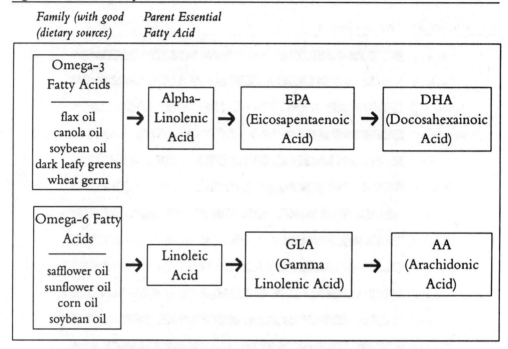

Family (with good (dietary sources)	Parent Essential Fatty Acid		
Omega-3 Fatty Acids flax oil canola oil soybean oil dark leafy greens wheat germ	Alpha-Linolenic Acid	EPA (Eicosapentaenoic Acid)	DHA (Docosahexainoic Acid)
Omega-6 Fatty Acids safflower oil sunflower oil corn oil soybean oil	Linoleic Acid	GLA (Gamma Linolenic Acid)	AA (Arachidonic Acid)

POLYUNSATURATED AND ESSENTIAL FATTY ACIDS

When a fatty acid has two or more double bonds between the carbon atoms, it is referred to as a polyunsaturated fatty acid. If the first double bond on the molecule is at the third carbon from the methyl end, it is an **omega-3 fatty acid**. If the first double bond appears on the sixth carbon from the methyl end, it is an **omega-6 fatty acid**. (Most monounsaturated fats are omega-9 fatty acids, the most important of which is oleic acid, a major component of olive oil.) Each of these two fatty acid families includes a parent *essential fatty acid* (the kind we must have but our bodies cannot manufacture). In the omega-3 family, alpha-linolenic acid is the essential fatty acid, and in the omega-6 family, linoleic acid is the essential fatty acid. We must receive food sources of these two essential fatty acids for survival.

In addition, there are longer chain fatty acids (fatty acids with more carbons in their chain) which can be made in our body tissues by the action of enzymes or obtained directly from food. In the omega-3 family, eicosapentanoic acid (EPA) and docosahexaenoic acid (DHA) are made from alpha-linolenic acid (both are found in fish, fish oils and other seafoods). In the omega-6 family, gamma-linolenic acid (GLA) and arachidonic acid (AA) are made from linoleic acid (GLA is found in primrose, borage, and black currant oils; AA is found in animal fats).

Polyunsaturated fats tend to be liquid at room temperature. The principal dietary sources of omega-3 and omega-6 polyunsaturated fats are as follows:

Sources of Omega-3 Fatty Acids:
- flax, canola and soybean oils
- flaxseed and walnuts
- fish and seafood
- soybeans and tofu
- dark green leafy vegetables
- wheat germ

Sources of Omega-6 Fatty Acids:
- safflower, sunflower, corn, soybean and walnut oils
- sunflower, sesame, poppy, pumpkin seeds and walnuts
- wheat germ
- many other plant and animal foods in varying concentrations.

Polyunsaturated fats have received both praise and criticism regarding their effects on health and disease. On the one hand, omega-6 fatty acids lower blood cholesterol levels and omega-3 fatty acids lower triglyceride levels and blood pressure. On the other hand, polyunsaturated fatty acids can go rancid very quickly, sometimes resulting in the formation of harmful chemicals that can contribute to disease processes. We can help to ensure that the maximum health benefits of these valuable fatty acids are realized by consuming appropriate amounts and storing them with care.

Cholesterol and other Sterols

Sterols are another group of lipids that are very important to human health. There are over 30 sterols found in nature, the most widely recognized being cholesterol. This sterol is an essential part of our cells. Since our bodies produce about 800 mg per day, we do not need dietary sources of cholesterol. Too much dietary cholesterol can cause an increase in our blood cholesterol levels, thus increasing our risk for coronary artery disease.

Health experts recommend an intake of not more than 300 mg of total dietary cholesterol per day for the general population (over 2 years of age) and even less for those on cholesterol-reducing diets. Cholesterol is found only in animal foods, so the next time you see "no cholesterol" on the label of vegetable oil or peanut butter, realize it's no big deal. The most concentrated sources of cholesterol are organ meats and eggs; one egg has over 200 mg of cholesterol. Contrary to what many people believe, there is little difference in the cholesterol content of meat, poultry or fish. A food does not have to be high in saturated fat to be high in cholesterol, as cholesterol is stored primarily in lean tissue.

Plants also contain sterols, such as beta-sitosterols which have been shown to inhibit cholesterol absorption, potentially offering some degree of protection against coronary artery disease.

THE FUNCTIONS OF FATS AND OILS

In our concerns about the undesirable health consequences of an *excessive* consumption of fats and oils, we have lost sight of the fact that fats perform vital functions in our bodies. Both essential and non-essential fats play important roles in promoting health.

THE ROLE OF NON-ESSENTIAL FATS

Fats are our most concentrated sources of energy, providing nine calories per gram, as compared to four calories per gram for either protein or carbohydrate. They serve as our main energy stores, supply insulation for the body, protect our vital organs and provide physical "padding." Fats also aid in the absorption and transportation of fat-soluble vitamins, including vitamins A, D, E and K.

THE ROLE OF ESSENTIAL FATTY ACIDS

Essential fatty acids are critical to the formation and function of healthy cell membranes and the proper development of eye and brain tissue. They are also involved in energy production and in the metabolism of cholesterol and triglycerides. Essential fatty acids from both the omega-3 and omega-6 families are metabolized to produce hormone-like substances called eicosanoids. These substances help to regulate numerous vital body functions such as blood clotting, blood pressure, immune response and reactions to injury. Eicosanoids formed from omega-3 fatty acids tend to lower blood clotting, blood pressure and inflammatory responses in our bodies. Eicosanoids formed from omega-6 fatty acids play a role in response to shock or injury and can have the opposite effect of those from the omega-3 family on blood clotting, blood pressure and inflammatory responses. These two families compete against one another, and optimal functioning of all body systems is dependent on the balance of eicosanoids from both families.

Essential Fatty Acid Balance

Historical sources suggest that humans evolved on a diet containing a much higher proportion of omega-3 to omega-6 fatty acids than the average diet of today. In the past, we obtained abundant omega-3 fatty acids from wild plants and from the fish and game which consumed these plants. Today modern refining and hydrogenation have extended the shelf life of fats and oil, but in the process, omega-3 fatty acids have been reduced and damaged. Foods rich in omega-3 fatty acids are highly perishable and therefore have been rejected for use as ingredients in most commercial foods. In addition, people consume far greater quantities of foods rich in omega-6 fatty acids; consider the fried foods, commercial baked goods, convenience foods, high-fat snacks, margarines, shortenings and vegetable oils that are all a common feature in the American diet.

The reduction of omega-3 fatty acids in the diet is now being recognized as a factor that can have a negative impact on health. Indeed, high levels of certain omega-6 fatty acids relative to omega-3 fatty acids may increase our risk for immune and inflammatory disorders (arthritis, lupus and atopic dermatitis), coronary artery disease, asthma and headaches. Although it is too early to make specific recommendations regarding the role of essential fatty acids in the prevention and treatment of such diseases, many developed countries have set standards for a minimal intake of both omega-6 (linoleic acid) and omega-3 (alpha-linolenic acid) fatty acids. Recommended Dietary Allowances (RDAs) have not yet been established for essential fatty acids, however the 1989 edition of the RDAs acknowledges that this possibility should be considered in the near future.

Nutrition experts use the ratio of omega-6s to omega-3s (omega-6: omega-3) to assess the balance between essential fatty acids in the diet. Research scientists and national governments from around the world recommend ratios varying from 1:1 to 10:1, although opinions differ considerably as to the level that is more effective in promoting health and preventing disease. Many leading experts are currently suggesting a ratio of 2:1 to 4:1 as being optimal.

Although this may all seem quite confusing, achieving a healthy balance of omega-3 and omega-6 fatty acids in a vegetarian diet is really not so difficult. Simply select foods that are rich in omega-3 fatty acids (flax oil, flaxseeds, canola oil, walnuts, soybeans, soy oil, tofu, leafy plants and wheat germ) on a daily basis. Use oils that are rich in omega-6 fatty acids less often (safflower, sunflower and corn oils).

Are Plant Sources of Omega-3 Fatty Acids Sufficient for Human Needs?

Vegetarians and vegans have no direct sources of the longer chain omega-3 fatty acids (EPA and DHA) in the diet, thus must convert the parent fatty acid (alpha-linolenic acid) to EPA and DHA in the body. There has been some debate as to whether this conversion takes place adequately to meet human needs. Scientific studies show that although the conversion is slow, it is sufficient to meet the needs of most people. Having a favorable balance of omega 6:omega 3 fatty acids assists the conversion process. It is important to note, however, that certain factors can adversely effect a person's ability to carry out this important conversion process: high intakes of saturated fat, trans-fatty acids, cholesterol and alcohol, in addition to inadequate intakes of energy and protein or a deficiency of certain nutrients (e.g., zinc or copper). There may also be conversion problems for people with diabetes or other metabolic disorders and for those who inherit a limited ability to produce conversion enzymes (possibly where fish has been a major component of the diet for centuries). In addition, infants have less capacity to convert essential fatty acids. It is therefore recommended that they get 1% of energy as alpha-linolenic acid when it is the only source of omega-3s. Breast-fed infants receive ample DHA and EPA from their mother's milk.

Considering the potential for insufficient fatty acid conversion and the possible health benefits of reducing the ratio of omega-6 to omega-3 fatty acids in the diet, it would seem prudent to achieve a minimum intake of alpha-linolenic acid of 1 percent of calories (2–2½ grams per day) in diets which do not contain fish.

Unsaturated Fats and Free Radical Reactions

Free radicals are unstable molecules which are highly reactive. When they react with other molecules, new free radicals are often formed, producing chain reactions. The oxidation of fats is one such chain reaction. A single free radical can trigger a reaction altering literally hundreds of fatty acid molecules.

When this happens in the body, it can cause irreparable damage to cell membranes and genetic material. Fatty acid molecules can also decompose to yield a range of products which are highly toxic to body tissues. This kind of reaction can also occur in foods, particularly those foods that are rich in polyunsaturated fats. Air, light or heat can initiate oxidation in such foods causing deterioration and rancidity.

There has been tremendous interest in the impact of free radicals on health and during recent years. Free radicals have been associated with over 50 diseases. In some cases, free radicals play a role in the cause of disease, while in others they are simply products of the disease.

In cardiovascular disease, oxidation of fats can damage blood vessels and contribute to the accumulation of plaque along their walls. Oxidation products have also been implicated in both the initiation and promotion of some cancerous tumors. In rheumatoid arthritis, the end products of fat oxidation increase as the disease gets worse. Although there are still many questions regarding the role of free radicals in disease states, we can expect some important answers from research that is presently under way.

PROTECTION FROM FREE RADICALS

If the oxidation of fats were to go on with nothing to stop it, it would eventually destroy our body cells completely. Fortunately, many foods contain substances called antioxidants that can protect us from the ravages of fat oxidation. Some antioxidants can stabilize free radicals. Other antioxidants serve to prevent the chain reaction by tying up chemicals that increase the rate of oxidation. Plant foods contain antioxidants such as beta-carotene, vitamins C and E and selenium, along with their polyunsaturated fats. When oils are extracted from these foods, as in the case of commercial oil refining, these natural antioxidants are greatly reduced. Food manufacturers generally add synthetic antioxidants to help prevent rancidity and increase the shelf life of these foods.

There has been considerable discussion on the role of antioxidants in reducing free radical reactions in our bodies. Some experts advise supplemental antioxidants, particularly for individuals who are at high risk for disease such as smokers, people living in polluted areas and those with a high family incidence of cancer or coronary artery disease. Others feel that we need to learn more about the usefulness of such supplements before making any recommendations.

The one thing they all seem to agree on is that it is important to eat foods that are naturally rich sources of antioxidants such as fruits, vegetables and whole grains every day.

Some scientists suggest that we limit our intake of polyunsaturated fats to not more than 10 percent of total calories in order to reduce our exposure to the products of fat oxidation. Although there is currently little solid evidence to either support or contradict this recommendation, there are few benefits to consuming a greater percentage. By the same token, we need some polyunsaturated fats in our diets to ensure that we get enough essential fatty acids.

THE PROCESSING OF FATS AND OILS

Virtually all of the concentrated fats and oils that we consume are processed in some way. The first step is the extraction of oils from the whole food, such as corn, olives or sunflower seeds. Further refining helps to rid the oil of offensive odors, toxins and organisms, and to ensure a safe and acceptable product. As well, fats and oils are processed to alter their taste, texture and shelf life.

Some of the techniques employed in the processing result in changes that could have undesirable consequences for health.

Commercial Oil Production

Prior to World War I, the extraction of fresh oil from various foods was a cottage industry. Fresh pressed oils were delivered to the door each week and used shortly after delivery. Seeds were pressed without the use of heat, chemicals or deodorization. This way of processing oil did little damage to valuable omega-3 fatty acids and to protective natural antioxidants such as vitamin E.

After World War I, new methods of processing oils were developed which greatly increased their shelf life, and many of these techniques are still in use today. The first step is extraction, where oils are removed from seeds by mechanically pressing them or by mixing heated, dehulled and chopped or ground seeds with a solvent such as hexane. When solvent extraction is used, the solvent is later evaporated off the oil at temperatures of about 300°F. The primary objective in this first step is to produce a clean, crude oil product. In some cases the oil is filtered after mechanical pressing and sold as unrefined oil.

More often, the oil undergoes further refining. Degumming removes a variety of substances including phospholipids such as lecithin and minerals such as calcium and magnesium. An alkaline refining treatment removes free fatty acids that can cause rancidity and decreases the quality of the oil. Refining also helps to remove toxic substances that are naturally present in many plants. Phospholipids and minerals are further reduced during this procedure. Often, oils have a strong yellow or reddish hue that is considered undesirable, so it's bleached out. In the bleaching process, oils are heated to temperatures of about 175° to 225° C and mixed with a substance that will absorb unwanted pigments. During this phase, some of the polyunsaturated fatty acids may undergo oxidation.

The final process, deodorization, removes undesirable odors and tastes from the oil. Deodorization also reduces the content of many other substances including pesticide residues, toxins and products of oxidation formed during the bleaching phase. It also decreases fat-soluble vitamins such as vitamin E and beta carotene (vitamin A). In the deodorization, oils are heated to 425°F to 500°F C for an hour or more. These high temperatures can result in some structural changes in the fatty acid molecules, and small amounts of trans-fatty acids are produced. (See explanation of trans-fatty acids on page 112.)

These processing methods produce tasteless, odorless, clear and stable oils that can sit on supermarket shelves for long periods of time without going rancid. On the down side, some of the substances that make oils valuable to us, including essential fatty acids and vitamin E, are damaged or diminished in the process.

WHAT ABOUT "COLD PRESSED" OILS?

The term "cold pressed" is used to describe oils that have been mechanically pressed slowly so that temperatures do not rise above 140°F. In order to avoid damaging the essential fats or reducing other valuable constituents, it is important that the oil is also unrefined. These oils should be made from organic seeds (non-organic seeds contain higher levels of pesticide residues which are partially removed from refined oils during deodorization) and stored in opaque bottles to protect them from light. Unfortunately, the use of the term "cold-pressed" is not regulated, and some oils labeled as such have undergone further refining such as bleaching and/or deodorization which can damage unstable essential fatty acids. Producers of oils that are truly "cold pressed" often provide on their label a description of the process used and the temperature reached during that process. These oils are more intense in taste and color than the refined oils. Recent research has demonstrated that these unrefined, cold pressed oils contain 25–50 percent more vitamin E than refined oils, 45 percent more beta-sitosterols and a significantly lower level of trans-fatty acids.

There are several truly "cold pressed" or mechanically pressed, unrefined oils on the market today which are available in natural food stores. Most of these oils are highly perishable and should be kept in the refrigerator or freezer. The exceptions are virgin and extra-virgin olive oil. The oil extracted from the first pressing of olives is called extra-virgin. This oil has a full flavor and aroma and contains most of the beneficial substances that are naturally present in the olives. Virgin olive oil can come from the first or second pressing and is of somewhat lower quality. Because these olive oils are made up mainly of the more stable monounsaturated fatty acids, they can be safely kept at room temperature for several months and are therefore widely available on supermarket shelves. Pure or "light" olive oil comes from the second pressing; since it is higher in solid particles, it must undergo further refining, which lowers its quality.

For many oils, the refining process is just the first stage of their transformation. A sizable proportion of these oils will go on to become hydrogenated or partially hydrogenated.

Hydrogenation of Oils

Hydrogenation is a commercial process that converts liquid oils into hard fats by the addition of hydrogen. Oils can be hydrogenated to varying degrees depending on the hardness desired. The most common examples of hydrogenated fats include shortenings, margarines and partially hydrogenated vegetable fats used for frying and in processed foods.

Hydrogenation is looked upon favorably by food producers as it improves the spreadability, shelf life and "mouth feel" of fat. It also increases its melting point, allowing for high-temperature cooking and frying. However, hydrogenation is regarded less favorably by health experts because it results in the conversion of a portion of the unsaturated fat molecules to trans-fatty acids and a lesser portion of unsaturated fats to saturated fatty acids.

TRANS-FATTY ACIDS

A trans-fatty acid molecule has the same chemical formula as a "normal" fatty acid molecule, but its hydrogen atoms are in a different spatial arrangement. One of the results of the hydrogenation of mono- and polyunsaturated fats is the creation of trans-fatty acids. The high temperatures used in the deodorization phase of the refining of unhydrogenated oils also converts a limited amount of fatty acids (about 2 percent) to the trans form. When an unsaturated fat molecule is changed to a trans form, its melting point increases and it becomes solid at room temperature. Thus, it offers the same benefits for food production as saturated fats, but is cheaper and quicker than converting unsaturated fats to saturates.

A fatty acid molecule with a trans configuration is still technically an "unsaturated fat." However, it behaves quite differently both in foods and in our bodies. Essential fatty acids with a trans configuration can no longer perform the critical functions of these nutrients in our bodies. In addition, these essential fatty acid "impostors" can interfere with the formation of long chain omega-6 and omega-3 fatty acids and increase the body's need for "genuine" essential fatty acids. Trans-fatty acids also increase LDL (bad cholesterol) and decrease HDL (good cholesterol), thereby increasing the risk of coronary artery disease.

The chemical structure of trans-fatty acids makes them a bit of a nightmare when it comes to food labeling. There seems to be little consensus between countries on how to deal with trans-fatty acids on labels. In the United States, trans-fatty acids are lumped together with monounsaturated fats. Although the bulk of trans-fatty acids are monounsaturated, there is no distinction made on food labels between those that are generally health-supporting (cis form) and those that are potentially very damaging (trans form). Since monounsaturated fats are looked upon very favorably, the consumer might naturally assume that a product rich in monounsaturated fats is a healthy choice, while in fact it could be loaded with damaging trans-fatty acids. It would be far better if trans-fatty acids were listed separately on food labels.

FATS AND OILS IN A HEALTHY VEGETARIAN DIET

Turning toward the practical aspects of the fats in our diets, there are two principle considerations:

1. What *quantity* of fat will best support health?
2. How can we be sure to get top *quality* fats in our diets?

The Question of Quantity

We have been told that we need to cut back on fat, but even the experts have difficulty agreeing just how much. The World Health Organization (WHO) suggests that adults receive between 15 and 30 percent of their calories as fat. They add, however, that the 30 percent upper limit is an interim recommendation meant to accommodate nations with high-fat intakes, and that further benefits would be expected by reducing fat towards 15 percent of total energy. An upper limit for cholesterol of 300 mg/day is also suggested.

When determining what a healthy level of fat intake would be for you, there are a couple of points to consider. First, what is the quality of fat in your diet, and second, what is your state of health? If you are in good health, and most of the fat in your diet comes from whole plant foods and fresh pressed oil (including good sources of omega-3s), you likely can maintain excellent health on a diet that is higher in fat than someone who emphasizes high-fat animal foods and heavily processed foods laden with hydrogenated oils. If you are selecting foods with high-quality fats, the standard recommendation of not more than 30 percent of calories from fat would seem reasonable. In contrast, if you are consuming a diet rich in saturated fats, trans-fatty acids and cholesterol, you would be well advised to aim for the lower end of the WHO recommendation – approximately 15–20 percent of calories from fat. Similarly, if you have high blood cholesterol or are at risk for coronary artery disease, maximum benefits appear to occur at or even slightly below the 15 percent fat level.

There are also specific times during the life cycle when our needs for total fat and specific essential fatty acids increase. During infancy, a greater proportion of calories should come from fat (as is found in breast milk). It is also important for the pregnant and lactating mother to ensure that her diet contains sufficient essential fatty acids. Many experts suggest that children receive a slightly greater proportion of fat than adults, and a range of 25–35 percent of calories is generally considered appropriate.

FAT IN THE NORTH AMERICAN FOOD SUPPLY

It is most revealing to take a look at sources of fat in the American food supply. The average person does not get much fat from vegetables, fruits, grains and legumes. In fact, all of these foods combined provide less than 5 percent of the total fat in the North American food supply. About 50 percent of the fat in our foods comes from meat, fish, poultry, dairy products and eggs, and over 40 percent comes from fats and oils.

The greatest concentration of fat is found in pure fat foods including vegetable oils, butter, margarine, shortening and lard. These foods are *"visible fats,"* or fats that we can see. One hundred percent of their calories come from fat, and they provide about four to five grams of fat per teaspoon. Many foods contain *"hidden fats,"* or fats that we don't see. Over 90 percent of the calories in salad dressings, cream cheese and heavy cream come from fat. Foods providing over 75 percent of calories from fat include high-fat meats (such as bologna, liverwurst, bacon, wieners, salami and sausage), nuts, seeds and their butters, avocados, olives and regular cheeses. Other foods high in hidden fats include regular meat, full-fat dairy products, deep-fried foods, snack foods (such as chips and buttered or microwave popcorn), crackers, chocolate bars and rich baked goods. These all get about 50–60 percent of their calories from fat.

Don't be deceived by a low percent of fat declaration on a food label. This tells you only how much fat there is as a percent of *weight*, not as a percent of calories. For example, whole milk is 96.5 percent fat-free and only 3.5 percent fat by weight (indicated as 3.5% M. F. or Milk Fat). However, about *50 percent of the calories* in whole milk come from fat, because most of milk's weight is water which is calorie-free.

HOW MUCH FAT IS BEST?

One way of controlling your fat intake is to estimate the maximum amount of fat you should get per day and select foods that provide no more than that amount. The first step is to estimate your energy (calorie) requirements. Table 6.1 lists estimated energy needs according to sex, age and activity level. Simply multiply your ideal weight in pounds by the calories per pound (cal/lb) for your age, sex and activity level as indicated in Table 6.1. For example, if you are a 28-year-old, moderately active female, with an ideal weight of 128 lbs, your energy needs would be roughly 2176 calories (128 x 17 = 2176).

Table 6.1 Estimating your caloric requirements per pound body weight

Activity Level	Female 19–24	Male 19–24	Female 25–49	Male 25–49	Female 50–74	Male 50–74	Female 75+	Male 75+
Light	16.5	18	16.5	17.5	15.5	16	15	15.5
Moderate	17.5	20.5	17.5	20	16.5	18	17	16
Heavy	19	24	19	24	18	22	18	20

The second step is to estimate the amount of fat, in grams, to include in your diet. Table 6.2 provides this information based on your energy needs and the percent of fat you desire in your diet.

Table 6.2 Maximum Fat Per Day (in Grams)

Caloric Intake	10%	15%	20%	25%	30%
	Desired Percentage of Fat				
1400–1600	16–18	23–27	31–36	37–45	47–54
1600–1800	18–20	27–30	36–40	45–50	54–60
1800–2000	20–22	30–33	40–44	50–55	60–66
2000–2200	22–25	33–37	44–50	55–62	66–75
2200–2400	25–27	37–40	50–54	62–67	75–81
2400–2600	27–29	40–43	54–58	67–72	81–87
2600–2800	29–31	43–47	58–62	72–78	87–93

Finally, you'll need to keep tabs on how much fat you are actually eating. This does not have to be a daunting task, but something you do occasionally to estimate the level of fat in your diet and to familiarize yourself with the fat content of various foods. Table 6.4 provides a short list of foods and the amount of fat, in grams, that these foods contain per serving. More precise information can be found on food labels and in nutrient composition books. Remember that the figures given are based on the serving size listed and will need to be adjusted when you eat larger or smaller portions.

FAT IN THE VEGETARIAN DIET

Vegetarians tend to consume less fat, on average, than do omnivores. However, being vegetarian does not necessarily mean you will have a low-fat diet. Table 6.3 compares the fat content of the menus from Chapter 3. The fat content of the omnivore and the first lacto-ovo vegetarian menus are similar. Vegetarian diets that are lower in eggs, high-fat dairy products and high-fat processed foods more easily meet the current recommendations for total fat and essential fatty acids. Well-planned vegan diets generally provide a healthy quantity of fats.

Table 6.3 Fat Content in Various Menus

Diet Pattern	omega-6:omega-3 ratio	percent calories from fat	Cholesterol (mg)
Omnivore Menu No. 1	9:1	33%	374
Lacto-ovo Vegetarian Menu No. 2	11:1	34%	481
Lacto-ovo Vegetarian Menu No. 3	6:1	28%	55
Vegan Menu No. 4	5:11	18%	0
Recommended levels	1:1–10:1	30 or less (15–30% WHO)	300 mg/day or less

Table 6.4 Fat in Food

Food/(Serving Size)	Fat grams/ serving	Fat as percent Calories
Fats and Oils		
All (1 tsp)	4–5	100
Fruits and Vegetables		
All, except those below (½ cup or 1 med.)	trace	0–12
Avocado (⅙) or olives (10)	5	75–90
Legumes		
All, except those below (½ cup)	trace	1–6
Peanuts, dry roasted (1 oz)	14	76
Soybeans, cooked, or tofu, medium (½ cup)	6	45–56
Garbanzos, cooked (½ cup)	2	14
Grains		
Wheat, rice, millet, barley, cooked (½ cup)	trace	3–7
Oatmeal, quinoa (¾ cup)	2	15–16
Bread, whole grain (1 slice), or pasta (1 cup)	1–2	3–12
Crackers, snack type (e.g., Ritz) (4 crackers)	4	51
Crackers, rye crisp type (e.g., Zwieback) (2 pieces)	1	15
Nuts and Seeds		
All, except those below (1 oz)	13–19	73–88
Chestnuts, roasted (¼ cup)	½	7
Nut or seed butter (1 Tbsp)	8–10	78–85
Dairy Products		
Milk, whole, 3.5% M.F. (1 cup)	8	48
Milk, 2% (1 cup)	5	35
Milk, skim (1 cup)	trace	4
Cheese, 33% M. F. (1 oz)	9	74
Cheese, 15% M. F. (1 oz)	4.5	54
Ice cream, 10% M. F. (½ cup)	14	48
Meat, Chicken, Fish and Eggs		
Lean beef and pork (3½ oz)	7–12	30–45
Regular beef and pork (3½ oz)	16–30	50–73
Poultry, white meat, no skin (3½ oz)	4.5	23
Poultry, light and dark with skin (3½ oz)	14	51
Fish, low-fat varieties (3½ oz)	½	6–9
Fish, high-fat varieties (3½ oz)	8–10	40–62
Egg (1 large)	5½	64
Sweet and Salty Snack Foods		
Potato chips (1 oz), or microwave popcorn (3 cups)	10–12	54–61
Fruit pie (⅙th of pie)	11	39
Cake, chocolate, iced (¹⁄₁₂th of cake)	10	42
Chocolate bar, plain (1 oz)	8	56
Granola bar, plain commercial type (1 bar)	4	35
Cookies, oatmeal, commercial type (2 cookies)	5	32

TRIMMING THE HIGH-FAT VEGETARIAN DIET

If your diet is too high in fat, you may need to make an effort to bring it down to a healthier level. Take a good look at where the fat in your diet is coming from, then develop a plan to reduce this fat. Remember that our food supply includes both visible fats and hidden fats. First, focus on cutting back on the visible fats, then go to work on the foods containing hidden fats.

To Cut Back on Visible Fats
- Use less margarine or butter on your foods.
- Pass up the fried foods and opt for baked, steamed or broiled.
- Cut down the amount of fat used in your recipes.
- Replace concentrated fats with low-fat alternatives (for example, use low-fat soy or dairy yogurt in place of mayonnaise).
- Flavor foods with salsa, fresh lemon juice, wine, broth, flavored vinegars and a variety of herbs and spices instead of fat.

To Reduce Hidden Fats
- Switch from high-fat dairy products to low-fat alternatives or low-fat plant-based options (for example, instead of ice cream try fruit sherbet, rice-based frozen dessert or low-fat frozen yogurt).
- If you use eggs, do so in moderation.
- Reduce your consumption of high-fat commercial foods or replace them with low-fat options (for example, replace high-fat snack crackers with rye crisps). Many snack foods, cookies, crackers, granolas, granola bars and baked goods derive well over 40 percent of their calories from fat.
- Be conscious of how many nuts and seeds you are using. Although these are a valuable part of your diet, they are high in fat and should not be used in excess.

When you reduce the amount of fat in your diet, it doesn't mean that you have to reduce the amount of food that you are eating. Indeed, if your weight is not a problem you may need to increase the volume of food you are taking in to help compensate for the loss of the concentrated calories found in fat.

CAN A VEGETARIAN DIET BE TOO LOW IN FAT?

From the menus provided in Chapter 3, it seems as though vegans and the vegetarians who limit high-fat dairy foods and eggs do very well in terms of the quantity of both total fats and specific fatty acids in their diet. What about the vegetarian or vegan who decides to minimize fat as much as is possible? It is safe to remove concentrated fats and oils from the diet, provided that sufficient essential fatty acids (EFAs) are consumed in whole foods. However, when high-fat plant foods such as nuts, seeds and tofu are also avoided, it becomes difficult to meet needs for EFAs. If you wish to reduce your total fat intake, aim for the lower end of the WHO recommended range – 15 percent of calories from fat. Vegetarian or vegan diets supplying less than 15 percent of calories from fat have proven effective in treating atherosclerosis. However, limiting fat to this extent is not necessary for healthy adults and is not suitable for children.

ACHIEVING ADEQUATE ESSENTIAL FATTY ACIDS

The World Health Organization recommends that polyunsaturated fats make up 3–7 percent of the energy in the diet. They do not specify the amount needed from each family, however many experts advise a minimum of 3 percent omega-6s and 0.5–1 percent omega-3s. An adult consuming 2000 calories could achieve the recommended minimum 3 percent of omega-6s with 60 calories of pure linoleic acid (6½ gm) and a minimum of 0.5 percent of omega-3s with 10 calories of pure alpha-linolenic acid (1.1 gm). (Remember that 1 percent of omega-3s [20 calories] may be preferable.) Obtaining this amount of omega-6s is easy on almost any varied vegetarian or vegan diet, other than one that is severely limited in fat. The task is not so simple with the omega-3s. Food sources of omega-3s are not as plentiful in the food supply. Each of the following provide the minimum 1.1 grams of omega-3s:

- ½ tsp flax oil or 2 tsp flaxseed
- 1 Tbsp canola or soybean oil
- 3 Tbsp walnuts
- 6 oz firm tofu or 12 oz medium tofu
- 1 cup cooked soybeans*

Other plant foods such as dark green leafy vegetables and wheat germ are less concentrated sources of valuable alpha-linolenic acid. In order to obtain sufficient omega-3 fatty acids from these foods, you would need to consume just over 1 pound (9 cups) of raw broccoli or kale, 3–3½ pounds (24–32 cups) of lettuce (darker greens have slightly more) *or* 20 tablespoons of wheat germ. Thus, while these foods can add valuable omega-3s to the diet, it would be a challenge to meet your needs with these sources alone.

The Question of Quality

When it comes to the quality of fat, there is a stark contrast between the high-quality fats found in plant foods, and the poor-quality, refined and chemically

*Other soyfoods such as soymilk and tempeh contain omega-3 fatty acids in varying amounts, depending on processing techniques and the fat content of the product.

altered fats that are so prevalent in our food supply. While we have been conditioned to carefully examine food labels for quantity of fat, we seldom give a second thought to matters of quality. The highly refined vegetable oils that sit on supermarket shelves have been likened to white flour which has been stripped of valuable vitamins and minerals. Worse yet are the oils that have undergone further processing to render them solid. Added to the standard animal-centered fare, rich in saturated fat and cholesterol, the overall quality of fat in the American diet is seriously lacking.

Adopting a vegetarian diet, especially one with limited amounts of high-fat dairy products and eggs, generally results in a decrease in total fat and saturated fat in the diet. But it does not guarantee that the fats we choose will be of any better quality. There is no law against spreading a thick layer of margarine on your morning toast, ordering French fries from a fast food restaurant for lunch, opting for a veggie pot pie with a traditional shortening crust for dinner, and frequently snacking on commercial cookies and crackers containing hydrogenated vegetable oils. There is nothing to stop us from indulging in sizable quantities of refined oils that are extremely high in omega-6 fatty acids, but almost void of omega-3 fatty acids. Indeed, to ensure that a vegetarian diet provides an appropriate balance of high-quality fats, we must select food with care.

When attempting to improve the quality of fat in your diet, begin by making fresh whole foods the foundation of your meals. Emphasize plant foods, including those that are rich in omega-3 fatty acids such as flaxseeds, walnuts, soybeans, tofu and dark, leafy greens, and limit high-fat dairy products and eggs. Nuts, seeds and their butters, avocados, olives, soybeans, garbanzos and tofu are all excellent sources of good-quality fats. If your diet contained no concentrated fats and oils or prepared foods containing fats, you could be confident that these wholesome plant foods would provide all the essential fats that your body requires. Just as you can get all the carbohydrates that your body needs from whole foods without any concentrated sugars or sweets, so you can get all of the fat that your body needs without using *any* extracted fats and oils.

When you do use concentrated fats and oils, select those that have undergone minimal processing, unrefined, truly "cold pressed," organic oils are best. Look for those stored in opaque containers to help avoid deterioration caused by light. Whether from whole foods or vegetable oils, the fat in most plants is primarily unsaturated. The more unsaturated a fat, the more quickly it undergoes oxidation which can result in the production of toxic chemicals. When this occurs in a food, it develops a most objectionable flavor and odor and becomes rancid. Perhaps this is nature's way of telling us that a food has lost its freshness and is no longer wholesome. When we obtain good-quality oils or food that is rich in essential fatty acids, especially those of the omega-3 family, we must handle these foods with care.

Nuts and seeds that are naturally preserved by a hard shell or coat will keep for about a year in a cool, dry place. Once this coat has been removed, they will keep up to four months in the refrigerator. Walnuts may not keep as long due to their high omega-3 fatty acid content. Ground flaxseed and wheat germ should always be kept in the freezer as they go rancid very quickly. Unrefined oils, with the exception of olive oil which is primarily monounsaturated fat, should always be refrigerated. Buy these oils in small quantities to use within a month. Oils can be frozen for later use if desired.

Step by Step: Improving the Quality of Fats in Your Diet

STEP 1. AVOID HYDROGENATED FATS

Hydrogenated and partially-hydrogenated fats are our main sources of trans-fatty acids. These fats have an altered chemical structure which can have negative consequences for health. Of all fats, these appear to be the most damaging. As much as is possible, avoid using products that contain hydrogenated or partially hydrogenated fats, including shortening, hydrogenated margarines and processed foods containing these fats. Be aware that hydrogenated fats are used extensively in most commercially prepared foods, including crackers, cookies, cakes, pastries, frozen convenience foods and snack foods. A small bag of potato chips or corn chips carries a whopping 6 to 9 grams of trans-fatty acids (1½ to 2 teaspoons). Don't be fooled by a declaration of "all-vegetable oil" on the label. This vegetable oil is often at least partially hydrogenated. Be sure to read the list of ingredients! Remember that ingredients are listed by weight, from the highest to the lowest. Hydrogenated vegetable oils are also frequently used in restaurants for deep frying. When eating out, pass on the fries and opt for a baked potato or rice. When preparing baked goods at home, experiment with vegetable oils and nut butters instead of using hard fats.

STEP 2. LIMIT FOODS RICH IN SATURATED FATS

Most Americans consume excessive amounts of saturated fats which can increase blood cholesterol levels and interfere with the use of essential fatty acids in the body. To reduce saturated fat in the diet, limit your use of butter, cheese and other high-fat dairy foods, eggs and tropical oils. If you use dairy products, replace high-fat items such as whole milk and sour cream with non-fat or low-fat items such as skim milk and non-fat yogurt. Try scrambled tofu instead of scrambled eggs for breakfast, and substitute ground flaxseeds or commercial egg replacer for eggs in baking (see Chapter 12). Go lightly on spreads such as margarines. Try mixing butter, soy lecithin spread or soft (preferably non-hydrogenated) margarine with a good quality oil (ideally one which is rich in omega-3 fatty acids such as flax or canola oil).

STEP 3. CUT BACK ON REFINED OILS

Although refined oils offer major advantages over hydrogenated and saturated fats, they are still not our best sources of fat. They provide little nutritional value other than pure fat, as most of the valuable vitamins, minerals and phytochemicals have been removed in the refining process. Many of these oils (especially corn, safflower and sunflower) are very high in polyunsaturated fats from the omega-6 family, and when used in excess can lead to serious essential fatty acid imbalance and reduction in HDL (good) cholesterol. To reduce your consumption, be conscious of how much refined oil you use in cooking and try to cut back as much as possible. When sautéing foods, try a few tablespoons of water, broth or wine instead of oil. Avoid deep fried foods. Bake, broil, microwave or barbecue instead. Experiment with tasty, fat-free marinades. In most recipes cooking oil can be reduced by about ⅓ to ½ without affecting the quality of the product. When baking, refined oils can be completely or partially replaced with applesauce, nut or seed butters, lecithin or soft tofu.

STEP 4. SELECT UNREFINED, MECHANICALLY PRESSED OILS

Whenever possible, select unrefined, organic oils (i.e. high quality, "cold pressed" oils) that have been mechanically pressed. Extra-virgin olive oil, which is widely available on supermarket shelves, is a good choice. This oil can be used for salads, marinades, pestos, and in cooking (using moderate heat). It does not need refrigeration but should be stored in a cool, dark place. Other high-quality, cold pressed oils are available in natural food stores. These oils must be refrigerated or frozen. The less they are subjected to heat, light and air, the better; however, most of these oils can be used in baking and for cooking at low temperatures (except those that are very high in omega-3 fatty acids). Frozen oils can be used in baking pie crusts, cookies and other items that normally call for hard fats.

STEP 5. SELECT GOOD SOURCES OF OMEGA-3 FATTY ACIDS EACH DAY

To improve the omega-3 content of your diet, include good sources of this nutrient in your daily menu. The best omega-3 sources for the vegetarian include flaxseeds and flaxseed oil, canola oil, walnuts, soybeans, tofu, dark green leafy vegetables and wheat germ. Foods rich in omega-3 fatty acids should be stored in the refrigerator or freezer as they are very perishable. Flaxseed oil is the richest source of omega-3 fatty acids and can be used in salads, sprinkled on pasta, vegetables and popcorn and added to cooked foods such as mashed potatoes. If you use butter or non-hydrogenated margarine, mix in flax oil at a ratio of about 2:1 butter or margarine to oil to help improve its fatty acid profile.

STEP 6. RELY ON WHOLE FOODS FOR THE BULK OF YOUR FAT

The highest-quality fat comes from fresh, whole foods, and wherever possible, rely on these foods instead of concentrated fats and oils. Whole foods come carefully packaged by nature to protect them from damaging light, heat and air. There is an abundance of excellent fat in foods like nuts, seeds, soybeans, olives and avocados. These foods provide phytochemicals, including antioxidants, beta-sitosterol and essential fatty acids, and thus are deserving of our respect. Nuts and seeds can be added to salads, cereals, baking and many main dishes. Put out a big bowl of unshelled nuts after dinner and get cracking! Try spreading nut or seed butters on your morning toast instead of butter or margarine. Soyfoods add wonderful variety to your menu. Pour some soymilk on your cereal, pack a soy burger for lunch and bake some "tofu fingers" for dinner. Avocados and olives can be added to salads, sandwiches, dips and main dishes. Wheat germ makes a healthful addition to hot cereal and baked goods. Remember that fats and oils are essential for good health, so make the effort to choose those of the highest quality.

FIBER: THE GIFT FROM PLANTS

iber has hit the front pages, not only because of its role as an intestinal tract cleanser, but more recently as a scavenger of harmful dietary components. Fiber is proving to be a valuable part of the defense against colon cancer, bowel disorders, coronary artery disease, hypertension, obesity and diabetes. The steady diet of many North Americans – refined cereals, bagels with cream cheese and burgers on white buns – provides very little of this complex of protective substances. *Fiber is found only in plant foods.* Foods of animal origin contain no fiber at all,* and refined grains and flours have been robbed of most of their original fiber content.

For those who have switched to vegetarian diets, an increased consumption of plant foods automatically results in more dietary fiber than is found in a meat-centered diet. Consequently, the concerns vegetarians have about fiber might differ from those of people with diets high in animal foods and refined grains. What are the important fiber issues from a vegetarian viewpoint?

At one extreme, some vegetarians may still consume diets with *insufficient* fiber, if they rely on refined foods and replace meat, poultry and fish with dairy products and eggs. At the other extreme, some vegetarian diets may provide *too much fiber*, particularly for specific age groups such as children and the elderly, In addition to determining optimal levels, we must give consideration to the various types of dietary fiber, each with different metabolic and health benefits.

*There are rare exceptions, such as the membranes (chitin) in some shellfish.

The Roots of Fiber

Fiber and whole foods have long been a part of medical wisdom and folk remedies. During the early part of the 19th century, Sylvester Graham, an evangelical preacher, advocated an increased use of whole grains and developed a version of the crackers that still bear his name. Later in that century, Dr. John Harvey Kellogg, managing a health sanitarium in Michigan, inspired a return to the use of high-fiber foods. Kellogg encouraged the use of plant-based diets for healing. At the same time, he launched the well-known line of breakfast cereals.

By the late 1800s, Americans were heading in a different direction from that advocated by Graham and Kellogg. The milling of grains, introduced in 1875, resulted in the removal of the bran (outer coating of whole grains) and germ (which contains essential, perishable oils). Consumers enjoyed the lighter flours and baked goods, while producers were delighted with the extended shelf life. Removal of the bran and germ meant substantial decreases in nutrients: many B vitamins, vitamin E, the minerals iron, zinc and magnesium – as well as 80 percent of the fiber (see Figure 7.1). Midway through the 20th century, four of these nutrients (three of the B vitamins and iron) were returned to refined flours, through the process of enrichment. In the 1990s a fourth B vitamin, folate, will probably be added to the list. Perhaps other missing nutrients will be added back over the next 50 years. But why not simply eat whole grains right now?

Figure 7.1 Some Nutrients in Breads

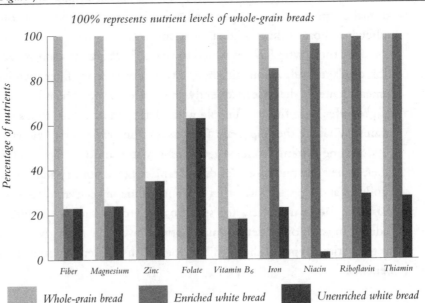

100% represents nutrient levels of whole-grain breads

The World Health Organization Study Group estimates that the daily diet of early man as a hunter-gatherer provided approximately 40 grams of fiber; later, peasant agriculturalists consumed 60 to 120 grams per day. High levels, in the range of 70 grams per day, are observed in diets of people in some developing countries today. By contrast, while American consumption of meat and other animal products rose through the early part of the twentieth century, fiber intake plummeted to the current level of 10 to 18 grams a day. As fat replaced fiber in our diets, the chronic diseases that are today's most noticeable killers became widespread, and bowel disorders increased. As the century draws to a close, the attention of health professionals is drawn to dietary fiber.

What is Fiber?

Fiber is a complex mixture of substances derived from the cell walls of plants. It is made up of long chains of glucose and glucose-like molecules, joined together by bonds that our digestive enzymes cannot break down. Whenever we eat vegetables, fruits, legumes, whole grains, nuts and seeds, we're taking in fiber. There are two categories of fiber – soluble and insoluble – with both types represented in each plant food. For example, oat bran has become well-known for its substantial contribution of soluble fiber; in addition, oats contain various types of insoluble fiber.

SOLUBLE FIBER

Mucilages, pectins and gums are forms of soluble fiber found inside and around plant cells; they help to "glue" plant cells together and protect them from drying out. Soluble forms of fiber dissolve or swell when put into water. This effect can be observed if ground psyllium seeds, a source of mucilage found in many commercial laxatives, are placed in water. The same is true for ground flaxseed. Pectin is the substance in apples, berries and oranges which causes jams, jellies and marmalades to gel. Oats and oat bran contain a gum, giving oatmeal its sticky consistency. The gums from kidney beans are evident in the thickened water which develops when beans are cooked and canned. Other rich sources of soluble fiber include guar gum (used to stabilize frozen desserts), agar (the vegetarian "gelatin" of seaweed origin), other seaweeds and legumes.

INSOLUBLE FIBER

Cellulose, hemicellulose and lignin are structural components found throughout the plant kingdom. These compounds generally will not dissolve in water, and so are called insoluble fiber. They do, however, attract and soak up water. Wheat bran is high in all three types of insoluble fiber. Legumes, seeds, root vegetables and vegetables of the cabbage family contain substantial amounts of cellulose; as they age, their lignin content increases.

Dietary Fiber: Just Passing Through?

As it moves through our stomachs and small intestines, fiber isn't digested. It's not a vitamin or a mineral. How is it that this substance can so profoundly affect our health?

In part, the beneficial action of fiber results from its ability to attract and hold water as it passes through the intestine. Fiber and water supply mass to the feces, creating a large, soft stool which stimulates the intestinal muscles. This allows the stool to move through the large intestine easily and quickly. In its journey it takes with it many substances which could otherwise trigger disease processes.

Fiber in Relation to Health and Disease

Because of this cleansing action, fiber plays a significant role in the prevention of a great many diseases. Listed below are just a few of the reasons we need dietary fiber.

FIBER, DIVERTICULITIS AND HEMORRHOIDS

Diets *low in insoluble fiber* result in small, hard feces; the intestine has to work hard to move such stools through its entire length (up to 29 feet). The intense muscular contractions may damage the walls of the lower intestine, resulting in diverticula (small pockets or bulges) in approximately half of elderly Americans. In some individuals, diverticula become inflamed, creating diverticulitis. The final passage of such stools is characterized by extra pressure and the stool is abrasive, hence the frequent occurrence of hemorrhoids. High-fiber diets have a preventive effect by providing soft, bulky stools that pass swiftly and easily and that help to keep intestinal walls strong.

FIBER AND COLON CANCER

Colon cancer, a leading cause of cancer deaths in North America, has been linked to a lack of dietary fiber. Exactly how fiber exerts its protective role is not entirely clear. However it appears that fiber decreases the effects of potential carcinogens (cancer-causing agents) on the inner wall of the large intestine in the following ways:

1. The larger, more liquid stool dilutes the carcinogens and decreases the time for contact.
2. Fiber binds the carcinogens and decreases synthesis of toxins.
3. Fiber supports the presence of more health-promoting strains of bacteria in the colon.

4. The products of intestinal fiber fermentation help limit the growth of cancer cells.

Both insoluble and soluble fiber have parts to play in decreasing our intestinal contact with carcinogens, thus consuming a wide variety of whole grains, fruits, vegetables and legumes is protective. Recent Finnish research demonstrated that when people switched to a vegan diet, within a week there was a marked reduction in four enzymes associated with the production of carcinogens in the intestine, indicating a further protective effect of plant-based diets.

FIBER AND CORONARY ARTERY DISEASE

When researchers first suggested that oat bran could lower blood cholesterol, many people in the medical field found it difficult to believe that fiber, which is not absorbed into the bloodstream, could affect the amount of a substance circulating in the blood. However, further studies proved those researchers to be correct. Oat bran really does lower blood cholesterol and thus reduces risk of coronary artery disease. It appears that soluble fiber can prevent the absorption of excess cholesterol and cause it to be excreted through the feces. This includes cholesterol in the foods we eat as well as the cholesterol we secrete into the intestine in the form of bile acids. Soluble fiber in other foods – the pectin in fruit, guar gum and the gums in legumes – has also been found effective in lowering cholesterol. Since plant-based diets tend to be lower in total fat and cholesterol as well as being higher in fiber, there is a multiple benefit.

FIBER AND CONTROL OF BLOOD-SUGAR LEVELS:
FOR DIABETICS AND NON-DIABETICS

Soluble fiber is a useful dietary component for controlling blood-sugar levels by promoting a slow and gradual delivery of dietary carbohydrate instead of sharp rises and falls. The accompanying release of insulin, the hormone that helps us to utilize sugar, is more gradual as well. These effects are of interest to many people who wish to avoid low-energy periods mid-morning or mid-afternoon due to drops in blood sugar. Endurance athletes find a pre-game meal of foods high in soluble fiber, such as lentils, to be preferable to sugar drinks and candy bars, because it assists with normal blood sugar maintenance. One British double-marathon winner uses oatmeal as her pre-race meal. Dr. James Anderson of the University of Kentucky, Dr. David Jenkins in Toronto and their co-workers have shown that diets high in soluble fiber support better diabetic control and in many type II diabetics, a decreased need for insulin. Additional insulin-related benefits have been shown for individuals with atherosclerosis, hypertension, and obesity. Legumes, as rich sources of soluble fiber, are particularly valuable in diets designed to control blood sugar levels.

AND THAT'S NOT ALL

The litany of benefits grows as we learn more about the health-promoting roles played by various types of fiber. For the average, bulge-battling North American adult, generous amounts of dietary fiber can be a great help with weight control. The bulk provided by high-fiber foods increases feelings of fullness and reduces hunger and caloric intake. Although the information presented here may have already converted you into a fiber fan, several questions still need to be addressed before you put your high-fiber theories into practice. One question that might have occurred to you already is:

Why Not Just Use Fiber Supplements?

The term "fiber supplements" can refer to either fiber tablets or a concentrated form of natural fiber such as wheat bran. Deriving your fiber from a variety of whole food sources has a number of advantages over the use of a refined, low-fiber diet, accompanied by such supplements.

1. For insoluble fiber to work in producing a softer stool, the fiber particles should be quite large. The finely ground insoluble fiber found in supplements appears to have lost the protective function provided by the longer strands of fiber naturally present in whole grains.

2. Many foods that contain dietary fiber contain substantial amounts of water closely associated with the fiber. Unlike dry fiber or bran, fruits and vegetables are 80 to 90 percent water by weight; cooked grains are 70 to 85 percent water. The presence of this water helps fiber to become effective in maintaining intestinal health.

3. Wheat bran is high in a substance called phytate which can bind essential minerals such as calcium, iron and zinc. Highly refined diets may provide marginal levels of zinc and other minerals, and the addition of wheat bran may make the situation worse. An equivalent amount of fiber from a variety of plant foods will be lower in mineral-binding phytate (see section on pages 129–31).

4. When an individual relies on a single fiber supplement such as wheat bran to provide the fiber he needs, he will miss the health benefits of other types of fiber found, for example, in fruits, legumes or nuts. Fiber supplements, either as single purified sources of fiber or commercial laxatives, are no substitute for the rich combination of fibers provided by nature. We don't yet understand what every individual type of fiber does. Nature has put together a complex

blend in each food. Many of the elements have unique roles to play in some aspect of health maintenance.

Returning to our earlier question, can we simply continue with highly refined diets and add fiber pills? Certainly we can include *some* refined foods without ill effect, and fiber pills can help with constipation. But our best bet is a return to an increased intake of whole foods, with their full complement of the various types of dietary fiber.

The Extremes: Too Much or Too Little Fiber

TOO LITTLE FIBER

A vegetarian diet which relies on refined baked goods, white rice and includes only 2–4 servings of fruits, vegetables and low-pulp juices is likely to be in the same range as the typical American diet (10 to 18 grams of fiber per day). A shift to whole grain products and the inclusion of legumes and more vegetables or fruits quickly doubles the fiber intake. This brings the total fiber consumed up into a health-promoting range, as well as providing a wide variety of types of fiber.

TOO MUCH FIBER

When children are fed diets excessively high in roughage and raw foods, growth may be compromised because such a large volume of food is required to get enough calories. For example, to obtain the 50 calories found in ¼ cup of tofu, a child would have to consume 2 cups of raw cauliflower or 5 cups of alfalfa sprouts! Children, with their small stomachs and appetites, need concentrated energy sources to support growth. Cooking of some highly fibrous foods is helpful; it does not change the amount of fiber in a food, but the fibers become smaller, softer and more compact, leaving space in the stomach for additional food. For the same reason, cooked vegetables and fruits may also benefit those elderly vegetarians whose total food intake is small.

FIBER, PHYTATE AND MINERALS

Phytates are the storage forms of phosphorus associated with fiber in seeds, grains, legumes, nuts and other plant foods. In the past, phytate has been regarded as a problematic substance due to its ability to bind minerals and decrease protein digestibility. These views were supported by many studies in which raw wheat bran or baked goods high in wheat bran were given as the primary source of dietary fiber. Findings from these studies have limited relevance when applied to vegetarians whose dietary fiber comes from a variety of raw, cooked and processed sources. For this and several other reasons, some of the ideas based on early research are being replaced, and phytate is being seen in a more positive light.

Unlike earlier techniques, modern analytical methods used by Dr. Barbara Harland of Howard University, Washington, D.C., and others allow researchers to differentiate between phytate and its breakdown products. During many aspects of food preparation, phytate-splitting enzymes called phytases become active. The products of phytate breakdown have diminished mineral-binding tendencies. Whereas wheat bran is high in mineral-binding phytate, a great many other raw and prepared plant foods are less likely to bind minerals than was formerly thought. Along with phytate breakdown, mineral availability increases during the following processes:

- presoaking of beans
- raising of yeasted bread doughs
- sprouting of seeds or legumes
- cooking cereals
- roasting of nuts
- fermentation (as in the production of tempeh, miso and natto from soybeans)

Thus, ideas based on the many "wheat bran" studies are not directly applicable when we are looking at the effects of balanced vegetarian diets on mineral absorption. While early research on fiber and phytate focussed on concerns about mineral losses, our perspective is changing. In fact, phytate is being hailed as friend rather than foe, as it carries excessive iron through the intestine and out of the body, protecting susceptible individuals from iron overload. Also, phytate appears to play a role in the defense against colon cancer. Fiber and associated phytates also provide benefits in regulating the absorption of glucose from starch.

For these reasons, there is little cause for the concern expressed by early researchers regarding mineral absorption by people on vegetarian diets. Naturally, these diets must include mineral-rich plant foods, and special care must be taken not to overload certain age groups, such as children, with bulky, high-fiber foods and high-phytate foods.

In summarizing the effects of fiber and phytate on the availability of minerals from plant foods, we can quote the World Health Organization Technical Report 797:

Studies from the eastern Mediterranean region suggest that very high intakes of unleavened bread, where the cereal phytate has not been destroyed by the endogenous phytase in the grain, do lead to problems of mineral malabsorption. However, this seems to be a problem of food preparation rather than of the diet as such. In human physiological studies, exchanging full grain cereals for refined starches low in fiber does not lead to calcium, zinc or iron malabsorption, because the whole grain provides an additional intake of the minerals that compensates for any reduced mineral availability. Oxalate-rich foods such as spinach do, however, limit mineral absorption. The intake of fiber from a mixed diet providing the maximum proposed adult limit of 32 g of NSP [32 grams of Non-Starch Polysaccharides, equivalent to 54 grams total dietary fiber] has been shown to allow the maintenance of mineral balance, but this conclusion may not apply to fiber-rich foods made by the addition of bran, which contains extra phytates as well as fiber.

The WHO study group goes on to state that there appears to be no advantage to intakes of dietary fiber in excess of 40 grams per day, and proposes approximately 54 grams as an upper limit. A diet composed of whole grains, products made from whole grains, vegetables and a variety of other plant foods will supply the necessary diversity in fiber.   •

Recommended Intakes of Fiber

The newest recommendations from expert committees around the world suggest that adults aim for 25–40 grams of dietary fiber per day. Fiber intakes in excess of 40 grams per day may be beneficial in treating specific medical conditions such as diabetes and high blood cholesterol. These recommendations are based on the use of whole foods rather than a diet made high in fiber through the addition of wheat bran or fiber supplements.

Table 7.1 shows fiber intakes of four sample diets. Note that the two menus on the right provide as much fiber at breakfast as the entire day of the menu on the left.

Guidelines for Increasing Your Fiber Intake

1. Choose whole grain products instead of refined breads and cereals.
The bread you use for your morning toast, lunch bag sandwiches and evening snack can be a great fiber booster. If made with wheat, rye, or other grains, and perhaps added nuts or seeds, you'll include many types of fiber in a single food. Crackers, pastas or pancake mixes can also be good sources of fiber if they are made with whole grains; in addition they will retain their original balance

Table 7.1 Approximate Fiber Content in Grams of Various Meals

Typical Low-Fiber	Refined Vegetarian	Vegetarian, Moderate	Vegetarian, High-Fiber
Breakfasts			
bacon and eggs (0)	French toast (1.2)	1 c bran flakes (5.0)	1 c multigrain cereal (5.3)
2 slices white toast & jelly (1.2)	syrup (0)	1 slice whole wheat toast (1.6)	1 slice multigrain bread with nut butter (3.0)
4 oz. juice (0.2)	½ c berries (2.0)	1 banana (1.8)	½ grapefruit (2.5)
1 cup milk (0)	1 cup milk (0)	1 cup milk (0)	1 cup soymilk (1)
Total = 1.4 g	Total = 3.2 g	Total = 8.4 g	Total = 11.8 g
Lunches			
beef burger and bun (1.5)	cheese & lettuce on white bread (1.4)	hummus and pita bread (4.0)	tofu "cheese" whole wheat with sprouts and tomato (3.5)
fries & ketchup (2.5)	green salad (1.5)	carrot sticks (2.0)	1½ cups lentil soup (4.0)
milk shake (0)	½ c grapes (0.5)	1 apple (3.0)	1 pear (4.3)
Total = 4.0 g	Total = 3.4 g	Total = 9.0 g	Total = 11.8 g
Suppers			
½ 10 in. pepperoni pizza (1.5)	broccoli quiche (1.8)	spinach lasagne (4.0)	chili (5.0)
lettuce salad (1.0)	1 cup white rice (0.6)	½ cup baked squash (3.0)	1½ cups brown rice (4.9)
	½ c vegetables (3.6)	¾ c coleslaw (2.5)	kale and carrot salad (3.0)
1 piece chocolate cake (0.5)	½ c apple crisp (2.0)	1 c fresh fruit salad (2.0)	1 orange (2.5)
Total = 3.0 g	Total = 8.0 g	Total = 11.5 g	Total = 15.4 g
Total fiber for the day			
8.4 g	14.6 g	28.9 g	39.0 g
Suggested health promoting range: 25–40 g			

of nutrients. Food labels designate a high source of fiber as one that provides 20 percent or more of the Daily Value (DV) of 25 grams; a good source provides 10 to 19 percent. Chapters 11 and 12 give practical tips to help you increase your intake of whole grains and other high-fiber foods.

2. Eat plenty of fruits and vegetables.

You may have become accustomed to eating your standard fruits and vegetables in certain quantities or with certain meals. Dare to break those patterns! You can build a meal around broccoli. How about trying a new fruit or vegetable every month? Learn about preparing unfamiliar foods from cookbooks, neighbors or from your grocer.

3. Include legumes and nuts.

There is great variety in the legume family, including quick-to-cook red lentils and slower cooking alternatives. Occasionally when you spend a day or an evening at home, put a big pot of beans, peas or lentils on to cook. (See Legume Wizardry on pages 229–30.) Supermarkets generally offer a wide range of canned beans, instant dried bean mixes and deli products such as hummus, bean salads, lentil soups, bean tortillas and nut butters. Make your selections from this group with a focus on high-energy foods – nuts, seeds and tofu or low-fat legumes (most legumes rather than soybeans).

Fiber and Digestibility

Boost your fiber intake in gradual steps. We all have helpful intestinal bacteria that assist in digesting our food. The amount and type of bacteria present depends on the kinds of food we eat; it takes time for the right bacteria to become dominant when you change your diet. Here are some suggestions to ease the transition:

a) Start with the legumes that are easiest to digest. These tend to be the smaller ones, such as split peas, lentils, adzuki beans and mung beans. Gradually introduce the bigger beans to your diet.

b) Increase your use of legumes gradually over a period of a month or two. Start with small servings once or twice a week, and gradually increase both serving size and frequency.

c) Soak beans before cooking, as the gas-producing potential of legumes is reduced when they are presoaked. Discard the soaking water and cook using fresh water.

d) For optimal digestibility, legumes should be cooked well until they can be mashed on the roof of your mouth with your tongue. Dried beans that have been stored for a long time require increased cooking time and will give you more gas compared to fresh legumes.

e) Chew your food. Thorough chewing begins the process of good digestion, starting with a starch-digesting enzyme present in the saliva.

Emission Control

Often people are somewhat cautious about eating too many beans, owing to their reputation in the gas department. It helps to understand the origins of intestinal gas, so that you can eliminate potential digestive difficulties. Both the types of food you eat and the population of bacteria in the intestine affect gas production. Some of the most healthful foods have the potential to be the gassiest: high-carbohydrate foods, beans and vegetables from the cabbage family. Even potatoes and refined wheat products such as bagels and pasta can lead to flatulence. Most of the starches and sugars in these foods are absorbed in the small intestine; some pass into the large intestine along with pectin, hemicellulose and short, fiber-like molecules. Here bacteria feed on these carbohydrates; a product of this bacterial action can be gas. Other bacteria which *consume* gas may be present as well, a reason for the different responses you might experience.

Scientists are beginning to understand how to shift the populations of bacteria. In Japan, for example, certain beverages and foods are consumed because they support the growth of specific health-supportive types of bacteria known as bifidobacteria. Specific soy products, such as soyflour and textured soy protein, can be particularly helpful in this regard. You may become aware that certain foods and combinations do (or don't) work for your intestinal well-being. For example, the milk sugar lactose cannot be digested by 70 percent of the world's population and can cause gas and discomfort. Fructose in soft drinks and sorbitol in diet soda are poorly absorbed, leading to flatulence. On the other hand, rice has little tendency for gas production.

The same meal may affect two people differently. Also, the same person is likely to find that in two to three weeks he or she adjusts to a different way of eating with a shift in intestinal bacteria and improved intestinal motility. Populations from different parts of the globe have centered their diets on carbohydrates for generations without ill effects. As we realize the substantial health benefits of these foods, we start to wonder what these people know that we don't! To minimize those moments when you don't know whether to look at each other or blame the dog, use these tips from people around the world.

The Gas Crisis: International Solutions

Ingredients in traditional dishes from around the world frequently have benefits beyond adding flavor! For example the Japanese use a seaweed called kombu to help with digestion. Kombu is added during the cooking of legume dishes and is removed before the dish is served.

In India, an herbal extract called asafoetida (or hing) is sometimes added to cooked foods for adults. Fennel, which is often added to curries, bean dishes and teas is also found to be helpful for digestion.

Latin Americans prevent their gas problems with a herb similar to parsley, called epazoate. Epazoate, which grows wild on the west coast of North America, is used as a seasoning for bean dishes and is a component of many chili powders.

Herbs that have long been used as aids to digestion by Europeans and Asians are peppermint, chamomile and ginger.

In America a product called Beano is available in health food stores and pharmacies. It takes the wind out of gassy foods like beans, wheat products, oat bran and foods from the cabbage family. Three to eight drops can be added to your first spoonful of the food. The enzymes of Beano break down fiber-like molecules so that we absorb them as sugars in the intestine. Presto! Less gas. Beano does not change the flavor of the food, and has no side effects. (Just one precaution: do not use Beano if you have a sensitivity to galactose.)

It typically takes a few weeks to adjust to new ways of eating. You may also find that you do have more gas, generally odorless, on a higher fiber diet. This is actually a normal part of a well-functioning intestine and is not to be confused with intestinal discomfort. Medical journals, having advocated a return to diets high in carbohydrates, beans and the vegetables of the cabbage family, are following up with articles giving tips to help people through the adjustment phase, such as "Give Status to Flatus and Class to Gas," "Unsilent Passage," "Wind" and "How to Quiet the Rumble."

So for your short- and long-term health, accept the gift that only plants can give and boost your fiber intake

THE VEGETARIAN FOOD GUIDE: PUTTING IT ALL TOGETHER

The next step towards great vegetarian eating is to combine all of our information about protein, calcium, iron, zinc, essential fatty acids and fiber into a complete guide that helps us make our daily food choices.

Food guides are products of the twentieth century. The first American food guide was published in 1916, at the beginning of an exciting era when essential vitamins and minerals were identified and found to influence health. Over the years, food guides have changed to accompany the new, evolving science of nutrition.

Our Vegetarian Food Guide has been modeled on the Food Guide Pyramid, with foods grouped together because of similar strengths in the nutrients they provide. Serving sizes and numbers of recommended servings are similar to those in the Pyramid for all the food groups except one. The exception is the Milk and Milk Alternates group. In the Pyramid, 1 cup milk = 1 serving. In the Vegetarian Food Guide, ½ cup milk = 1 serving. This approach leads to more appropriate serving sizes for the calcium-rich plant foods that can be used as milk alternates. At the same time, the *number* of servings from this group is *doubled*. The food guide that follows is designed to meet nutrient needs and yet allow for food preferences, economic constraints and differing caloric needs.

THE VEGETARIAN FOOD GUIDE*

Select a *variety* from the following food groups each day.

Breads, Cereals, Rice & Pasta: 6–11 servings

Whole grains are recommended.

Serving sizes:

Breads:	Bread, 1 slice
	Small roll, biscuit, tortilla, chapati, roti, bannock, scone, 1
	Large bun bagel, large pita bread or English muffin, ½
Hot & cold cereals:	Cereal, cooked, ½ cup
	Cereal, ready-to-eat, 1 ounce
Pasta & grains:	Pasta, rice, quinoa or other grain, cooked, ½ cup
Other:	Pancake, waffle or muffin, 1 small or ½ large
	Wheat germ, 2 Tbsp
	Crackers, 2 large or 4 small

Vegetables: 3–5 servings

Serving sizes:

Vegetable (such as potato or carrot), 1 medium
Vegetable, fresh, frozen or cooked, ½ cup
Vegetable juice, ¾ cup
Salad, 1 cup

Fruits: 2–4 servings

Serving sizes:

Fruit (such as apple, banana, orange, peach or citrus fruit), 1 medium
Small fruit (such as apricot or plum), 2
Fruit, fresh, frozen or cooked, ½ cup
Fruit juice, ¾ cup

Many vegetables and fruits are excellent sources of vitamin C. Some that will provide more than 30 mg of vitamin C in a ½ cup serving are broccoli, brussels sprouts, cauliflower, collards, peppers, snow peas, cantaloupe, citrus fruits and juices, guava, kiwi fruit, papaya, strawberries and vitamin C-fortified juices.

* See pages 160 and 169 for guides designed for children and recommendations for pregnancy and lactation.

Beans & Bean Alternates
(Beans, Peas, Nuts & Eggs): 2–3 servings

(Pregnant and lactating Women: 3–4 servings)

For increased iron absorption, eat a vitamin C source (vegetable or fruit) at the same time.

Serving sizes:

Legumes (beans or lentils), cooked, ½ cup
Tofu or tempeh, ½ cup
Meat analogs (such as tofuburgers), 1 patty
Nuts or seeds, 3–4 Tbsp
Nut or seed butter, 2–3 Tbsp
Soymilk, 1 cup
Egg, 1 large

Milk & Milk Alternates: 4–6 servings

(Teens, young adults [to age 24 years], pregnant & lactating women: 6–8 servings)

Bonus: With some of these foods you get "2 for the price of 1," in that they count as servings from other groups as well as this group.

Serving sizes:

Seeds & nuts:	Sesame tahini, 2 Tbsp
	Almond butter, 3–4 Tbsp
	Almonds, ⅓ cup
Vegetables:	Green vegetables (kale, collards, Chinese cabbage, bok choy, okra, broccoli), cooked, 1 cup
	Greens (kale, Chinese cabbage, broccoli), raw, 2 cups
	Seaweed (hijiki), dried, ⅓ cup
Legume foods:	Tofu made with calcium, supplying 15% of the DV per serving*
	Legumes (soybeans, baked white beans, navy, Great Northern, navy, black turtle beans), cooked, 1 cup
	Legumes (chick-peas, pinto, butter, kidney), 1½ cups
Other foods:	Blackstrap molasses, 1 Tbsp
	Figs, dried, 5
	Calcium-fortified foods (such as tortillas) and beverages providing 15% of the DV per serving*
Dairy products:	Milk or yogurt, ½ cup
	Cheese, ¾ oz
	Process cheese, 1 oz

*If the product you purchase provides 10 percent of the Daily Value (DV) per serving, you could use 1½ servings.

Essential Oils

The tip of the American Food Guide Pyramid is devoted to Fats, Oils and Sweets, with a suggestion that these foods be used sparingly. From this category, the only substances you actually require are the essential fatty acids (omega-3 and omega-6 fatty acids). Omega-6s are very easy to come by in seeds, nuts, oils and a variety of other foods from the five food groups on the preceding pages. You will easily get enough in all but *very* low-fat diets (under 10 percent of calories from fat). Significant amounts of omega-3s are present in far fewer foods, so it's important to ensure sufficient intake. Each of the following supplies the minimum omega-3 fatty acids to meet your daily needs:

- flaxseed oil, ½ tsp
- canola or soybean oil, 1 Tbsp
- walnuts, 3 Tbsp
- firm tofu, 6 oz

For other sources and more information, see the section *"Achieving Adequate Essential Fatty Acids"* on page 118 of Chapter 6.

In addition, make sure you have sources of the following:

Vitamin B_{12}

For those using few or no animal products: Fortified foods or a supplement supplying an average of 2 µg vitamin B_{12} per day or 3 µg during pregnancy and lactation.
For ovo-lacto vegetarians: See Table 5.1 on page 97 for amounts of vitamin B_{12} in cow's milk, yogurt, cheese and eggs.

Vitamin D

Sunlight option: Sunlight on hands and face will supply adequate vitamin D. For people with light skin, 10–15 minutes of sunlight; for people with dark skin, ½ hour or more (for more details, see pages 85 to 87).
Fortified food or supplement option: Fortified foods or a supplement supplying 5 µg vitamin D for people above 25 years of age and 10 µg of vitamin D for those under 25 years of age, and for pregnancy, lactation, those at northern latitudes (such as Alaska) or confined indoors. The higher amount (10 µg) may be beneficial for people above 50 years of age.

Water

Drink 6–8 glasses of water daily (this includes herb tea, juice, soups and non-caffeinated beverages)

More About the Five Food Groups in the Vegetarian Food Guide

Note that one of the keys to successful use of a food guide is the selection of a *variety* of foods. For example, riboflavin is found in some foods that you probably wouldn't use every day, such as mushrooms, sweet potatoes, avocados and figs. Riboflavin is also provided by foods that may show up fairly regularly in your diet, because they are such concentrated sources of nutrients: wheat germ, broccoli, almonds, beans and nutritional yeast. When you focus on the most nutritious foods, but also choose variety, you'll maximize your nutrient intake.

BREADS, CEREALS, RICE AND PASTA

This group is the basis of a healthy vegetarian diet, contributing calories (*energy*), protein, B vitamins and minerals. Whole grain products are recommended as they provide fiber and more of the vitamins and minerals. As with the other food groups, there is a range in the number of servings suggested from this group, The minimum number of servings (six) is suitable for those with lower caloric requirements such as people limiting their caloric intake, those with low activity levels and the elderly. Does six servings sound like a lot? It's really not. For example, a cup of cooked cereal at breakfast, a sandwich with two slices of bread at lunch, and a cup of rice or pasta at supper adds up to six servings. Teens and people who are bigger or more active will need more servings. Athletes with very high energy requirements may exceed 11 servings from this group.

VEGETABLES

Vegetables provide an abundance of vitamins A (beta carotine), C and others, minerals, fiber and phytochemicals. Leafy greens are especially valuable as contributors of folate; many have available calcium as well. Your diet will be enriched by other parts of plants as well: stems (celery and asparagus), roots (carrots, turnips and beets), tubers (potatoes and yams), flowers (broccoli and cauliflower) and seeds (peas and corn). Some vegetables are actually the fruits of plants: cucumbers, squash, eggplant, okra and tomatoes.

FRUITS

Fruits are a low-calorie, sweet way of packing in vitamins A and C, folate, minerals and soluble fiber. Fresh fruits provide a wonderful alternative to high-calorie desserts.

BEANS AND BEAN ALTERNATES

Beans, peas and lentils are the protein powerhouses of the food guide. They contain iron, zinc, a range of B vitamins, both insoluble and soluble fiber, and some are fairly good calcium sources as well. Foods made from legumes, such as tofu, tempeh or meat analogs, are an easy and delicious way to increase your protein intake. Remember that iron absorption will be increased substantially when you eat a source of vitamin C at the same time.

Nuts and seeds provide protein as well as being concentrated energy foods (another way of saying they're high in fat). In addition, walnuts are rich in essential fatty acids, almonds and sesame seeds are sources of calcium and cashews contain zinc. Nut and seed butters are valuable in vegetarian diets as nutritious spreads and are sometimes used in recipes to replace oils.

To increase your intake of beans and bean alternates:

• load up on legumes by using them in soups, stews, pasta sauces, loaves and patties, and in sandwich fillings such as hummus;

• use tofu more often; scramble some for breakfast, add it to sandwiches for lunch and toss it into your stir-fry at dinner;

• spread nut or seed butter on your toast instead of butter or margarine;

• snack on nuts and seeds during the day, use them in baking and add them to salads.

Foods from this group can also be counted as "milk alternates" choices.

MILK AND MILK ALTERNATES

The foods in this group are rich sources of calcium. Several milk alternatives are found in the preceding groups as well, for example:

• calcium-fortified tortillas are in the bread group too;

• tofu made with calcium, almonds and tahini can also be counted as servings from the bean group;

• green vegetables (kale, collards, bok choy, Chinese cabbage, okra or broccoli) are a part of the vegetable group as well as being a milk alternates.

Calcium-fortified foods and beverages that provide 15 percent of the DV (150 mg calcium) are equivalent to one serving from this group (check labels). For those who use dairy products, ½ cup of milk or yogurt is a serving. *Unfortified* non-dairy beverages, such as soy- or rice-based beverages are *not* options from this group. Even though they may be used in the same ways as cow's milk as a drink or in cooking, they are not nutritionally equivalent.

The recommended intake from this group is 4–6 servings. Youths, whose bone density is still increasing, need more: 6–8 servings. Pregnant and lactating women also need 6–8 servings, and many experts recommend intakes in the higher range for post-menopausal women not on estrogen replacement therapy.

The most practical way to meet one's calcium needs through plant foods is to *choose tahini, almond butter, dark green leafy vegetables, tofu made with calcium and calcium-fortified products on a regular basis.*

Assessing Your Diet

How do you figure out whether you're meeting your needs from each group?

A handy way of checking off your day's food intake is the Score Sheet below, and on pages 143 and 144. The darkened squares indicate your recommended minimum from each group; white squares represent the additional recommended servings per day.

VEGETARIAN FOOD GUIDE SCORE SHEET

Grain Products	■■■■■■□□□□□
Vegetables	■■■□□□
Fruits	■■□□
Beans & Bean Alternates	■■□□
Milk & Milk Alternates	■■■■□□□□
Omega-3 Fatty Acids	■
Vitamin B_{12}	■
Vitamin D	■

Copy the Score Sheet and use it to assess your diet for a few days. This will give you an idea of the strengths and weaknesses of your current way of eating. If you find that you're short in a certain group, choose foods from that group and put them on your shopping list. If there are some foods that you don't know how to use, check the recipes in Chapter 12; these recipes have a special emphasis on highly nutritious ingredients. After scoring your diet for a while and making a few adjustments, you can relax and realize you're on the right track.

As we learn more about nutrition, we find more reasons to eat *whole* foods. Nature has packaged foods so that they provide a great many more health supportive components than we may have realized. Although the era of vitamin discovery is complete, new substances are being found in whole foods that appear to play powerful roles in the prevention of disease. These are the phytochemicals found in such foods as garlic, onions, licorice, tofu and cooking herbs. Scientists are also investigating the parts played by trace minerals towards our overall well-being. These substances are present in whole foods, but can be lost with processing.

Today's discoveries are making it increasingly obvious that vitamin pills can never replace real food. Supplements and fortified foods can sometimes help – for example, providing vitamin B_{12} to vegans. Organic foods are good choices; in buying these products we support our health, environmentally friendly industries *and* the planet. These foods are becoming more available and less expensive, with increasing consumer demand.

Overall, fresh and tasty plant foods are superbly designed to nourish us – at every stage of the life cycle.

USING THE VEGETARIAN FOOD GUIDE SCORE SHEET

To show you how to use the score sheet, here we rate the lacto-ovo vegetarian menu (No. 3) from page 44.

(number of servings)

Grain Products ☑ ☑ ☑ ☑ ☑ ☑ ☑ ☐ ☐ ☐ ☐

dry cereal, 1 cup	(1)
toast, 1	(1)
pita bread, 1	(2)
spaghetti, 1½ cups	(3)
	(TOTAL: 7)

Vegetables ☑ ☑ ☑ ☑ ☑

cherry tomatoes, 4	(1)
carrot, 1	(1)
tomato-vegetable sauce, 1 cup	(2)
green salad, 1 cup	(1)
	(TOTAL: 5)

Fruits ☑ ☑ ☑ ☐

orange juice, ¾ cup	(1)
apple, 1	(1)
banana, 1	(1)
	(TOTAL: 3)

Beans & Bean Alternates ☑ ☑ ½ ☐

almond butter, 1 tbsp	(⅓)
hummus, ½ cup	(1)
cashews, ¼ cup	(1)
lentils, ¼ cup	(½)
	(TOTAL: 2½+)

Milk & Milk Alternates ☑ ☑ ☑ ☑ ☐ ☐ ☐ ☐

calcium-fortified orange juice	(1)
2% milk, 1 cup	(2)
almond butter plus tahini and garbanzo beans	(1)
	(TOTAL: 4)

Omega-3 Fatty Acids ☑

flaxseed oil, 1 tsp in salad dressing

Vitamin B_{12} ☑

fortified cereal providing 35 percent of the DV

Vitamin D ☑

vitamin D fortified milk and sunlight, combination

VEGETARIAN FOOD GUIDE SCORE SHEET

And here's a sample analysis of the vegan pattern from page 46.

(number of servings)

Grain Products ☑ ☑ ☑ ☑ ☑ ☑ ☑ ☑ ☑ ☐ ☐

multigrain cereal, 1 cup	(2)
toast, 1	(1)
sandwich, 2 bread	(2)
rice, 1½ cups	(3)
muffin, 1 small	(1)
	(TOTAL: 9)

Vegetables ☑ ☑ ☑ ½ ☐

carrot, 1	(1)
salad, 2 cups	(2)
onions, ¼ cup	(½)
	(TOTAL: 3½)

Fruits ☑ ☑ ☑ ☐

orange juice, ¾	(1)
apple, 1	(1)
figs, 3	(1)
	(TOTAL: 3)

Beans & Bean Alternates ☑ ☑ ☑ ½

soymilk, 1 cup	(1)
tofu, ¼ cup	(½)
lentils, 1 cup	(2)
	(TOTAL: 3½)

Milk & Milk Alternates ☑ ☑ ☑ ☑ ½ ☐ ☐ ☐

tahini, 1 Tbsp	(½)
blackstrap molasses on toast and in baking, 1 Tbsp	(1)
tofu made with calcium, providing 15% of the DV	(1)
kale in salad, 1 cup	(½)
figs, 3	(½)
calcium-fortified soymilk providing more than 15% of the DV	(1)
	(TOTAL: 4½)

Omega-3 Fatty Acids ☑

walnuts, 3 Tbsp

Vitamin B_{12} ☑

Red Star T6635+ nutritional yeast in sandwich

Vitamin D ☑

a short walk in the sunlight during lunch break

VEGETARIAN NUTRITION IN THE GROWING YEARS

The growing years are characterized by physical changes that result in unique nutritional requirements. During pregnancy and lactation, infancy, childhood and adolescence, our needs for many nutrients are greater (per pound of body weight) than at any other time in our lives. Although the essential dietary goals of optimal health and well-being stay consistent throughout the various stages of life, the food patterns that best support these goals naturally differ. During the adult years, a primary focus is the prevention of chronic disease (e.g., low-fat, high-fiber diet), while during the growing years greater emphasis must be placed on adequate growth and development (e.g., concentrated sources of energy and nutrients). By recognizing these fundamental differences in our nutritional needs, the positive health consequences of a vegetarian diet can be fully realized at every stage of life.

Regardless of whether you are just beginning to cut back on animal foods or are a vegetarian or a vegan, you can be assured that a plant-centered diet can support good health. The guidelines offered in this chapter will help to ensure that the special needs of growing bodies are met in a simple and enjoyable manner.

PREGNANCY AND LACTATION

You're pregnant and there are few things that matter more to you right now than having a healthy baby. You may be wondering if your plant-centered diet is adequate to support this little person who shares your food. Relax. With a little good sense, you can obtain all the nutrients you need for both you and your baby.

It's best to begin your pregnancy well-nourished, but if your diet is less than ideal, there's no better time to improve it. Consider it an investment in the future.

Vegetarians enjoy some advantages when it comes to pregnancy and lactation, including a lower risk for obesity and hypertension. In addition, the vegetarian diet is usually loaded with nutrient-dense whole grains, fruits and vegetables, and contains few processed, high-fat extras.

Lacto-ovo vegetarians are at no greater risk for nutritional shortages during pregnancy than are omnivores. In planning a prenatal diet for the lacto-ovo vegetarian, the nutrients that need special consideration are iron, zinc and possibly protein. In comparison to the pregnant omnivore, lacto-ovo vegetarians seem to have less trouble meeting their needs for folic acid and calcium. Those who consume minimal amounts of dairy products would be well advised to follow the guidelines for vegans given in this chapter.

Vegan women who plan their diet carefully can also readily meet their nutritional needs. Attention must be given to those nutrients commonly provided by dairy foods, including calcium, vitamin D and vitamin B_{12}, in addition to the nutrients that may be of concern for lacto-ovo vegetarians. The recommended nutrient intakes during pregnancy and lactation are provided in Appendix 2 (see page 256). Restrictive vegan diets (as described on pages 34–35) have been linked to low birth weight in infants, thus some care is needed in planning a vegan diet during this time. On the other hand, vegans have been reported to have healthy pregnancies with no significant differences in birth weight, congenital abnormalities or other complications as compared to omnivorous women.

Nutrition Guidelines for Pregnant Vegetarians and Vegans

1. Aim for a weight gain of 25–35 lb during pregnancy.

A weight gain of 25–35 lb is associated with the healthiest outcome for both the mother and baby. Adolescents and women with large body frames should aim for the upper end of this range, while short women with smaller frames should aim for the lower end. For those who are underweight, a gain of 28–40 lb is suggested. Women who are overweight do not need to gain "fat stores" for lactation, thus a gain of 15–25 lb is generally sufficient. It is important to note that many people assume that they are overweight, when in fact they are within their healthy weight range. Check with your doctor or health care provider before you decide to limit your weight gain. You may be limiting your nutrient intake unnecessarily. *Do not try to lose weight during pregnancy – it's not worth the risk!*

In order to produce the desired weight gain, about 100 extra calories per day are needed during the first trimester and about 300 extra calories per day in the last two trimesters, in addition to normal food intake. A hundred calories amounts to little more than three figs or a dozen almonds each day, while 300 calories can be easily obtained from a ½ cup serving of trail mix or a peanut butter and banana sandwich. Those who are underweight or who are not gaining weight adequately will need additional calories.

If you are experiencing "morning sickness" and have a poor appetite during the first trimester, do your best to include complex carbohydrate and protein foods when you do eat. Limit sweets and fatty foods, eat several small meals a day and drink plenty of water.

2. Eat a wide variety of nutritious foods, as outlined in the vegetarian food guide.
During pregnancy your need for nutrients goes up substantially although your need for calories increases by only a small amount. What this means is that you can't afford to eat a lot of "junk" that provides little nutritional value. Instead, focus on wholesome foods, as outlined in the vegetarian food guide.

To make the food guide work for you, be sure that you achieve the recommended number of servings every day. Select a wide variety of foods from within each of the groups; the more variety you include, the better balance of nutrients that you will receive. Try not to skip meals, as you need a good supply of vitamins and minerals throughout the day.

A suggested meal plan, based on the food guide, with the additions recommended during pregnancy, is provided at the end of this section.

3. Include one extra serving from the beans and bean alternates group every day.
An extra serving from the beans and bean alternates group is recommended during pregnancy, bringing the total to three to four servings per day. This will help to increase your intake of protein, iron and zinc, which are necessary to a normal healthy pregnancy. These nutrients are important for the growth of your uterus, and your expanding blood volume, as well as the development of the fetus (review Chapter 3 for more information on these nutrients).

The following food combinations are examples of three to four servings of beans and bean alternates:
- ½ cup tofu and 1 cup kidney beans
- 3 Tbsp almond butter and 2 soy burgers

- ¼ cup cashews, 1 cup pea soup and ½ cup tempeh
- 1 egg, ½ cup pinto beans and 1 cup soy milk

4. Include two to four additional servings of milk (½ cup servings) and/or milk alternates each day.

An additional two to four servings from the milk and milk alternates group are recommended, bringing the total to six to eight servings per day. An increase in calcium intake during pregnancy helps ensure proper formation of your baby's bones and teeth, as well as proper nerve, muscle and blood functioning. It is also important for your bone health.

The necessary calcium can be obtained by consuming a minimum of six servings from the milk and milk alternates group, in addition to the smaller amounts that you receive from other foods throughout the day. The following examples provide the equivalent of at least six servings from the milk and milk alternates group:

- 2 tbsp tahini, 1 Tbsp blackstrap molasses and 1 cup tofu (made with calcium)
- 3 cups of calcium-fortified non-dairy milk (read label) or cow's milk
- 1 cup steamed kale, 1 cup baked beans, ⅓ cup almonds and 5 figs
- 1 cup broccoli, 1 cup black turtle beans, ¼ cup hijiki seaweed and 1 cup yogurt

Those who have difficulty eating six to eight servings of calcium-rich foods may need to take a calcium supplement.

Sufficient vitamin D is necessary to assist in the absorption and retention of calcium. During pregnancy, a day's supply of vitamin D can be obtained from 20 minutes of sunlight for people with light skin and one hour for those with dark skin. You can also get vitamin D from fortified cow's milk *or* from fortified non-dairy milk and margarine (read labels). For those with limited exposure to sunlight or those living in northern latitudes, a vitamin D supplement supplying not more than 10 µg (400 IU) per day is recommended.

5. Increase your intake of omega-3 fatty acids to at least 1 percent of total calories.

During pregnancy and lactation, you need more essential fatty acids to help ensure that the brain and eyes of the fetus and young infant develop normally. This can be achieved by increasing your current intake of omega-3 fatty acids to at least 1 percent of calories. For someone consuming 2400 calories a day, sufficient omega-3 fatty acids could be obtained from the following foods:

- 1 tsp flaxseed oil
- 1 Tbsp canola oil and 1 cup cooked soybeans
- 1½ cups cooked broccoli, 4 Tbsp walnuts and 4 oz firm tofu

6. Include a reliable source of vitamin B_{12} in the diet every day.

Vitamin B_{12} needs are increased during pregnancy and lactation to allow for the expanding blood volume and the growth and development of the baby. For lacto-ovo vegetarians, 3 cups of cow's milk or one egg and 2 cups of milk provide all the vitamin B_{12} required.

Vegans can obtain enough vitamin B_{12} using one tablespoon of Red Star T-6635+ yeast (flakes) or vitamin B_{12}-fortified foods. Aim for a total of approximately 3 µg per day. Do *not* rely on other plant foods which have traditionally been considered vitamin B_{12} sources, as many of them contain vitamin B_{12} analogs (see Chapter 5). *If adequate vitamin B_{12}-fortified foods are not used, a supplement is necessary.*

7. A prenatal vitamin/mineral supplement is recommended for vegetarians and vegans who are at risk for under-nutrition, who have a nutrient deficiency or who for any reason are unable to follow the vegetarian food guide carefully. A folate supplement of 400µg per day and an iron supplement of 30 mg per day are recommended for all pregnant women.

Prenatal vitamin and mineral supplements provide some protection against nutrient shortages during pregnancy and thus are often prescribed for vegetarians and omnivores alike. An adequate intake of most nutrients can be obtained from a well-planned diet, although it is difficult to meet RDA pregnancy levels for some nutrients such as zinc, folate and iron. It is possible that RDA levels are higher than necessary for some nutrients, and this is an area of intense research and debate. The National Academy of Sciences recommends that all pregnant women take a folate supplement of 400 µg (0.4 mg) and an iron supplement of 30 mg per day.

There are a number of situations in which you would be well-advised to take a daily prenatal vitamin/mineral supplement. Some of the more common reasons (including the appropriate course of action) include:

- you have entered pregnancy undernourished, underweight or otherwise nutritionally compromised. *Take a prenatal vitamin/mineral supplement;*
- you do not consume the necessary amounts of vitamin B_{12}-fortified foods or animal products to get the vitamin B_{12} you require during pregnancy. *Supplement with 3.0 µg vitamin B12 per day;*
- you do not use adequate quantities of vitamin D-fortified foods or have limited exposure to sunlight. *Supplement with 10 µg (400 IU) vitamin D per day;*
- you are unable to consume the amounts of foods recommended in the food guide because of nausea, lack of appetite or any other reason. *Take*

a prenatal vitamin/mineral supplement;

• you do not eat sufficient calcium-rich foods. You need 6 to 8 servings of milk and milk alternates per day (1 serving = ½ cup calcium-fortified soymilk or cow's milk). *Use a daily supplement of 500–1000 mg elemental calcium, depending on your dietary intake.*

Remember that a supplement does not compensate for a poor diet, so if you do use one, continue to make a healthful, balanced food intake your priority. Higher dose supplements are not advised unless medically indicated, as they provide no added benefit and can interfere with the absorption of other nutrients.

Apart from iron, folate, calcium and vitamin B₁₂, single nutrient supplements can be toxic to the developing baby and are therefore best avoided unless medically indicated.

8. Avoid alcohol during pregnancy.

Pregnant women who drink alcohol on a regular basis increase the chances of their babies being born with fetal alcohol syndrome (FAS). This devastating condition can result in central nervous system disorders, mental retardation, growth deficiencies and abnormal facial features. Although the risk to the infant increases with the amount of alcohol consumed, safe lower limits are not known. For this reason, alcohol should be completely avoided during pregnancy.

9. Keep caffeine consumption under 300–400 mg per day.

Caffeine passes easily across the placental barrier and is poorly metabolized by the unborn baby. During the last trimester of pregnancy, caffeine is poorly metabolized by the mother as well. The effects of caffeine on the baby are not clearly understood, although research indicates that caution is warranted. Caffeine is found primarily in coffee, tea (both black and Oriental green teas), cola beverages, chocolate and some medications. Three hundred milligrams of caffeine is found in approximately three cups of regular coffee or seven colas.

Caffeine-free, grain-based beverages made from ingredients such as roasted malt, barley, chicory and carob may be useful substitutes. Although decaffeinated coffee contains minimal caffeine, it is often processed with harsh chemicals and thus there are some concerns regarding its effects during pregnancy. Herbal teas such as rosehip, mint, lemon and fruit teas are tasty alternatives. Some herbal teas – for example goldenseal, Scotch broom, sassafras, devil's claw and pennyroyal – are unsafe for use during pregnancy. If you do use herbal teas, make sure that those you select are safe.

10. Minimize your intake of environmental pollutants.

There are a number of things that you can do to minimize your intake of environmental pollutants during pregnancy. These steps are also important to reduce the possible residues in your breast milk:

• Choose organically grown fruits, vegetables and grains whenever possible. Otherwise, be sure to wash your produce well.

• Choose low-fat dairy products.

• If you use fish, avoid those from polluted waters. Small fish have less residues. Also, avoid fish oil supplements.

Additional Considerations for Breast-Feeding, nutritional needs during

When you breast-feed your baby, your nutrient needs continue to be higher than normal and are similar to what they were during the second and third trimesters of pregnancy. An additional 400–500 calories per day are generally required for those who are normal weight. This amount could be provided by a cup of lentil soup, a multigrain roll and a glass of orange juice. If you are underweight, an extra 800–1000 calories per day may be necessary. This would be most easily achieved by increasing food intake by about 200 calories per meal (e.g., a glass of calcium-fortified orange juice or soymilk and a slice of bread with tahini) and adding an extra snack (perhaps a bowl of cereal). If you don't get enough to eat, your milk supply could suffer.

You'll also need extra fluids while you are breast-feeding. Try to remember to drink a big glass of water whenever you are nursing.

You should continue to limit your intake of caffeine while you are breast-feeding. Alcohol does not need to be as strictly avoided, although it is quickly transferred to breast milk, so your intake should be minimal. Some babies are sensitive to strong flavors such as garlic, onion or hot spices, so you may have to limit these as well. If your baby has colic, eczema or chronic congestion, it could be caused by something you are eating, particularly if there is a history of allergies in your family. The food most commonly associated with these kinds of reactions is cow's milk. Try eliminating it from your diet for three days, and see if there are any improvements. Other foods to consider are those that other family members are sensitive to. It may take a little perseverance to track the culprit down.

Supplements may be necessary for those women who have a nutritional deficiency or who are unable to follow the vegetarian food guide. Prenatal supplements can be finished, then an adult multivitamin and mineral supplement is quite acceptable. Make sure that it contains vitamin B_{12}, vitamin D, iron and zinc. Vegan breast-feeding mothers must be especially careful to get a reliable source of B_{12}. Some mothers will also require a calcium supplement.

Table 9.1 Planning an adequate prenatal diet

sample pattern	food choices that meet sample pattern
Breakfast	
3 grain products	1 cup oatmeal
1 fruit	1 tsp ground flaxseed (mixed in oatmeal)
2 milk and milk alternates	½ cup milk
	(fortified non-dairy or cow's)
	1 orange
	1 slice toast
	1 Tbsp blackstrap molasses
	1 Tbsp tahini
Lunch	
3 grain products	2 slices whole grain bread
2 vegetables	½ cup tofu
2 milk and milk alternates	(tofu salad sandwich)
1 beans and bean alternates	1 cup Chinese cabbage salad
	1 slice banana loaf
Dinner	
2 grain products	1 cup millet
2 vegetables and 1 fruit	1 cup curried garbanzos
1 milk and milk alternates	1 cup broccoli
2 beans and bean alternates	sliced melon
Snacks	
1 grain product	1 whole grain muffin
2 fruits	1 banana
1 milk and milk alternates	5 figs
	1 oz fresh walnuts

The totals provided by this sample plan are:
9 grain products
8 vegetables and fruits
6 milk and milk alternates
3 beans and bean alternates
Be sure to drink at least 6 glasses of water a day.

INFANCY: UP TO TWO YEARS OF AGE

The first two years of life are filled with discovery. So many new colors, textures and flavors are welcomed by the adventurous infant. As parents, we must seize the opportunity to build a foundation for health that includes a wide variety of wonderful foods.

It is our responsibility to ensure that the foods we choose provide all the nutrients that are needed for proper growth and development. We must begin with a basic understanding of the unique needs of human infants and a little common sense.

During the first year of life, our babies grow at an unprecedented rate, tripling their birth weight. Their requirements for most nutrients (per pound of body weight) are two to three times that of adults. When we consider the small stomach capacity of a baby and this tremendous rate of growth, we can understand their need for a steady supply of energy and nutrients.

A vegetarian or vegan infant can be very well-nourished; the parent or care-giver must simply be informed about the kinds of food patterns that work well and those that don't. One must pay particular attention to the energy, protein and B_{12} in the baby's diet. It is also important that the diet not be too bulky, as this can reduce overall energy intake. Certain foods that are higher in energy and nutrients, such as tofu, nut and seed butters, are especially valuable for the vegan infant. As vegetarian and vegan diets increase in popularity, new products will appear on the market to help make food preparation easier for vegetarian and vegan parents.

Poorly planned or overly restrictive diets can have serious consequences for the growth, development and overall health of an infant. The following guidelines will help to ensure that your vegetarian or vegan baby grows up to be a happy, thriving toddler.

Nutrition Guidelines for Vegetarian and Vegan Infants (birth to two years of age)

1. Infants should be breast-fed for a minimum of six months, and preferably for a full two years.

Breast milk is specifically designed to meet the needs of the human infant, just as the milks of other mammals are specifically designed to meet the needs of their young. The more scientists learn about the unique composition of human milk, the more they realize that an equivalent can never be formulated in a lab.

Breast milk provides much more than simply an ideal balance of nutrients for your infant. It provides special substances that will protect your baby from infection. Breast-feeding helps to create a bond between you and your infant, and its benefits can continue to provide these advantages well into the second year of life and beyond.

2. If breast-feeding is not chosen, not possible or if it stops before a year of age for the lacto-ovo vegetarian infant, and two years of age for the vegan infant, commercial infant formula is recommended.

Commercial infant formula is the most acceptable alternative to breast milk. Experts advise using the iron-fortified variety from birth until the introduction of high-iron solid foods, as iron deficiency is the most common nutritional problem in infants. If you stop breast-feeding, or breast-feed your baby fewer than three times a day, a commercial, iron-fortified infant formula should be used as the replacement.

The American Academy of Pediatrics advises that whole cow's milk be avoided during the first 12 months of life. The primary reason is that the ingestion of cow's milk in infancy often leads to iron-deficiency anemia (cow's milk is low in iron, reduces its availability and can cause blood loss in infants). There is also concern that one of the constituents of cow's milk may be a trigger for insulin-dependent diabetes mellitus in susceptible infants. This constituent is found in milk and milk products, as well as in some infant cow's milk formulas (one study found it in powdered formulas but not in the liquid varieties). For this reason it has been suggested that babies who are at high risk of developing diabetes should be breast-fed during their first year.

Low-fat milks are not suitable for babies under 12 months of age, and skim milk should not be used as the main source of milk for babies under 24 months of age. Vegan babies should continue to be given infant formula for a full two years and beyond. *Fortified or unfortified soymilk, tofu milk, rice milk, nut milk and skim cow's milk should not be used as the primary milk source during the first two years of your baby's life.* These milks will not provide the nutrients necessary for optimal growth and development of your infant and could lead to malnutrition.

3. Vegetarian infants between 12 and 24 months of age should consume at least 20 oz of breast milk, cow's milk or formula per day.
Milk continues to provide important nutrients for your baby in the second year of life. It helps to ensure that he or she receives sufficient calcium and high-quality protein to support normal growth and development.

If your baby is a lacto-ovo vegetarian, breast milk or whole or 2% cow's milk are appropriate choices. Other animal products such as yogurt, cottage cheese and eggs provide additional protein. Plant foods such as legumes, tofu, vegetables and grains also contribute significantly to the protein needs of the lacto-ovo vegetarian baby.

For the vegan infant, breast milk or formula should be continued to help ensure an adequate balance of nutrients (at least 3 good feeds will amount to approximately 20 oz. of milk). Plant foods supply all of the additional protein needed by the 12–24-month-old vegan. Your baby should be given a wide variety of protein-containing foods, as described in the "Getting Enough to Grow On" guidelines on pages 159–60. By following these guidelines, your infant will receive 25–35 grams of protein per day (providing all necessary essential amino acids) which is well above the 16 grams per day recommended by the National Academy of Sciences. Legumes are an especially important part of the baby's diet. Tofu is the undisputed star among the legume family for our little ones. It not only provides protein, but it is high in fat (with essential fatty acids), low in fiber and loaded with valuable vitamins and minerals, including calcium (check the label).

If for any reason lesser amounts of breast milk or formula are consumed during the first two years of life, it is recommended that food combinations be provided at each meal that supply high-quality protein. Soy products (such as tofu and tempeh), quinoa and amaranth have amino acid profiles similar to cow's milk and are therefore important protein sources for the vegan infant. Other plant foods can be combined to offer similar protein quality. Plant proteins tend to be slightly lower in their digestibility, thus vegan babies require slightly more protein than lacto-ovo vegetarian babies. Examples of "all-plant" combinations that work well for the older baby include pea soup with bread, tofu with rice, and bean stew with millet (refer to Chapter 3 for more information on protein complementation).

4. Breast-fed infants who are not exposed to sufficient sunlight should be given a D supplement of 7.5 µg per day (birth to 6 months) and 10 µg per day (over 6 months). The United States RDA recommends that breast-fed infants (birth to 6 months) who are not exposed to sunlight should receive a daily vitamin D supplement of 5.0 to 7.5 µg (200–300 IU). Infants over 6 months of age should be given a supplement of 10 µg (400 IU) per day. To make enough vitamin D, infants need a total of approximately two hours of sunlight per week to hands and face (more for babies with dark skin).

It is a matter of debate whether or not human milk can provide sufficient vitamin D for an infant with little or no sun exposure. Nursing mothers who do not receive sufficient vitamin D from food sources or sunlight will have *very* low levels of this nutrient in their milk. Cases of rickets reported in American breast-fed infants appear to be a consequence of both minimal sun exposure and low maternal vitamin D intake. Mothers who receive sunlight and/or vitamin D-fortified foods will have vitamin D in their milk, but whether or not it is sufficient to meet infant needs is less certain.

Formula-fed infants don't need a vitamin D supplement as infant formula is fortified with this nutrient.

5. Breast-fed infants require an additional source of iron by six months of age. Infants on regular infant formula need extra iron by at least four months of age.

The iron stores of breast-fed babies start to decline at about six months of age, and even earlier for babies who were premature. With the small amounts of highly absorbable iron from breast milk and the iron stores from birth, many infants can maintain normal iron levels until they are nine months old or more. However, even marginal iron deficiency can slow development and cause irritability. Thus, it is generally recommended that a good source of iron be provided by six months of age for breast-fed infants.

The American Academy of Pediatrics (AAP) and most pediatricians advise the use of iron-fortified formula from birth for infants who are not breast-fed. For those who do use an unfortified formula, extra iron is needed by no later than four months of age. Iron-fortified formula or an iron supplement (at a dose of about 0.5 mg/lb body weight) can be given until the baby begins solid foods. The first food generally recommended is iron-fortified infant cereal, which is easy to digest and provides abundant available iron. Begin with single grain infant cereals such as rice, barley or oats, so that food allergies can be easily identified if they occur. Mixed cereals can be used after the infant has been given each grain separately. Iron-fortified cereals can continue to provide high-quality iron up to two years of age and beyond. Sprinkle them on cold cereal, and add them to muffins, pancakes or other baked goods.

If you do not wish to use commercial infant cereal, you'll need to provide an alternate source of iron for your baby. One way of doing this is by adding iron drops to cooked whole grain cereals. Tofu, prune juice, fortified cream of wheat and quinoa also provide significant amounts of iron. The absorption of iron from these foods will improve significantly if they are given with a vitamin C source. To achieve the daily recommended allowance for iron without supplements, your baby will need a combination of iron-rich foods such as 2 tbsp of tofu, 2 tbsp of quinoa, ¼ cup of prune juice and ¼ cup of wax beans. Other high-iron vegetarian foods are listed in table 3.8 (page 60).

6. Breast-fed vegan infants should receive a vitamin B_{12} supplement of at least 0.5 µg per day for the first year and 0.7 µg per day for the second year.

As a vegan mother, your breast milk can be very low in vitamin B_{12}, especially if you are not using a supplement or vitamin B_{12}-fortified foods. For this reason, your baby should receive a vitamin B_{12} supplement of at least 0.5 µg per day from birth until at least two years of age, or until such time that enough vitamin B_{12} is provided by fortified foods.

If you are a lacto-ovo vegetarian, you don't need a supplement unless your intake of milk and eggs is limited. You can get enough vitamin B_{12} from

3 cups of milk (or equivalent dairy products) or 1 egg and 2 cups of milk per day.

If your baby is formula-fed, a vitamin B_{12} supplement is not necessary as formula is fortified. Vitamin B_{12} supplements can be discontinued if your breast-fed infant begins to consume at least 3 oz of formula each day in addition to or in place of breast milk.

7. Fat and energy should not be restricted during the first two years of life, unless medically indicated.

Breast milk, the ideal food for infants, derives approximately 54 percent of its calories from fat; 1 cup of breast milk contains about 175 calories. This could well be nature's way of telling us that babies need food that is concentrated in both fat and energy. Vegetarian, and particularly vegan, diets are sometimes low in fat and energy, and are often high in fiber. Be sure to take this into account when planning your infant's diet, so baby receives enough calories, fat and protein. As you begin to introduce solid foods, follow these suggestions to help keep fat and energy at a healthy level for your infant:

- *Include plenty of low-fiber, high-protein foods in the diet.* Tofu, smooth nut and seed butters and creams, soy yogurt, soy cheese and other soy products, in addition to dairy products and eggs for the lacto-ovo vegetarian, are good choices.
- *Do not restrict fat during this time.* Low-fat or skim milk, other "low-fat" food products and foods made with fat substitutes are not appropriate for infants. Use some high-fat foods such as tofu, avocado, wheat germ, smooth nut and seed butters and good quality vegetable oils in food preparation.
- *Avoid excessive fiber in the diet.* Concentrated fiber products such as raw wheat bran, bran cereals and bran muffins should be limited. Use mainly whole grain breads and cereals (for example, brown rice, millet, quinoa and oatmeal bread), as they contribute important minerals to the diet. Some refined breads, pastas and cereals can help limit total fiber in the diet. Use moderate amounts of raw vegetables and fruit.
- *Serve regular meals with snacks in-between for infants above ten months of age.* Infants have very small stomach capacities, and thus should be fed frequently. Choose snacks carefully, making sure that they contribute to the infant's overall nutrient needs. (Younger infants are still receiving enough milk between meals so that regular snacks are not as important.) A few energy-packed favorites include spreads (hummus, tofu spreads or nut butters) on crackers or rusks; bread with cheese (soy or dairy); homemade, wholesome cookies, muffins or squares; rice, cornmeal, quinoa or

other whole grain puddings with fruit, and yogurt (soy or dairy).

8. Solid foods should be delayed until four to six months of age.
Not so long ago, a baby's first bite of solid food was considered a real developmental milestone. Parents were often told to begin solid foods by one or two months of age, and the babies usually ended up with more food dribbling down their faces than into their bellies. We now understand that most infants have no need for solid foods before six months of age. Some infants are ready for solids by four or five months of age, particularly if they are growing very quickly. When your baby is ready for solids, he or she will let you know with the following signs:

- Your baby will be constantly hungry, even after nursing eight or ten times in a day or drinking 40 oz of formula.
- He or she will be able to sit up and give signs of satiety like turning the head away.
- The birth weight will have at least doubled.
- Your baby will be able to move solids to the back of the mouth and swallow without spitting most of it back out.

There are no hard and fast rules regarding the order of introduction for solid foods after six months of age, although the sequence usually recommended is infant cereals, vegetables, fruits, then protein-rich foods. This sequence takes into consideration both the nutritional value of these first foods and the maturity of the infant's gastrointestinal system. Each infant is unique in his or her ability to chew and handle foods at various ages (don't wait till your baby has teeth; he or she can chew without them). Some infants are ready for mashed vegetables and fruits by six months, while others are not ready for these types of foods until they are eight months old.

Suggestions regarding specific quantities of foods needed between 12 and 24 months are provided in the "Getting Enough to Grow On" guidelines on pages 159–60.

9. Avoid giving foods to infants that may cause choking or asphyxiation.
Your baby may have difficulty chewing and swallowing foods that are small, hard or seedy. Always supervise your infant while he or she is eating, as choking can occur suddenly. Make sure children are seated during meals and snacks. Eating on the run greatly increases the risk for infants. The following foods are commonly associated with choking in babies and should be avoided or prepared as outlined to reduce the danger of choking:

During the first 12 months avoid:
- raw, hard fruit and vegetable pieces (cook for a few minutes to soften)
- grapes (later, grapes can be cut in half)

- fruits with seeds (these can be mashed and strained)

During the first three to four years avoid:
- popcorn, nuts and seeds (smooth nut butters and creams may be given)
- potato or taco chips
- small candies
- whole tofu dogs (slice in half or quarters, lengthwise)
- chewing gum

10. Honey and corn syrup should not be fed to infants under one year of age.
Infant botulism is a rare but very dangerous form of food poisoning. It can happen when an infant eats a food containing *Clostridium botulinum* spores, which can produce a deadly toxin in the infant's gastrointestinal system. The foods eaten by infants that most commonly contain these spores are honey and corn syrup. In order for the *Clostridium* spores to produce the toxin, their environment must be non-acidic and anaerobic. In the early months of life, a baby's gastrointestinal system fits both of these criteria. As the baby gets older, and is eating a variety of solid foods, his or her gastrointestinal tract becomes acidic (usually by six or eight months of age), and the toxin can no longer be produced.

Getting Enough to Grow On: a guide for the 12–24-month-old infant

The second year of life is an important time of transition for a baby. Parents need to take special care to ensure that their baby receives a balance of foods that will make this transition a healthy one. The 12–24-month-old infant should receive the following foods each day:

Milk and Milk Alternates
2½ cups of formula or breast milk or a combination of the two.
It is important to continue breast-feeding or formula for the vegan infant. Lacto-ovo vegetarian babies can be safely switched to whole cow's milk at 12 months of age.

Other milk alternates can be given, but should not be used as a replacement for breast milk, formula or whole cow's milk (2% milk is acceptable for the baby who is getting higher-fat foods such as cheese and eggs on a regular basis, and is growing very well).

Breads and Cereals
4–6 oz iron-fortified infant cereal, plus
2–4 child-size servings of other breads and cereals per day
1 child-size serving = ½ slice of bread
      ¼ cup rice, quinoa, enriched pasta or
        other cooked grain
      ½ cup cold cereal

Vegetables
2–3 child-size servings per day
1 child-size serving = ½ cup salad or raw vegetable pieces
       ¼ cup cooked vegetables
       ⅓ cup vegetable juice

Fruits
2–3 child-size servings per day
1 child-size serving = ½–1 fresh fruit
       ⅓ cup fruit pieces or fruit juice

Bean and Bean Alternates
2 child-size servings per day
1 child-size serving = ¼ cup cooked legumes
       1 oz tofu
       4 tsp nut or seed butter
       1 egg

CHILDREN: TWO TO TEN YEARS OF AGE

The years of childhood provide an excellent opportunity to introduce a world of interesting and enjoyable foods to impressionable little ones. By giving your children a wide variety of wholesome vegetarian foods, they'll reap the benefits twice over. First, as children they'll have less likelihood of becoming obese than their omnivorous peers. Second, as adults they'll be at reduced risk for several chronic degenerative diseases (including coronary artery disease and cancer) than the population at large. One common criticism of vegetarian and vegan diets is that they may place children at risk for nutritional deficiencies. The reality is that insufficient nutrition is more a function of poor diet design than of whether a diet is vegetarian or omnivorous. Research studies have clearly demonstrated that well-planned vegetarian and vegan diets can support normal growth and development in children.

In planning a vegetarian diet for your child, you have to consider how their needs differ from the needs of an adult. Small children have limited stomach capacities and high requirements for nutrients. A plant-centered diet, containing mainly fruits, vegetables and whole grains, can be too low in calories and other nutrients and too high in fiber to meet a child's needs, particularly during the preschool years. Vegetarian diets can be well-designed to provide more concentrated sources of energy and nutrients, so that an appropriate balance of foods is achieved.

Children who are raised from birth as vegetarians generally accept a wide variety of healthful foods without any problem. If you adopt a vegetarian style of eating a number of years after your children are born, there may be a little resistance, especially if your original diet was based on highly refined foods and "meat and potato" type meals. Do not despair. There are a number of things that can be done to help ease the transition to vegetarianism for youngsters:

- *Involve children in food selection and preparation.* Children love to help stir, knead, roll, decorate and do just about anything else in the kitchen that you think they're ready for.
- *Consider your child's preferences when planning menus.* Try to include something that they really enjoy at each meal.
- *Serve vegetarian versions of traditional favorites.* Pizza, spaghetti, lasagne, chili, burgers, hot dogs, stews and stir-frys are all popular items.
- *Stock the cupboards and refrigerator with a variety of foods that are both wholesome and appealing for children.*
- *Don't restrict fun foods excessively.* It can be tough enough on a child to be vegetarian in the midst of friends who love cheeseburgers and chicken nuggets, so do allow your version of "treats."
- *Keep offering new foods, even if they are rejected.* A child who turns up their nose at something one day could end up adopting it as their favorite meal a month later (it really does happen!).
- *Respect a child's right to dislike a few foods.* Children can't be expected to love everything, nor is it necessary for good nutrition.
- *Let your children decide when they have had enough to eat.*
- *Work on making meals a pleasant time.* Set a pretty table, light a candle and encourage positive family interaction.

As parents, we are responsible for providing our children with safe and adequate food. The whole thing can seem a little overwhelming at times, especially when the children go through periods of food refusal or strange eating behaviors. Be assured that if you provide a variety of nourishing foods in a pleasant atmosphere, your child will manage to get enough to eat.

Nutrition Guidelines for Vegetarian and Vegan Children

1. Include a variety of foods from all five food groups, as outlined in the vegetarian food guide for children.

Children learn to enjoy the foods that they grow up with. If they are served whole grains, a wide variety of vegetables and fruits, legumes, tofu and other healthful foods as described in the vegetarian food guide, they will likely accept and enjoy these kinds of foods all their lives.

Offer something from every food group at each meal whenever possible. This will help to ensure that a balance of nutrients is provided throughout the day.

Select a variety of foods from within each food group so that your children become familiar with many different tastes and textures.

Grain products

• Instead of always having the same type of sliced bread, buy a variety: rye, pumpernickel, pita bread, chapatis, bagels, multigrain rolls and oatmeal scones.

• Try many different grains such as millet, quinoa, spelt, barley, amaranth, and kamut.

• Offer your children a variety of pasta including whole grain, vegetable and pastas made from different grains.

Vegetables and fruits

• Plant some unusual vegetables or go to an ethnic store to buy them. Involve your children and make it a real adventure.

• Try artichokes, eggplant, zucchini, collards, kale, daikon or broccoflower (a cross between broccoli and cauliflower).

• Children often love to try unusual fruits such as mangos, Chinese pears and pomegranates.

Beans and bean alternates

• Experiment with all kinds of tofu, and use it in everything from appetizers to dessert.

• Try other soy products such as tempeh, miso and soy burgers.

• Get familiar with many different kinds of legumes. Try black beans, red lentils, pinto beans, adzuki beans, mung beans and lima beans.

Milk and milk alternates

• Introduce milk alternates such as tahini, collards, almond butter and tofu early on and make them a part of the normal fare.

• If dairy products are used, include cottage cheese and other cheeses, yogurt and puddings.

2. Preschoolers should receive 16–20 oz of calcium-rich milk per day. Appropriate drinks include breast milk, formula, fortified soymilk and cow's milk (or milk from another mammal such as a goat). School age children should receive four ½-cup servings of milk (2 cups total) or milk alternates (see the vegetarian food guide on page 168) per day.

Milk continues to be a valuable source of calcium, vitamin D, riboflavin and other nutrients after the first two years of life. During the preschool years, it is recommended that a nutritious milk be selected, providing plenty of calcium and protein. Suitable milks include breast milk, formula, fortified soymilk and cow's milk. One option during the preschool years is breast milk. In many cultures, children are breast-fed into the third and fourth years of life. Although this is not a common practice in our culture, it is deserving of consideration. Breast milk offers a wonderful balance of nutrients and immune protection for your child as long as it continues. Even though the amount of breast milk consumed during this time may be fairly small, it should be taken into account when determining quantities of other milks needed.

For lacto-ovo vegetarian children, 2% or 1% cow's milk is suggested, depending on the needs of the individual child. If your child is overweight, a lower-fat milk may be appropriate. Cheese, yogurt, and milk alternatives such as tofu made with calcium, legumes, greens, and nuts and seeds provide the necessary calcium, but they do not contain vitamin D, so it is important that a reliable source be provided (sunshine, fortified foods or a supplement).

For vegan preschoolers two to five years of age, commercial soy-based infant formula or a calcium- and vitamin D-fortified soymilk is recommended (in addition to or in place of breast milk). By using soy formula, your child's risk for nutritional deficiencies will be reduced, as it is fortified with a broad range of nutrients necessary for growth and development. Fortified soymilks are also acceptable choices (full-fat varieties are suitable for most vegan preschoolers). Unfortified soymilks, rice milks and nut milks are *not* appropriate milk substitutes during the preschool period as they do not provide sufficient nutrients to meet the needs of a preschooler.

Calcium-fortified non-dairy milks are also the most suitable milk for the older vegan child. Fortified non-dairy milks that are commonly available include soymilk, tofu milk, rice milk and potato milk. Soymilk provides a good supply of protein while rice, potato and tofu milks have much smaller amounts. Soymilk is also often fortified with vitamins A and D. Other soymilks fortified with vitamin B_{12} are just coming onto the market. Many fortified non-dairy milks are low in fat, thus it is important that your child receive adequate fat to meet their needs for energy and essential fatty acids if these milks are used.

3. Provide a variety of protein-rich foods in your child's diet each day.
It is important for children to receive protein-rich foods every day. By following the "Getting Enough to Grow On" guidelines on pages 167–68, your preschool child will receive 30–45 grams of protein a day and your 6– to 10–year-old will receive 45–55 grams protein a day. This is well above the recommended dietary allowances (RDAs) of 16–24 grams for 2– to 5-year-olds and 24–28 grams for 2– to 10-year-olds. When sufficient calories are provided from a variety of nutritious plant foods and foods with little nutritional value are kept to a minimum, protein needs are virtually assured.

As a lacto-ovo vegetarian, your child will get plenty of protein from animal foods such as milk and eggs and protein-rich plant foods such as legumes, nuts and seeds.

The vegan child will meet all of his or her protein needs by consuming plant foods. Legumes are particularly valuable for children who do not consume animal products. Make tofu, tempeh, textured soy protein, soymilk, and a wide assortment of colorful legumes a regular part of your child's meals. Nuts and seeds can be made into butters, creams and sauces with a blender or food processor and used in preparing vegan lasagnes, casseroles and baked goods.

4. Provide foods that are concentrated in fat and energy and low in fiber as part of the regular daily fare.

Vegetarian and vegan diets can be very high in bulk, making it difficult for small children to meet their needs for energy. When this occurs protein is used as energy, rather than for building body tissues, and growth can be compromised. This situation is most often seen when foods rich in fat and protein are restricted. Small children need nutritious, energy-packed foods throughout the day. The following suggestions will help to ensure that the vegetarian or vegan child gets enough fat and calories:

• *Provide three meals a day plus regular snacks in-between.* For many children it is difficult to pack in enough food at a meal to tide them over until the next meal.

• *Don't restrict fat excessively.* Allow liberal use of tofu and other soy products, avocados and nuts, seeds and their butters. Avoid whole nuts and seeds until four years of age due to danger of choking. Include some fats and oils in baking and cooking. Milk, yogurt, cheese and eggs provide concentrated fat and energy for lacto-ovo vegetarian children.

• *Don't overdo raw foods.* Use some cooked vegetables and fruits and their juices. Make sure legumes have been well cooked.

• *Avoid the use of concentrated fiber foods in the form of wheat bran or fiber supplements.* Choose whole grain breads and cereals, but do not add extra fiber to foods. Whole grains can be cooked to increase their digestibility. Use refined grains such as pasta, crackers and couscous in lesser quantity, because of their inferior mineral content.

• *Offer plenty of low-fiber, protein-rich foods.* Great choices include tofu, nut butters and creams, soy cheese and yogurt, in addition to dairy products and eggs for the lacto-ovo vegetarian.

• *Make a special effort to provide children with appealing and wholesome snacks.* Offer nutritious squares, muffins, loaves and cookies, crackers and cheese (soy or dairy) or nut butters, yogurt (soy or dairy), and trail mixes for older children.

5. Provide your child with plant foods that are good sources of iron and zinc every day. Iron deficiency is the most widely recognized nutritional deficiency in North American children. Vegetarian and vegan children may receive insufficient iron if their diet is low in iron-rich foods and high in inhibitors of iron absorption such as phytates and oxalates.

Lacto-ovo vegetarian children may not get enough iron if dairy products are used as the main source of protein. Dairy foods are not only poor sources of iron, but they inhibit its absorption. It is not uncommon for a child to consume cheese, yogurt, ice cream, or other dairy foods at almost every meal and with snacks, in addition to drinking 3 or 4 glasses of milk during the day. When dairy products are the central focus of the diet, it can be difficult to make room for iron-rich legumes, tofu and greens. If your child consumes dairy foods, limit them to the number of servings recommended in the vegetarian food guide for children.

To help ensure that your child receives sufficient iron, frequently include iron-rich foods such as tofu, prunes, legumes or dark greens along with a good source of vitamin C in the diet. Infant cereal is an excellent source of iron. It can be added to other hot cereals, pancakes and baked goods. Remember to use cast-iron cookware when possible.

Although we seldom hear of problems relating to zinc deficiency, it is one of the nutrients for which we have difficulty meeting the RDA. Insufficient zinc in a child's diet can cause a lack of appetite, delays in development and slow wound healing.

To help ensure that your child's diet contains sufficient zinc, serve legumes, nut butters, wheat germ, miso and tofu on a regular basis. Rather than refined breads and cereals, select whole grains most of the time, as they provide two or three times as much zinc. Preschoolers who are drinking 20 oz of formula each day are getting about one third of their zinc requirements from the formula alone.

6. Include at least 3 servings of vegetables and 2 servings of fruits in the diet each day. The value of vegetables is well-known to one and all, but many people still don't manage to eat their daily quota. Perhaps this situation would be remedied if we could interest our children in these fabulous foods during their formative years. Vegetables and fruits provide an abundance of vitamins, minerals and phytochemicals.

For love of vegetables:

• *Encourage an interest in vegetables by growing some in your own garden or even on your balcony.* If that isn't possible, bring children on an excursion to a farm and let them see how these foods grow.

• *Get children accustomed to dark greens early on.* Broccoli is often a favorite. Use a variety of dark greens in salads, stir-frys, casseroles and spaghetti sauces.

• *Be adventurous!* Try all kinds of different vegetables and show your enthusiasm when you bring home something unusual. If you go into ethnic stores, ask how to prepare unfamiliar vegetables – you'll get some great ideas!

• *Preserve the nutritional value and bright color of vegetables by cooking them in a minimum of water, steaming or stir-frying them.* Children often prefer their vegetables tender-crisp rather than mushy, so try not to overcook them.

• *Make these healthy foods fun.* Children love vegetables and dip. They make a great snack, even before dinner. Fancy shapes and patterns are most inviting for little ones. Vegetable pieces can also make wonderful pictures on a plate (faces are a favorite).

For love of fruit:

• *Go for variety!* There are so many flavorful fruits to choose from, it's not hard to find a dozen or two that will stimulate even the fussiest eaters.

• *Serve vitamin C-rich fruit often.* Whole fruits such as oranges, grapefruits, kiwi, cantaloupe and strawberries are your best choices. Fruit juices can be used, but only in moderation (e.g., not more than 8 oz per day). Juice can cause chronic diarrhea in small children and displace other foods in the diet when used in excess. Do not use fruit "drinks" in place of juice, even if they do have vitamin C added. Vitamin C is usually all they have; the rest is sugar, flavor and color.

• *Make fruit fun.* Kids love fruit kabobs, fruit salads and fruit platters (arrange the fruit in a flower shape).

• *Offer dried fruits for a change.* Dried fruits are convenient, portable and nutritious. Try something different like dried peaches, pears, apples or your own homemade fruit leather. Unfortunately, dried fruits aren't so great for the teeth – remember to brush afterward, if possible.

7. Include a source of omega-3 fatty acids in the diet.
Omega-3 fatty acids are very important to normal growth and development and good food sources should be included in your child's diet each day. The following chart provides a small list of omega-3-rich foods and the quantities of each required to meet minimum daily needs (see pages 104–8 for further information on omega-3 fatty acids in foods).

Omega-3 Fatty Acids — Getting Enough

Food Sources	2–5-year-olds	6–10-year-olds
flaxseed oil	⅓ tsp	½ tsp
canola and soybean oil	2 tsp	1 Tbsp
firm tofu	4 oz	6 oz

8. Include a reliable source of vitamin B₁₂ in the diet every day.

Vitamin B_{12} is not supplied by plant foods to any significant degree. Thus, a special effort must be made to ensure that vegetarian and particularly vegan children receive reliable sources of this nutrient.

Lacto-ovo vegetarian children can obtain enough vitamin B_{12} from dairy products and eggs.

For vegan children, fortified foods or supplements must be used to supply this vitamin. Significant dietary sources include Red Star T-6635+ nutritional yeast, vitamin B_{12}-fortified cereals, meat analogs and tofu milk. Be sure to read the labels.

One and a half teaspoons of Red Star T-6635+ nutritional yeast flakes per day supplies sufficient B_{12}. The reference daily value (DV) for vitamin B_{12} on food labels is 6 µgs, thus a product that provides 25 percent or more of the DV will meet the daily requirements for a 2– to 10-year-old child.

The Question of Supplements

Lacto-ovo vegetarian children can be well-nourished without the use of supplements, providing that a balance of foods as described in the vegetarian food guide for 2– to 10-year-olds is followed.

For vegan children, needs for all nutrients can be met if vitamin B_{12}-fortified foods are used. Otherwise, a supplement of vitamin B_{12} is necessary. A regular children's multivitamin/mineral supplement generally contains enough vitamin B_{12} – read the label. Vegan children will also need a vitamin D supplement if there is limited exposure to sunlight. If insufficient servings from the milk and milk alternates group are consumed, then a supplement of approximately 500 mg elemental calcium per day is recommended.

If a supplement is used, it is best to select one which contains a variety of vitamins *and* minerals including vitamin B_{12}, vitamin D, zinc and iron in amounts which approximate the RDAs (see Appendix 2). Many children's supplements contain no minerals except iron. Read the label. Avoid single nutrient supplements other than calcium, unless medically indicated.

Getting Enough to Grow On: A Guide for 2– to 10-year-olds

Children need smaller, more frequent servings of food. Appetite can fluctuate considerably in this age group, and there are going to be times when your child will eat more or less than what is suggested in the guide. Child-size servings are recommended for 2– to 5-year-olds in all groups but the milk and milk alternates group. These servings are approximately half of the portion recommended for the older child or adult. For additional examples of foods in each of the food groups, see the vegetarian food guide.

Milk and Milk Alternates: 4–6 servings per day
2–5 years: Give preschoolers 16–20 oz of cow's milk, soy formula or fortified soymilk per day. Milk and milk alternates servings should mainly come from these beverages.
6–10 years: Adult-Size Servings
one serving = ½ cup cow's milk, infant formula or fortified non-dairy milk
           1 oz dairy cheese or ½ cup of yogurt
           ¼ cup or 2 oz tofu (made with calcium)
           1 cup calcium-rich green vegetables (see food guide on page 138 for specifics)
           3 Tbsp almond butter, 1½ oz almonds, or 2 Tbsp tahini

Grain Products: 6–11 servings per day

2–5 years: Child-Size Servings	6–10 years: Adult-Size Servings
one serving = ½ slice of bread	*one serving* = 1 slice of bread
¼ cup cooked grain	½ cup cooked grain
¼ cup hot cereal	½ cup hot cereal
⅓ cup cold cereal	¾ cup cold cereal

Vegetables: 3–5 servings per day

2–5 years: Child-Size Servings	6–10 years: Adult-Size Servings
one serving = ¼ cup vegetables	*one serving* = ½ cup vegetables
⅓ cup vegetable juice	¾ cup vegetable juice

Fruits: 2–4 servings per day

2–5 years: Child-Size Servings	6–10 years: Adult-Size Servings
one serving = ¼ cup fruits	*one serving* = ½ cup fruits
½ whole fruit	1 whole fruit
or 1 small fruit	or 2 small fruits
⅓ cup fruit juice	¾ cup fruit

Beans and Bean Alternates: 2–3 servings per day

2–5 years: Child-Size Servings	6–10 years: Adult-Size Servings
one serving = ¼ cup legumes	*one serving* = ½ cup legumes
¼ cup or 2 oz tofu	½ cup or 4 oz tofu
1½ Tbsp nut/seed butter	3 Tbsp nut/seed butter
1 small egg	1 large egg

Include a source of omega-3 fatty acids in the diet.

ADOLESCENTS: AGES 11 TO 17

Many teens today are making the decision to cut meat out of their menu. Their motivation often comes from concerns about the environment or animal rights rather than from a desire to improve the nutritional quality of their diet. This doesn't mean that food is not of prime importance. It just means that the criteria for food selection may be a little different than it is for the average health-conscious vegetarian adult. The two main criteria for food selection by teens generally are:

1) *How fast can it be ready?*

2) *Does it taste good?*

The most acceptable answers to these questions are that *it is ready* and *it tastes great*. In other words we're talking instant, delicious food. Our society is fairly well set up for instant and delicious, but not often for vegetarian.

Many teens who grew up eating the standard North American fare simply stop eating meat when they become vegetarian. Instead of a hamburger and fries for lunch, they opt for a double order of fries. When chicken, potatoes and corn arrive on the dinner table, they eat only the potatoes and corn. There are a few problems with this kind of approach. First, parents tend to be less than supportive because they see their teenager eating very poorly. Second, this inadequate eating pattern can take its toll on the teen, causing him or her to feel run down and eventually develop nutritional deficiencies.

The solution that will usually satisfy parents and teens alike is to venture into the world of nutritional alternatives to meat. The possibilities are endless. Parents generally become a little less resistant to the whole idea if they know that their teenager is getting a well-balanced diet. In many cases, they begin to enjoy vegetarian meals, and some even end up becoming vegetarians themselves. The result could well be a healthier family.

Of course, there are also teens who have been raised on a vegetarian diet. This group generally does very well. Some studies show that these vegetarian teens are not only well-nourished, but they eat less junk, less fat and more fiber than meat-eating peers. A large study by John Sabate, looking at Seventh-Day Adventist teens, showed that these vegetarians actually outgrew their omnivorous peers by an average of one inch.

The nutritional needs of a vegetarian teen are no different than the needs of any other teen. Many physical changes are taking place, and the demands for nutrients are high. There are several things that a parent can do to help a vegetarian teen be well nourished:

• *Keep a variety of super-fast and wholesome foods handy.* Stock up on fresh fruits, trail mixes, nutritious baked goods, and soy or dairy yogurt and cheese, as well as whole grain breads and cereals.

• *Encourage teens to contribute to meals by helping with meal planning and preparation.* Teens can be expected to prepare whole meals or make a salad or a nutritious dessert. This will give them a head start for managing on their own. The recipes provided in this book are a great place to start.

• *Offer vegetarian versions of popular dinner favorites.* Many traditional items such as pizza, burgers, burritos, lasagne, chili and spaghetti can easily be made meatless.

• *Remember that your teenager is responsible for his or her own food choices.* Your job is to stock the pantry with a wide variety of healthy foods.

• *Encourage involvement in groups and activities that will increase their knowledge of vegetarianism and the vegetarian way of eating.* The Vegetarian Education Network (VE-Net) supports young vegetarians and publishes a newsletter (How on Earth) written by teens for teens. For information about VE-Net or newsletter subscriptions, write to: VE-Net, P.O. Box 3347, West Chester, PA 19381 or call (717) 529–8638. Another organization founded and run by teens is YES! (Youth for Environmental Sanity). This group promotes vegetarianism and educates teens about the environment with their popular YES! tour, which travels to schools in the United States, Canada and Mexico. Contact YES! at 706 Frederick St., Santa Cruz, CA 95062 or call (408) 459–9344.

• Join *Advocates for Better Children's Diets (ABCD).* ABCD is a coalition of 22 organizations including the American Dietetic Association (ADA), the American Heart Association (AHA), the Vegetarian Resource Group (VRG) and the Center for Science in the Public Interest (CSPI) who are working together in an effort to improve school lunches. They have developed recommendations to assist schools in complying with the Dietary Guidelines for Americans.

The guidelines that follow provide practical tips on nutrition for teens. Don't get too concerned if things don't go precisely according to plan. Teens seem to manage even under conditions that are less than ideal.

Nutrition Guidelines for Vegetarian and Vegan Adolescents

1. Eat a variety of foods as outlined in the vegetarian food guide.
The best way to ensure the necessary nutrients are provided is to include a wide variety of foods from each of the food groups outlined in the vegetarian food guide. (Note that the number of servings suggested in the milk and milk alternates group is greater for teens than for adults.)

2. Include 6 to 8 servings of milk and milk alternates every day (serving size is ½ cup of fortified soymilk or cow's milk).

The density of bones and defense against osteoporosis in later life depends, at least in part, on getting enough calcium and vitamin D during the teen years, when calcium needs are greatest.

Lacto-ovo vegetarians who use the recommended amounts of dairy products have little difficulty meeting the RDA for calcium. Vitamin D needs can be easily met by fortified cow's milk, margarine and sunshine.

Vegan teens can easily meet their calcium needs using calcium-fortified foods and beverages. (See milk alternates in food guide on page 138). Many calcium-fortified, non-dairy beverages also contain added vitamin D.

Unfortified non-dairy milks vary considerably in their calcium content, with many varieties having less than 20 mg per cup. Thus they cannot be depended upon as calcium sources. If an unfortified milk is used, vitamin D must be supplied by sunlight or a supplement (see Chapter 4).

There are a number of ways that a vegan adolescent can boost his or her calcium intake with a wide assortment of calcium-rich plant foods:

• *Use more tofu.* Tofu is a great food for teens; it's convenient and loaded with nutrients. Be sure to buy the type that is made with calcium. Tofu can be used for a quick breakfast scramble, an eggless "egg" salad sandwich or a quick tofu stir-fry for supper. Add cubes of tofu to soups, stews, spaghetti sauces and casseroles.

• *Try tahini (sesame seed butter).* It's great on toast, or in hummus, soups or baking.

• *Snack on almonds.* Almonds are also great for throwing into a stir-fry or on a salad. Use almond butter instead of peanut butter on sandwiches.

• *Learn to cook with legumes.* Legumes are simply indispensable! Add them to soups and stews. Mash some up to make burgers and taco or sandwich fillings. If you aren't so keen on soaking and cooking them, simply open a can (drain well to reduce any added salt).

• *Go for the green!* Broccoli and many dark green leafy vegetables such as kale, collards and Chinese greens can add plenty of calcium to a meal.

• *Give blackstrap molasses a try.* Blackstrap molasses is the only sugar that is concentrated in minerals. It can be used on toast or bread as a spread (great with tahini or another nut or seed butter) or in baking for cookies, loaves and muffins.

3. Use whole grain breads and cereals most of the time.

Breads and cereals form the foundation of our diets, so they should be chosen with care. Refined grains are nutritional wash-outs when compared to their whole grain counterparts. Teens who have been raised eating white bread, white rice and white spaghetti may find it tough making the switch. Here are a few pointers:

• *Don't give up on whole grain breads without giving them a fair try.* Buy something different like multigrain bagels, Russian rye or sunflower bread. Make a sandwich using a slice of whole grain bread and a slice of white bread.

• *Make sure bread is fresh when it's purchased.* A good bakery is worth seeking out. You might even try making your own with a variety of different grains (with a bread maker it's a real snap). To keep bread fresh, freeze it right away, and take out only what you'll be able to eat in a day.

• *If whole grain breads are still rejected, offer whole grain anything!* Other whole grain products like whole wheat and vegetable pastas, brown, red or wild rice, millet patties or whole grain cereals may be well accepted.

• *Be adventurous.* Cook something different like quinoa, tabbouleh salad or barley pudding. You may be pleasantly surprised by the response.

• *Use more whole grain flour in baking.* Whole grain flours and wheat germ can be used in baking cookies, muffins, squares or other goodies for a more nutritious treat.

• *Try healthy convenience foods.* How about a scrumptious blackberry scone, jumbo oat 'n nut cookies, some dairy-free strawberry yogurt or a bag of apple chips? The high quality and tremendous variety of health convenience foods on the market today will surprise you. If you haven't explored your local natural food stores, you are in for a real treat.

4. Include vegetables and/or fruits with every meal, and select them often for snacks as well (aim for at least 3 vegetables and 2 fruits every day).

Don't make French fries the daily vegetable. The more colorful vegetables and fruits are delicious and nutritious. One or more servings of vegetables or fruit should accompany every meal. Encouraging the consumption of fruits and vegetables is easier than you might think:

• *Keep a variety of fresh fruits on hand.* It's great to keep a big bowl out, ripe for the picking.

• *Before dinner, put out a plate of raw vegetables and dip for everyone to munch on.* Even teens who turn their noses up at cooked vegetables seem to be quite happy to polish off a platter of raw veggies and dip (go for something different like an eggplant dip).

• *Make two or more different vegetables with dinner.* Include at least one that you know your teen likes.

• *Get teens involved in growing vegetables.* It's great fun to experiment with growing foods organically. Teens can prepare all kinds of salads, stir-frys and other dishes with what they reap from the garden. Gardens also make excellent snacking grounds.

• *Keep a jug of pure fruit juice in a tightly covered container in the refrigerator at all times.* For a real treat, squeeze your own fruit juice at home.

• *Load up spaghetti sauces, soups and casseroles with all kinds of vegetables.*

• *Steam or stir-fry vegetables more often.* The crispy texture of vegetables is often more appealing to teens than well-cooked vegetables.

• *Make fruits your main theme for dessert.* Fresh fruit salads or platters, blueberry crepes or peach crisp all make wonderful endings to a special meal.

• *Keep plenty of dried fruit or fruit leather on hand as instant snacks (remember to brush afterwards).*

5. Include two to three servings from the beans and bean alternates group every day. When meat goes, we need to make sure that our diets include good sources of protein, iron and zinc – the key nutrients supplied by meat. Legumes and foods derived from legumes are ideal replacements, offering a number of important advantages over meat. Although they are good sources of protein, legumes are far less likely than meat to lead to excessive protein in the diet. They are generally very low in total fat and saturated fat and are cholesterol-free. Legumes also provide iron and zinc in addition to other important vitamins, minerals, phytochemicals and fiber.

Using legumes as a regular feature in the daily diet not only serves to boost the nutritional value of meals, but it makes them more interesting and satisfying.

Iron can be a problem for both vegetarian and non-vegetarian teens, especially for girls. Those who are watching calories, are very active in sports or have replaced the meat in their diet mainly with cheese and eggs may also have a tough time getting enough iron. A multivitamin/mineral supplement with iron and zinc may be appropriate in these cases.

Beans and bean alternates don't have to be boring or tasteless. Here are a few tips for turning teens on to beans (and bean alternates):

• *Replace the meat with beans in favorite stew, casserole or soup recipes.* Red lentils work especially well where hamburger was used: in spaghetti sauces, sloppy Joes, cabbage rolls and tamale pies. Try a meatless version of old-fashioned beef stew with pinto, navy, or other beans.

• *Become a tofu wizard.* Remember that tofu picks up the flavor of whatever seasonings or sauces that you use, so try it with family favorites like barbecue or sweet and sour sauce. Tofu is one of the most versatile foods imaginable. It can be a part of sandwiches, snacks, fancy main dishes and beautiful desserts.

• *Rely on old standbys.* Serve baked beans, chili, bean tortillas and vegetarian pizza more often. (Top the pizza with vegetarian sausages or pepperoni if desired.) These can be helpful foods for easing the transition.

• *Check out the fantastic selection of ready-made meatless options.* Vegetarian patties, sausages, loaves and luncheon slices are available in supermarkets, health food stores, ethnic stores and food co-ops. Some of these products are very meat-like. Many are delicious, and all are fast and easy to prepare.

• *Stir-fry meals more often.* Use almonds, cashews or other nuts, tofu, tempeh or firm beans such as garbanzos in place of the meat.

• *Try making loaves or patties from scratch.* These can be frozen for later use and are much cheaper than the store-bought versions. They are also surprisingly easy to make.

• *If you use eggs, they can be made into a tasty meal in a jiffy.* Use in vegetable quiches or frittatas. You may want to experiment with cholesterol-free egg substitutes as a heart-healthy option.

• *Use nuts, seeds and their butters.* Nuts are great for more than just snacking. Spread nut butter on morning toast, pack a tahini-carrot sandwich for lunch and make some cashew burgers for supper.

6. Include a source of vitamin B_{12} in the diet every day.
Teens who consume only plant foods or small quantities of dairy products and/or eggs will need to ensure that they have a reliable source of vitamin B_{12} in their diet. Vitamin B_{12}-fortified foods such as Red Star T-6635+ nutritional yeast, some cereals and meat analogs or a vitamin B_{12} supplement can be used.

For lacto-ovo vegetarian teens, regular consumption of dairy products and eggs will supply sufficient vitamin B_{12} to meet needs (see Chapter 5 for further details on vitamin B_{12}).

7. Don't skip meals.
Teenagers are notorious for skipping meals. Breakfast and lunch are the meals most commonly missed. This can lead to bouts of hunger that are too often filled with nutritional wash-outs like potato chips and chocolate bars.

The answer lies in nourishing "fast" foods. There are endless quick and easy ideas for breakfast and lunch, many of which can be packed and carried along (see Chapters 11 and 12).

8. Make snacks count.
Snacks are an important part of life for most teenagers. They can make or break an otherwise marginal diet. Any food that fits into the food guide is a good snack

choice. If there is a sweet tooth to contend with, try some of the treats in the recipe section. This doesn't mean extras like chocolate bars should be forever forgotten, but they should be only occasional treats.

9. Maintain a healthy weight by eating a balanced diet and exercising regularly.
Focus on overall health instead of a slim figure. If teens eat a well-balanced diet and exercise regularly, they are probably at a healthy weight.

For overweight teens who are eating a well-balanced diet, activity level is usually the key. Try for at least 30 minutes of aerobic exercise three or four times a week. Encourage walking or biking whenever possible (it's better for the environment than driving or taking a bus). Make an effort to cut back on fatty foods, especially fried foods and sweet desserts.

For those who are underweight, encourage the consumption of regular meals and snacks. Trail mixes, milk shakes, homemade muffins and other baked goods make great choices.

For some teens the choice to eliminate meat and/or milk from the diet may be a sign of an eating disorder such an anorexia nervosa. People suffering from this disorder attempt to achieve extreme thinness by restricting foods, particularly those that are concentrated in fat and calories. Becoming vegetarian provides a legitimate reason for these individuals to pass on fatty meats, dairy foods and eggs. It is estimated that some 50 percent of anorexics claim to be vegetarian. If your teenager has recently announced that she (about 90 percent are female) is a vegetarian and you think that an eating disorder may be her motive, here are some points to consider:

• Are there other signs of an eating disorder (i.e. weight loss, preoccupation with food, food restriction, concern about weight and shape, self-induced vomiting or laxative abuse, excessive strenuous exercise, constipation, social withdrawal or intolerance to cold)?

• Does she restrict or refuse all higher calorie vegetarian foods such as peanut butter, nuts, seeds, tofu, legumes and visible fats and oils (i.e. salad dressing, mayonnaise and other spreads) or foods cooked in oil?

• What are her reasons for becoming vegetarian? Is she really interested in animal rights and environmental issues or is it entirely to "improve" her diet?

If you do suspect that your teenager is suffering from an eating disorder, please seek help as quickly as possible. For more information contact: Anorexia Nervosa and Related Eating Disorders, Inc. (ANRED), P.O. Box 5102, Eugene OR 97405 or call (503) 344-1144.

The Supplement Question

A teenager's need for nutritional supplements depends entirely on eating habits and individual needs. Supplements are not necessary if the vegetarian foods guide is being followed, although they can be useful in a number of situations. If you decide to supplement, select a regular (rather than high potency or stress type) adult multivitamin/mineral supplement containing close to recommended levels of a wide range of nutrients, including iron, zinc and magnesium (see Appendix 2). A calcium supplement will also be necessary if the recommended numbers of servings from the milk and milk alternates group are not consumed. Calcium supplements should provide not more than 1200 mg of elemental calcium per day. If exposure to sunlight or consumption of vitamin D-fortified foods is low, a vitamin D supplement of 10 µg is also recommended.

VEGETARIAN DIPLOMACY

Y ou did it! You finally decided to take the plunge and give up meat forever. The compassion you feel for animals, your fellow man and the environment will be felt by those for miles around you. People will look at you and say, "There goes a person who really respects life. What a hero!" Your parents will beam with pride, and your friends will call on you constantly, just so they might be seen in your presence.

A likely story? Not on planet Earth. Let's face it, when you become a vegetarian, family and friends may be less than enthusiastic. After all, there are few social situations that don't involve food, and in our culture that usually means meat. Your vegetarian lifestyle could cause some inconvenience to say the least. Your Mom will worry about how to rearrange her Christmas dinner menu to accommodate your new diet. Uncle Nat will be ticked off when he finds out that his best fishing buddy isn't quite so enthusiastic about the trip this year. You may feel a little awkward trying to explain to your work buddies that you don't eat meat anymore, after they've just thrown a 12 oz T-bone on the grill at your surprise party.

Becoming vegetarian, you might imagine, would have people applauding your selfless contribution to global ecology, but instead it often makes them uncomfortable. This discomfort may not be all bad; it could get people thinking more carefully about their own food choices. But then again, you'd probably rather be laughing with the people you care about than causing them discomfort.

Your vegetarian diet could make your family feel as though you are turning your back on their values and traditions. Food has always been an important aspect of socializing in any culture. You have created a separation in one area that your parents thought would always bind you together. That can be very difficult for loved ones to understand.

Friends and acquaintances might perceive your vegetarianism as a judgment on their choices. Those who have not been exposed to many vegetarian foods may feel alienated from you because your food choices are so different.

It is quite possible that your decision to cut meat from your menu becomes a source of anxiety and frustration, particularly when you are among a group of omnivores. Thankfully, it doesn't have to be that way. Rather than causing tension for you and those around you, your vegetarian diet can help you share a whole new world of valuable experiences. Much depends on your attitude, humor, and social diplomacy.

This chapter guides you through a variety of social experiences that are common to vegetarians. The first part considers the questions with which vegetarians are often faced and offers some answers. These are meant to help boost your level of comfort and confidence in the event that such a question should come your way. The second part invites you to put yourself in a few difficult social situations. How do you think you would react? Consider the selection of responses offered in the text. The probable outcomes are also discussed. As you think about these situations and their outcomes, you will be preparing yourself to handle social challenges in an effective and positive manner.

THE QUESTIONS

One of the interesting aspects of becoming a vegetarian is hearing the questions of all those people who are just a little mystified by your choice. Your answer to each question will depend, at least in part, on the situation and how the question is asked. There are many people who have a real interest in the vegetarian option or curiosity about your experience. You might wish that you were given a couple of hours to prepare a meaningful response. Some people may be considering cutting back on or even giving up meat themselves, but just aren't so sure of how to go about it. This could be a real opportunity to share a few practical pointers or some deeper insights into the real connections between our food choices and our daily lives. Still others may just be kidding around, and in that case it would be fun to come back with an appropriately light-hearted response.

The questions most commonly posed to vegetarians are "*What do you eat?*" and "*Why are you a vegetarian?*"

Question No. 1: *What do you eat?*

"What do you eat?" is a polite way of asking the particulars about your diet. The person who is inquiring may be curious about the taste and variety of vegetarian foods or the time needed to prepare meals. When someone pops the question, you might assume that they are interested in more than what was on your dinner plate last night. The real questions could well look more like this:

QUESTIONS RELATING TO TASTE AND VARIETY

Isn't vegetarian food boring?

Do you eat beans every day? Don't you get a lot of gas?

Do you really like the taste of vegetarian food?

Don't you miss meat?

What do you eat on special occasions?

To many people, a proper meal consists of meat and potatoes. Their experience with vegetarian food may be limited to macaroni and cheese or canned beans – the quick, economical standbys that are used in a pinch, but would never do for Sunday dinner. What else is there for vegetarians? They would naturally wonder why anyone would voluntarily choose to eat this way.

QUESTIONS RELATING TO FOOD PREPARATION

Do you spend hours slaving over a hot stove every day?

Don't you have to plan far in advance to allow time to soak and cook beans?

Do you grow all your own vegetables and preserve them for the winter?

Don't you have a hard time finding all of those unusual foods?

Many people are under the impression that vegetarian cooking is far more time-consuming than cooking with meat. They might imagine that vegetarians spend hours in their kitchen every day grinding flour, baking bread and preparing beans.

The Answers

When someone asks "*What do you eat?*" try to get a sense of what they would really like to know. Share some of your experiences and adventures as you made the shift away from meat. Capture their interest by telling them about some of your favorite meals. Gourmet vegetarian dishes can rival the best meat dishes around. Did you know that Chef Ron Pickarski's vegan dishes have captured gold medals at the Culinary Olympics?

Here is a sample of the kinds of responses you might make:

"I eat almost everything that you do, except instead of meat, I use tofu, beans, nuts and seeds as my main sources of protein. With these, I make vegetarian roasts with gravy, patties, casseroles and some great ethnic food such as Indian curries, Middle Eastern falafels and African stew. For fast and easy meals, I make tofu stir-frys, pasta dishes, tacos or burgers using home-made or commercial frozen vegetarian patties. Being vegetarian has made me a lot more adventurous with food. The variety of foods I eat now is even greater than it was when I ate meat."

Or a more in-depth version:

"You'd be amazed at the incredible variety of foods available to vegetarians. When I first started to cut back on meat, I tried tofu and different kinds of beans. I wasn't overly impressed because I really didn't know how to cook them, so I decided to take a vegetarian cooking class. I soon figured out cooking great vegetarian food is no more difficult than cooking with meat; it's just different. It didn't take me long to learn the basic skills required for preparing wonderful vegetarian meals. Now I know how to turn tofu into scrambled "eggs," textured soy protein into a beautiful holiday roast and black beans into a wonderful, spicy Chinese soup. I've purchased some superb vegetarian cookbooks and tried all kinds of recipes from sushi to dairy-free cheesecake. I've also found at least a dozen different recipes that I can put together in less than a half hour (some in less than 15 minutes). Now I feel like a pro, and I truly love the food — I don't even care for overly sweet or fatty foods anymore. It's affected the way I feel too. I have more energy and better endurance than ever before."

There are the odd occasions when someone will pop the question in a light-hearted manner. You wish that you had the perfect crazy response, instead of standing there saying that you eat some good food too. How about saying something silly:

"I eat tofu of course. Scrambled tofu for breakfast, tofu sandwiches for lunch, stir-fried tofu or tofu burgers for supper and tofu cheesecake for dessert. Thank goodness there's tofu for us vegetarians."

Question No. 2: *Why are you a vegetarian?*

People are often curious about what could have motivated you to give up meat. Was it just an interest in improving your health, concern for the environment or was it something "strange" like a new religion or animal rights? Other people are quite intrigued by the idea of becoming vegetarian and simply want to learn more about the issues. Some of the questions they might be thinking about could look like this:

QUESTIONS RELATING TO RELIGION

Have you changed your religion?

Have you joined some sort of weird cult?

Are you into that New Age movement?

Some people associate vegetarianism with religious extremism. They figure that if you are a vegetarian, you are probably into something fairly radical.

QUESTIONS RELATING TO ANIMAL RIGHTS

You're not one of those animal rights activists, are you?

What do you suppose would happen to the farmers if we all stopped eating meat?

You do eat chicken and fish, don't you? After all, they aren't really meat.

Why on earth would you give up dairy products? They don't actually kill the cow.

People are very curious about those that choose to stop eating meat out of concern for animals. They may feel just a little guilty themselves, or they may want to prove to themselves that it's really no big deal.

QUESTIONS RELATING TO THE ENVIRONMENT

Do you seriously think that there is a connection between meat-eating and the state of the environment?

Isn't all that manure from the animals good for the soil?

Are you a back-to-the-earth hippie type who thinks they can save the world?

Many people can recall the odd mention of a connection between the environment, human hunger and our food choices. They may wonder if it has any basis in reality or if it is just a myth perpetuated by a small fringe group.

QUESTIONS RELATING TO HEALTH AND SAFETY

Can a vegetarian diet really protect us against heart disease and cancer?

How can you get enough protein and iron without meat?

Do you feed your kids that way too? Do you think it's safe?

If a vegetarian diet is so healthy, how come the vegetarians I know don't look so hot?

If you don't drink milk, how will you get enough calcium?

For many years vegetarians were thought of as health food nuts. Today an ever growing number of people are recognizing that a vegetarian diet can not only be healthful, but can help protect us against disease. However there remains some skepticism about the nutritional adequacy of vegetarian diets, especially in regards to children.

The Answers

When someone asks you "Why you are a vegetarian?" consider where they are coming from and what kind of response would be of real value to them. Think about ways of sharing the deep concerns about issues that finally convinced you to become a vegetarian. Your answer will likely be well received if it is presented in a sensitive, non-judgmental manner.

"Well, it all started when my doctor suggested that with my high blood cholesterol I'd be better off eating little, if any, meat. I decided to try a few meatless cookbooks, and one of them had a whole section on the advantages of vegetarianism. It presented some interesting details about the health benefits of vegetarian diets and discussed how our food choices affect the environment. I wondered if what I was reading had any basis in fact, so I decided to do a little further investigating. You just wouldn't believe some of the things I found out. There's one book I discovered that is just amazing. If you'd like to read it, I'd be very happy to lend it to you."

Or a more in-depth version:

"There are many reasons why I decided to become vegetarian. I think that a vegetarian diet is very healthy, and it is one thing that I can do to make a contribution to the environment. But the most important issue for me was our treatment of food animals. Before I became a vegetarian, I was chiding a friend for deer hunting, and he quickly replied that at least the deer he kills has had some sort of a life. He went on to add that he doubts that I could say the same for the animals that are killed for me to eat. I had never really thought of it like that before so I decided that it was time I learned more about the source of my food. The old story-book image of chickens pecking at the ground, pigs rolling in mud and cows wandering contentedly through the fields was soon shattered. When I found out that in the United States alone over 7 billion food animals are consumed every year, I began to understand why the conditions in which they live and die are less than ideal. I became uncomfortable with the whole scene and decided that going vegetarian was my only option. I know that many people don't take animal issues very seriously, but it has made a real difference in my life. I feel better about myself — I guess it really was an ethical dilemma for me. I appreciate that in our society, giving up meat is not an easy thing to do and many people are in situations that would make a vegetarian diet difficult. Perhaps these people could demonstrate their concern for the care of our food animals in other ways."

If the question is posed with a light-hearted tone, you may want to come back with a suitably swift response:

"I figured if it's good enough for Albert Einstein it's good enough for me!"

"I prefer not to eat anything that could bite back."

"I'd like to stay healthy enough to run a small organic vegetable farm when I'm a 100 years old."

SITUATIONS

The world may never be quite the same after you pledge your allegiance to the land of bean sprouts. People seem to look at you a little differently. They eye your sandwich, wondering what really lies between those two pieces of bread. Some even avoid any eye contact with you at the company barbecue for fear of having to sit beside you with their big smoked sausages.

The situations you face as a vegetarian are not always easy. In some cases, you may feel quite unprepared. After it's all over, you dream up a hundred ways that you could have better handled the situation. In the next section, we invite you to put yourself in the place of other vegetarians who have found themselves in some rather sticky situations. How would you react if you were in their place?

1. WIFE AND MOTHER TURNS VEGETARIAN WITHOUT FAMILY SUPPORT

You're the only vegetarian in the house. Your husband and two young teenagers are just not interested. You switched to a vegetarian diet after going to a lecture with a friend who has been sharing information with you for some time. Your husband isn't thrilled. The one thing that he's made absolutely clear to you is that he has no intention of giving up his meat or eating a bunch of weird food. The kids are on Dad's side. You are uncomfortable buying and cooking meat, but feel that there is little choice. Your dinner usually consists of potatoes and vegetables with a spoonful of cottage cheese. A couple of times a week, you prepare a meatless lasagne or chili which seems to go over all right. Lately you've been finding it harder to cook meat, and it's reached the point where it makes your stomach turn. You should:

a) Be thankful that your family will eat the two vegetarian meals a week without much of a fuss, and continue to provide them with the foods they want.

b) Tell your family that you cannot stand having meat in your house, and if they want it, they'll have to go out to a restaurant.

c) Tell your family that you are not comfortable cooking meat anymore, and ask them to take over that part of meal preparation.

PROBABLE OUTCOME

a) Passive, thankful response:

This is certainly the path of least resistance as far as your family is concerned, but it doesn't seem like such a great choice for you. If this is the route you take, plan to progress by increasing the vegetarian meals to 4 or 5 times per week. Your family will be far less likely to notice that the meal is meatless if it is fashioned after a traditional favorite such as spaghetti. To improve the variety in your own diet when your family eats meat, use vegetarian alternatives for yourself. Commercial burgers and wieners, canned beans and tofu can all be prepared in a flash.

b) No meat in my house:

This could be a disaster. If you want to have a amicable household, you have to respect one another's choices. When one person begins to tell the another what he or she can or cannot eat, that mutual respect is undermined. Try to work out a compromise that is acceptable to all family members.

c) Express discomfort; ask for help:

This is probably your best option. Often caregivers (whether they be women or men) are expected to make endless sacrifices for their families and forget about their own needs. It has become difficult for you to purchase and prepare meat, so discuss those feelings with your family and solicit suggestions from them. If the solutions come directly from them, everyone will be happier with the agreements reached. Indeed, you may be able to accomplish your goal without having to get angry or upset at all.

2. INVITED TO ANOTHER PERSON'S HOME FOR DINNER

You and your partner have been vegetarians for three years. When you began your new job at the dental office, you were delighted with the warm and friendly staff. Within a couple of weeks, another dentist invited the two of you over for dinner. Although you often eat lunch at work together, you usually bring instant pea soup and a salad, or a phony bologna sandwich with lettuce and tomatoes. As a result, your new friend has no idea that you are vegetarian.

You're not too sure how to handle the dinner invitation. You decide to:

a) Turn the invitation down, making up a good excuse.

b) Accept the invitation, not mention that you are vegetarian and bring a casserole with you.

c) Accept the invitation, not mention that you are vegetarian, and just show up for dinner.

d) Tell your new friend that you'd love to come to dinner, but that you'd like her to know that you are vegetarians. Offer to bring a part of the meal (a main dish would be great).

PROBABLE OUTCOMES

a) Turn invitation down:

This is an easy out, but accomplishes little. As soon as you offer an excuse, another, more convenient date will likely be suggested.

b) Accept invitation; bring casserole:

Bad move. You host would likely have much rather known of your dietary preferences. She could have prepared one of her favorite Chinese meals – hot and sour soup, vegetarian spring rolls, tofu in black bean sauce and steamed Chinese greens instead of splurging on fresh lobsters and filet mignon.

c) Accept invitation and show up:

If you don't mind eating meat occasionally, this option is fine, but if you are quite firm in you avoidance of certain animal foods, it is a major mistake. You could arrive to chicken poached in a white wine sauce, a wild rice pilaf and steamed vegetables. Perhaps you could get away with eating just the rice and vegetables. But, then again, the rice could have been cooked in beef broth and the vegetables seasoned with butter and bacon bits. The point is that there is no guarantee that any of the dishes prepared will be free of animal products. Remember that the entire meal has been prepared in your honor. Both you and your host will have a much more enjoyable evening if she knows what you are or are not willing to eat.

d) Say that you are vegetarians:

This is your best option. Although you may feel like you are imposing, it is common courtesy to let your host know that you are vegetarians. You'll quickly get an idea of how comfortable she is with vegetarian meal preparation. She may just say that's great, they have been trying to cut back on animal foods and will enjoy preparing an interesting vegetarian meal. If you sense some hesitation, offer to bring veggie burgers or a main dish to share.

3. RESTAURANT WITHOUT VEGETARIAN OPTIONS ON THE MENU

The whole office is going for lunch. As you are a fairly new addition to the team, no one is aware that you are vegetarian. One of your co-workers says, "Do you guys want to go for some real food today? I'm always hungry an hour after eating at that Chinese place," so you end up at the local steak house. You feel a kind of uneasiness coming on as you look at the menu – even the Caesar salad is made with anchovies. There is some French onion soup, but of course the broth base is likely beef. You:

a) Say that you have the stomach flu and can't eat.

b) Order the dish with the least amount of meat, and eat around it.

c) Ask the waiter if he could suggest any meatless options.

PROBABLE OUTCOMES

a) Can't eat; stomach flu:

All this will serve to accomplish is making you very hungry. Think about your motivation for hiding the fact that you are a vegetarian. Are you worried that these people will suddenly think less of you? Perhaps you aren't giving them enough credit. Maybe they've already decided that you're a decent person, and being vegetarian isn't likely to change their minds. They are going to find out sooner or later, so why not save yourself a few hunger pains and make it sooner.

b) Order meat and eat around it:

At least you'll leave with something in your stomach, but did you really want to pay for that piece of steak? There are few restaurants that will not accommodate a vegetarian, so it's quite unnecessary for you to go to that length.

c) Ask for meatless:

You've got the idea! It's very common for restaurants to get this kind of request. Don't forget that many movie stars, elite athletes and famous scientists are vegetarian. Some restaurants without a single vegetarian entrée on the menu make wonderful vegetarian meals. They'll cook up an awesome pasta dish filled with fresh vegetables or a colorful stir-fry with rice, and serve it with a great salad and some fresh bread. If the waiter seems less than confident about the options, arrange to speak privately with the chef, and let him know exactly what you would like. The main menu will generally give you a good idea of what could easily be prepared. If there are stir-frys on the menu, these can generally be done without the meat, as can many pasta dishes. If all else fails, ask for a baked potato with a large order of stir-fried vegetables. You may want to discuss the price as well, so you don't end up paying for a filet mignon.

Remember, when you do have a choice of where to eat, go for an ethnic restaurant (the more authentic the better). Oriental, Greek, Lebanese, African and Indian restaurants all generally provide vegetarian options. When you can, phone ahead.

4. INVITING OUT-OF-TOWN WORK ASSOCIATES TO DINNER

You have three out-of-town business associates at the office for a week. You decide to invite them all for dinner, then you go crazy for the next couple of days trying to decide what to cook. You:

a) Decide to break down and buy some fish for the occasion.

b) Make some really interesting vegetarian dishes for them to try. Tofu roast, quinoa casserole and some curried eggplant. You even whip up a nice carob pudding for dessert.

c) Opt for familiar foods, without the meat.

PROBABLE OUTCOME

a) Buy fish:
It's certainly an option, but absolutely unnecessary. You can make a lovely meal without having to buy fish.

b) Make unusual vegetarian foods:
Risky. Some people are funny about eating foods that they don't recognize. You'd be better off to try this kind of meal with good friends, but not with people that you hardly know.

c) Make familiar favorites:
Good choice. Chances are that no one will even notice that there is no meat on the table. Lasagne, spaghetti, chili, tortillas and crepes can all work very nicely. Be sure to have some special side dishes, fresh bread and a great dessert, like peach pie or a chocolate and fruit fondue.

5. MAKING A CELEBRATION DINNER
FOR YOUR EXTENDED FAMILY

Every year you take turns with your brother and two sisters hosting the Christmas feast. This will be your first year as a vegetarian host. Jerry has let you know in no uncertain terms that he expects turkey for dinner. Ellen reminded you that it's only once a year and that it wouldn't kill you to make this little sacrifice for the occasion. You don't want to cook a turkey, nor do you want to end up in a huge fight with your family. You decide to:

a) Give in and cook a turkey.

b) Tell your family that you just aren't comfortable cooking a turkey, but you would be happy to do everything else, if one of them brings the turkey.

c) Refuse to have a turkey in your house. Tell them that they can make whatever they want when it is their turn to do the meal, so it's only right that you get to make whatever you want when it's your turn.

d) Explain to your family that you would prefer to host a part of the celebration at your house that is separate from the Christmas turkey dinner.

e) Go to Mexico for Christmas.

PROBABLE OUTCOME

a) Make a turkey:

This option makes everyone happy except you. Sometimes in life we feel compelled to do things that go against our principles, simply because it will help to avoid difficult confrontations. In the end, there is no greater understanding of your concerns or feelings, and your family will probably conclude that you don't mind preparing meat for other people. Perhaps a compromise could be reached. It's obviously important for your family to have their traditional meal for the occasion, and it's just as important for you not to have to purchase and prepare the turkey.

b) Have someone else bring the turkey:

This is a reasonable compromise for everyone involved. Prepare some wonderful trimmings and a vegetarian main dish to share. A giant stuffed squash makes a beautiful centerpiece. You may just find that the vegetarian foods are the most popular part of the feast.

c) No turkey in your house:

Sometimes it isn't what you say that creates a problem, it's how you say it. Remember that if turkey is the highlight of Christmas dinner for your family, telling them that they won't be having it this year may not go over so well. It could create a lot of tension during the season when peace, joy and love are supposed to fill our hearts and homes. This is not to say that you should give in and have a turkey in your house when you are really very uncomfortable with that, but rather that there may be a better way of reaching that end.

d) Offer to do something else:

This is a great option for those that do not wish to have a turkey dinner in their home. There are so many ways to participate in the celebration other than hosting Christmas dinner. How about offering a Christmas eve games night at your house, and serve appetizers such as hazelnut paté with rye bread, stuffed mushrooms, fresh fruit kabobs, and some special Christmas baking. Another alternative is a brunch and skating party you could be starting a healthy new tradition for your family. In time, your family will become more comfortable with vegetarian meals, and the idea of Christmas dinner without the turkey may become a real possibility.

e) Go to Mexico:

This isn't a bad idea, but you'll be faced with the turkey problem again next year!

6. TEEN GETS RAZZED ABOUT WEARING LEATHER SHOES

Your teenager is a confirmed vegetarian. In fact, he was a vegetarian two years before you were. He brings tofu sandwiches to school and doesn't seem to care what other kids say about it. One day he comes home rather upset and confides in you that the kids have been bugging him at school about wearing leather shoes. They tell him that if he really cared about animals then he wouldn't wear leather. They even go so far as to say there isn't a whole lot of difference between wearing leather shoes and eating a big steak. He asks you for some advice. You tell him to:

a) Just ignore people like that.

b) If your son avoids meat but uses other animal products, remind his friends that it is not an "all or nothing" situation. Leather is a by-product from the slaughter of millions of cows. By avoiding meat, we will decrease its demand, thereby reducing these by-products. This will benefit both the animals and the environment. If animal by-products are decreased sufficiently, manufacturers will come up with more acceptable alternatives. Removing meat from the diet is a powerful statement in of itself.

c) If your son is near-vegan and avoids animal products beyond diet, he is making a strong statement against the slaughter of animals and he can take the opportunity to educate his peers in a very positive way. He can let them know that his most recent purchases do not contain animal products, but the shoes he already has will be worn until they fall apart. Explain that completely avoiding animal products is tougher than one might imagine. In our society, it is nearly impossible to exclude all animal products, short of moving to a deserted island. Soaps, shampoos, and creams often contain animal products. The strings of musical instruments and tennis rackets, films and videos, paints and steel all contain animal products. Even cotton clothing and the soles of non-leather shoes are often made using animal constituents. However, as more and more people refuse to purchase items containing animal products, our choices will improve.

PROBABLE OUTCOME

a) Ignore them:

This won't help your teenager effectively deal with similar difficult situations, nor will it help the teens who were bugging him understand the real issues.

b) Not an all or nothing situation:

At the very least, your son's peers will have a better appreciation of the connection between our food choices, animal welfare and the environment. They will likely understand that his avoidance of meat is in itself a significant contribution. This type of discussion just might get them thinking a little more about their own food choices, and leather shoes will be far less an issue.

c) Avoiding animal products:

Your son's friends will probably be amazed at how extensive the use of animal products is in our society. They will gain an appreciation for how difficult it is to completely eliminate these things from our lives. Chances are that they'll respect your son for his commitment to this cause. In communicating these thoughts, he will create a bond with others who are trying to make the world a better place.

7.   YOUR FIRST BUSINESS CONVENTION AS A VEGAN

It's the first convention you've attended since becoming a vegan. It was never too difficult as a lacto-ovo vegetarian, as most places are happy to prepare an omelet on short notice. You aren't so sure how easy things will be now that you have eliminated milk and eggs. It's nice to know that the airlines offer vegan meals in addition to the regular vegetarian options. You make sure to have your meals ordered when you book your flight. You are pleasantly surprised with the meal: lentil loaf with tomato sauce, rice, broccoli, a whole grain dinner roll and some fresh strawberries for dessert. You arrive at the convention center to find a little basket of fresh fruit in your room. What a bonus! Maybe it won't be so bad after all.

Next morning you go down for breakfast and order some oatmeal, unbuttered whole wheat toast, and freshly squeezed orange juice. Lunch is to be over a meeting, so you figure it will be a buffet. You are fairly certain that you'll at least get salad, potatoes and a roll. To your dismay, lunch is a catered sit-down meal. A ham quiche with a tiny side salad and a white roll arrives in front of you. Your stomach turns as the aroma of ham and eggs fills the air.

You decide to:

a) Eat the roll and salad, and check the agenda to see if another
similar affair has been planned, so that you can be sure to order ahead
next time.

b) Decide that you can wait until dinner to eat.

c) Tell the waiter that you are a vegetarian, and ask if you could get
something else to eat.

PROBABLE OUTCOME

a) Eat the roll and salad:

This is probably the easiest thing to do, but it's not necessarily your best option. The person two seats away could receive a beautiful vegetarian plate just as you are finishing your dinner roll. (You only have to experience that feeling once to clue in to the fact that it pays to ask.)

b) Wait until dinner:

Besides making you very hungry, you're likely to attract unwanted attention to the fact you're not eating.

c) Ask for something else:

What have you got to lose? Most good hotels are very accommodating. You'll often end up with a meal that will have those around you wishing that they had the same. The worst thing that could happen is that the waiter says he is very sorry, they can't prepare anything else. We have never actually seen this happen, so your chances of getting a reasonable alternative are pretty good.

GUIDELINES FOR GETTING ALONG

1. Care about animals and the environment, but respect other human beings.

Your concern for animals and the environment demonstrates a reverence for life and an understanding of the fragility of the earth. The value of these qualities is immense, but they must be carefully balanced with a deep respect for other human beings. Always consider the potential effects of what you say and do on the lives of those around you.

2. Take the time to listen to other people, and lift them up with your words.

It is easy to pass judgment on someone without really understanding them. When you do, both people lose. If we expect others to listen to our perspective, we must begin by listening to theirs. By listening to other people, not only do you get to know them better, but you can support and encourage them. Putting people down does nothing but hurt them and push them away. Instead, lift people up with your words.

3. Share your experiences in a positive way.

In our society, where meat is front and center of most social interactions involving food, the vegetarian can feel a little intimidated. Recall people like George Bernard Shaw and Gandhi who went forth proudly, as vegetarians with something to share.

Trying to impress people with long sermons about the sins of meat eating and expecting to convert them into peace loving tofu munchers will result in little other than disappointment. Instead, inspire them with your example of healthy living. You might want to invite friends for a great vegetarian meal or bring a delicious vegetarian, ethnic dish to the staff party. Share recipes and books with them. You might even ask them to join you for a vegetarian cooking class.

4. Learn to laugh at yourself and some of the predicaments you get into.
You can go through life with a doom and gloom attitude towards just about everything, or you can take a step back and realize that there is a little humor in most awkward situations. Loosen up and laugh a little. It will likely add as many years to your life as your vegetarian diet.

Although it may not be easy for you, try to forgive and forget. People can say hurtful things without even realizing it. Holding a grudge will not make you feel better, only more stressed.

5. Realize that you can't always make perfect choices.
Think about your goals in life, and set priorities accordingly. For many people, the number one priority is the people they love. As a vegetarian, your lifestyle choices could be very different than the rest of your family. You may find occasion to eat some meat, poultry, fish, milk or eggs in order to avoid offending someone that you care about. If you do, don't feel guilty about it – the most any of us can do is to follow our hearts. On the other hand, if you choose to forego certain animal foods completely, realize that it will have to become a priority in your life. You'll need to plan ahead, to check with restaurants and conferences, to let friends and family know when you will be sharing a meal with them, and to bring appropriate foods along when it's necessary.

6. Become well-informed.
If you want to be an advocate for a vegetarian lifestyle, become well-informed about the issues. Read all you can, take courses, go to lectures and listen to all kinds of opinions. Not only will you get a confidence boost, but you'll be better equipped to handle questions and concerns in a clear and logical manner.

FROM MARKET TO MEALS

With the utmost confidence, you bound out the front door, armed with your cloth shopping bags, determined to go out there and fill them to the brim with wholesome foods that will help to transform your meals into vegetarian masterpieces. Do you return home with little more than oatmeal, peanut butter and a few fresh vegetables?

Shopping for healthy vegetarian food might be a bit intimidating for those who aren't so sure what to buy or where to buy it. Grocery store shelves are lined with a vast array of products, many masquerading as nutritional powerhouses with appealing claims gracing their packages. Fear not! The new and unfamiliar foods that await you are simply adventures waiting to happen. Imagine discovering a veggie-burger that is better than any beef-burger you've ever eaten, fat-free veggie-back bacon that rivals the real thing or a divine, dairy-free frozen strawberry dessert. It is all there for the taking – you need only learn how to find it. In the end, the quality of food you bring home will be beyond what you'd ever thought possible.

Food Labels: Nutrition know-how at your fingertips

A food label can be your best ally – if you know how to use it. It pays to invest a little time into understanding label lingo and what a food producer can do with it. Never before have the labels on food products provided such consistent, quality information about the nutritional value of the foods you buy. Regulations from the FDA and the Food Safety and Inspection Service (FSIS) of the United States Department of Agriculture (USDA) ensure that almost every packaged food comes with nutrition labeling. This labeling includes two essential components, *the nutrition panel* and *ingredient list,* and two optional components, *nutrient content descriptors* and *health claims*.

1. THE NUTRITION PANEL

The nutrition panel appears under the title "Nutrition Facts." This panel provides most of the details you will require regarding the nutritional contents of a food. Serving sizes are uniform across all product lines so that nutrients in similar food items can be easily compared. Nutrition information is expressed as a percent of a dietary reference value called the "Daily Value" (DV). The DVs are based on the nutritional needs of an individual consuming a 2,000 calorie diet. Most panels include the following information per serving of the food: calories, calories from fat, total fat, saturated fat, cholesterol, sodium, total carbohydrate, fiber, sugar and protein, plus the percent of the DVs for all but sugar and protein. Daily Values for vitamin A, vitamin C, calcium and iron are also listed, while those of other vitamins and minerals need only be provided when a claim is made about them on the label.

2. NUTRIENT CONTENT DESCRIPTORS

Manufacturers are permitted to use terms that describe the nutrient content of a product in accordance with the new FDA regulations. These regulations ensure that whenever a description is used, it means the same thing on all food labels. For example, when a label states a product is "low-fat, low-cholesterol," it must contain *less* than 3 grams of fat, 20 mg cholesterol and 2 grams saturated fat per serving.

Food producers can use nutrient content descriptions in ways that are confusing to consumers. For example, the label on a jar of peanut butter may read "cholesterol-free," leading people to believe that other brands of peanut butter are high in cholesterol. In fact, no peanut butter (or any other plant food) contains cholesterol.

3. HEALTH CLAIMS

Claims that link a nutrient or food to the risk of a disease or health condition are now permitted under certain circumstances. There are eight diet and disease relationships for which claims are allowed. They include:
- calcium and osteoporosis;
- fat and cancer;
- saturated fat, cholesterol and risk of coronary artery disease;
- fiber-containing grain products, fruits and vegetables and cancer;
- fruits, vegetables and grain products that contain fiber (particularly soluble fiber) and risk of coronary artery disease;
- sodium and hypertension;
- fruits and vegetables and cancer;

• folate and neural tube defects.

Any product making a claim about the above relationships must provide a specified amount of the nutrient in question or, as in the case of fat and cholesterol, must not exceed the specified amount.

4. THE INGREDIENT LIST

A full list of ingredients must now appear on all packaged processed foods, including standardized foods such as bread and jelly which were previously exempt. New regulations provide for a more thorough description of ingredients such as food colors and protein hydrolysates (which must identify their source to assist people with allergies). Foods claiming to be "non-dairy" (i.e., non-dairy creamer) must identify caseinate as a milk derivative in the ingredient statement.

Ingredients are listed according to weight, with the ingredient present in the largest amount listed first. This list can often answer questions regarding nutrition claims or nutrition information. For example, a package of commercial cookies may claim to be low in saturated fat. This sounds good, but if you examine the ingredient list you see enriched flour (white flour) and vegetable oil shortening as the first two ingredients. As you may recall from chapter 6, shortening contains trans-fatty acids which are classified as monounsaturated fats, but are even more damaging than saturated fats. To help ensure that the product you are buying is everything it's cracked up to be, look for:

• Whole grain flour as the principle grain in the product (even multi grain products often have "enriched flour" or "wheat flour" as a first ingredient – both are refined white flours).

• The absence of shortening, lard, hydrogenated or partially-hydrogenated vegetable oil or other hard fats.

• Sweeteners that provide some nutritional value (i.e., concentrated fruit juices, dried fruits or blackstrap molasses).

• An ingredient list with words you recognize. Some unfamiliar words are harmless everyday items (e.g., sodium bicarbonate is baking soda), but a readable list provides some assurance that the product is wholesome.

Organic Options: A viable alternative?

More and more consumers are seeking out plant foods that have been grown without the use of synthetic fertilizers, pesticides, herbicides, fungicides or growth regulators – food otherwise known as organic food. Their reasons for making this choice are most compelling: to support environmentally responsible food production and to support human health. Organic farming practices are meant to create ecosystems which are sustainable: soil is replenished rather than depleted, and water systems are preserved rather than polluted. A reduction in the use of harmful chemicals in farming could decrease the risk of cancer in both the farm worker and the general population. Some studies have also suggested that organic foods may provide a greater concentration of vitamins and minerals than conventionally grown foods, although research is in very preliminary stages.

At present, regulations regarding the use of the term "organic" and "certified organic" vary considerably from state to state. In many states, any food that carries an organic claim must meet standards set out by government authorities. When the food is labeled "certified organic," it must meet additional standards established by independent certification agencies.

In 1990 a bill was passed that called for national certification standards for organic foods to be set by the USDA (The U.S. Organic Foods Production Act – Title 21 of the 1990 Farm Bill). In response, a 15-member National Organic Standards Board was created. This board is responsible for suggesting guidelines, which include: a national list of substances permitted or prohibited for use in organic farming; accreditation for state and private certification agencies; certification of organic farmers, processors, manufacturers and wholesalers, and all other regulations governing organic agriculture. As might be expected, there is considerable debate within the board and among concerned groups and citizens as to what should be deemed acceptable for use in organic agriculture. It appears at the present time that some controversial insecticides may be permitted for use, as may synthetic additives. However, remember that the USDA regulations are minimum standards acceptable and many states will continue to have more stringent requirements. Individual farmers will also be at liberty to choose to use or not to use those chemicals which are permissible. If you would like to have input into the national regulations governing organic foods, let your voice be heard by the USDA.

WHERE TO SHOP

There are many interesting places to find fresh, wholesome foods, so take the time to find out about all the options available to you. Chances are that you'll discover some amazing little store that you never even knew existed or stumble across a reputable organic farmer who delivers produce right to your door. Don't feel limited by the following list – it discusses many of the more popular choices, but there are certainly others.

NATURAL FOOD STORES

Begin your quest by seeking out a large natural food store or food co-op that specializes in vegetarian and organic foods (most of them do!). Many of the product lines they carry are made with whole grain flours, natural sweeteners, non-hydrogenated vegetable oils and are free of food colors, artificial flavors and preservatives. These stores also tend to offer a wide selection of bulk foods including less common grains and flours such as quinoa, spelt, kamut and bean flours; organic produce; hearty baked goods; fresh tofu, soymilks, yogurts and cheeses; nut butters; frozen, canned and dried convenience foods and wholesome snacks such as fat-free tortilla chips and fruit bars. A good natural food store can be a real ally in your efforts to put together fast and delicious vegetarian foods.

SUPERMARKETS

If you prefer to do your shopping at a large supermarket, you'll be happy to know that most of the items you need will be available right there. Although most supermarkets do not carry as many vegetarian or organic product lines as natural food stores, their stock is constantly growing (remember, the more demand they have, the more they will stock). In addition to their produce departments, many offer a great supply of bulk foods, interesting ethnic options, and vegetarian fresh, frozen and dried convenience foods. Don't hesitate to ask the manager about getting in special foods or purchasing in uncommonly small or large quantities. They are usually quite happy to accommodate you.

FARMERS MARKETS

If you are lucky enough to have a farmers market nearby, especially one that sells organic produce, do take advantage of it. Farmers markets tend to undercut supermarkets prices by least 30 percent or more on many items. The produce is usually locally grown, the goods are fresh, and the variety is superb, including great greens like collards and kale.

You may also have farmers in your area who sell directly to consumers or have "U-pick" options available. Some even offer shares in their farm, making payment in produce according to the number of shares you own, (resulting in a real community effort), and/or deliver produce to your door step.

ETHNIC SHOPS

Most cities have some ethnic grocery stores, and larger cities have ethnic stores of many kinds. When you find a good one, it's like finding a little treasure chest. Asian stores carry a wonderful selection of tofu, greens, seaweed, seitan (gluten) and Oriental sauces. Some of these items cost far less than you would pay at a natural food store or supermarket. Greek stores carry the best tahini in town, as well as a good assortment of legumes, olives, olive oil, Mediterranean herbs and pita bread. East Indian stores carry numerous flours, legumes, grains, and spice mixes: their curry pastes are great for spicing up vegetable or lentil dishes in one step. Many ethnic stores also carry delicious, vegetarian convenience foods.

CO-OPS AND BUYING CLUBS

Food co-ops are grocery stores that are owned and often operated by members. This reduces overhead costs, thus food prices are kept fairly reasonable. Members generally enjoy special discounts. Food co-ops are usually health-oriented and offer a wide selection of vegetarian and organic options. If you do not have access to a food co-op, you may wish to form a buying club of your own. To do this, you'll need to find a good wholesaler and at least three or four other people that are interested in participating (most wholesalers require minimum orders). The work of placing orders, picking them up and distributing them can be shared among club members.

BAKERIES

Although baked goods are widely available in most grocery stores, those fresh from a bakery will provide added enjoyment to your meals. Look for one that specializes in whole grain products. Many ethnic bakeries sell hearty rye and wheat breads, bagels and tortillas. If you prefer organic ingredients or wish to avoid dairy and eggs, be sure to ask. Another option for those who really appreciate fresh bread is to invest in a bread maker. You'll have complete control over the ingredients, making it ideal for people with food allergies.

WHAT TO BUY

After you've done your homework and you know where to shop, you'll want to decide just what your pantry should include. Begin by making a list of all the basics you will need for everyday cooking. Then write up your menu for a week. Add anything that is not already on your list. Soon your pantry will be complete. Keep a pad on your fridge so you can add items to your list when they get low. The shopping list on page 199 will help you to plan your first few shopping sprees.

Basic Shopping List

Grain Products

- ☐ Flours (whole wheat and others)
- ☐ Brown rice
- ☐ Dry cereal
- ☐ Whole grain breads
- ☐ Whole grain crackers, rye crisps
- ☐ Oatmeal, mixed grain cereals
- ☐ Pasta
- ☐ Wheat germ
- ☐ Other grains, as desired
- ☐ Popcorn

Vegetables and Fruits

- ☐ Fresh greens
- ☐ Garlic and onions
- ☐ Seasonal vegetables
- ☐ Seasonal fruits
- ☐ Canned tomatoes, sauce or paste
- ☐ Canned fruits
- ☐ Dried fruits
- ☐ Frozen vegetables
- ☐ Frozen fruit products

Beans & Bean Products

- ☐ Dried legumes (navy, pinto, black and kidney beans; garbanzos, lentils and split peas)
- ☐ Canned legumes
- ☐ Tofu, tempeh
- ☐ Instant dried legume dishes (e.g., hummus and soups)

Nuts, Seeds and Butters

- ☐ Nuts (almonds, walnuts, cashews, etc.)
- ☐ Nut butters (almond, peanut, etc.)
- ☐ Seeds (sesame, pumpkin, sunflower, flax)
- ☐ Seed butters (tahini)

Meat Analogues

- ☐ Vegetarian patties
- ☐ Other meat substitutes (tofu wieners, seitan, lunch slices, sausages, loaves, etc.)
- ☐ Frozen entrées
- ☐ Deli items (bean salad, sushi, etc.)
- ☐ Dried mixes (falafel and seitan mixes)

Non-dairy or Dairy Products

- ☐ Milk (non-dairy milk and/or low-fat cow's milk)
- ☐ Cheese (non-dairy or dairy)
- ☐ Yogurt (soy or dairy)

Sweeteners

- ☐ Blackstrap molasses
- ☐ Maple syrup
- ☐ Other sweeteners (e.g., date sugar,
- ☐ Sucanat, rice syrup, brown or white sugar)

Beverages

- ☐ Cereal grain beverages
- ☐ Fruit and vegetable juices
- ☐ Leaf and herbal teas
- ☐ Organic coffee

Miscellaneous

- ☐ Nutritional yeast (Red Star T-6635+)
- ☐ Seaweed
- ☐ Miso
- ☐ Eggs

Fats and Oils

- ☐ Oil (unrefined oils such as extra virgin olive, flax, canola or safflower oil)
- ☐ Soy spread, butter or soft margarine
- ☐ Vegan or regular mayonnaise

Seasonings and Condiments

- ☐ Bottled sauces (teriyaki, tamari, soy sauce)
- ☐ Vegetable broth powder, cubes or chicken
- ☐ style seasoning
- ☐ Vinegar (rice vinegar or apple cider
- ☐ vinegar), lemon juice
- ☐ Instant vegetarian gravy and sauce mixes

Herbs and Spices

- ☐ Basil, oregano, parsley
- ☐ Salt, pepper
- ☐ Sage, savory, thyme
- ☐ Chili powder
- ☐ Cinnamon, allspice, nutmeg
- ☐ Cumin, curry
- ☐ Dry mustard (Dijon type)
- ☐ Ginger

STORAGE TIPS

Now that you've arrived home with loads of wonderfully nourishing vegetarian food, you'll need to know how to care for it. In storing your food, there are three primary objectives:

1. *to keep food fresh and appealing*
2. *to prevent spoilage, mold, rancidity or infestations with bugs*
3. *to keep nutrients in*

Appropriate food storage is especially important when your diet is based on unrefined foods, as these foods are far more susceptible to rancidity and bug infestations than their refined counterparts. Items with little nutritional value, such as white sugar and white flour, will keep in your pantry for many months as they are of little interest to pests.

Whole foods come protected by nature. Take grains, for example. Intact wheat berries keep for a couple of years stored in a cool, dry place in a tightly covered container. Grind the berries into flour, and the storage time is reduced to a couple of months. Whole nuts in the shell are far better keepers than shelled nuts, which in turn last longer than chopped nuts. Fresh fruits come packaged in their skin. Remove that and the fruit quickly perishes. It is also important to note that foods containing natural fats, such as wheat germ and nuts, go rancid much more quickly than those containing little fat, such as wheat bran. Higher-fat foods should be stored in the refrigerator or freezer. Further guidelines for food storage are provided in Table 11.1.

When you expand your whole foods pantry, you'll quickly discover that you have such a wide variety of products that it can be a challenge to locate the ingredients for any given recipe. Taking the time to organize your pantry will help make food preparation a lot less stressful.

One simple way of doing this is to store foods in mason jars or other large, clear, air-tight jars. Buy about two or three dozen jars and label them. Arrange them on an open shelf, if possible, or keep them in your pantry. For bulkier items such as flour, you can use larger canisters or buckets. Keep spices in small tightly closed containers, preferably away from the warm stove area.

Many foods are best stored in the refrigerator as they go rancid quickly at room temperature. The refrigerator tends to dry things out, so make sure foods are covered. Lettuce and other greens keep especially well in plastic containers with tight fitting lids. Buy only as much fresh produce as you can use up in a week (excluding produce such as potatoes that are not stored in the refrigerator).

Whole grain flours should also be refrigerated. Bread, on the other hand, is better kept in the freezer to prevent moisture loss. Most fresh bread can be stored at room temperature for a few days.

A freezer can be a real asset. It allows you to store precooked beans, preserve in-season fruits and vegetables, stock up on bulk foods and purchase large quantities of perishables such as whole grain flours, wheat germ, nuts and dried fruits.

Table 11.1 Food Storage

Store in a cool, dry place	Store in the refrigerator	Store in the freezer
• whole grains and pasta	• nuts, seeds and their	• ground flaxseed
• legumes, textured soy	butters (or in freezer)	• wheat germ
protein	• non-dairy milks, cow's	• frozen patties, loaves,
• dry cereals	milk, yogurts, cheeses	• frozen vegetables,
• bread (keeps 3–4 days	• vegetables, vegetable	fruits, juices
at room temperature)	juices	• fresh herbs (Freeze in
• crackers dry goods	• opened condiments,	a plastic bag, crumble
• onions, garlic, potatoes	sauces, maple syrup	for instant use.)
and tomatoes	• whole grain flours	• breads, rolls, muffins,
• dried fruits, unripe	• active dry yeast	baked goods (for
fruits, bananas	• cold pressed oils	longer storage)
• honey, molasses	• tofu	
• milk powder (non-dairy	• fresh pasta	
or dairy)	• fresh herbs and ginger	
• olive oil, sesame oil,		
refined oils		
• nutritional yeast, spices		

MAKING THE MOST OF YOUR MEALS

Preparing a wonderful meal can bring a real sense of satisfaction. Begin by selecting the highest quality ingredients – fresh herbs and garlic with a squeeze of lemon and a touch of extra virgin olive oil can turn a ho-hum dish into a masterpiece. Choose a variety of colors and textures in the foods you prepare, and try not to overcook your vegetables. Finally, take the time to make meals look appealing: a sprig of parsley, an edible flower or a few carrot curls add a special touch.

Whether it's breakfast, lunch, dinner or snacks, you'll want your food to be interesting, tasty and nutritious. Don't fall into the rut of eating the same foods day in and day out. Experiment with all kinds of flavors, including those with which you aren't so familiar. The following pages will provide you with a host of practical suggestions for making the most of your meals.

BREAKFAST: A GREAT WAY TO START YOUR DAY!

Let's face it, most people don't set aside much time for the morning meal, if in fact they eat at all. Unfortunately, it's a bigger mistake than many people realize because those who eat a good breakfast enjoy a number of important advantages: they work harder, play harder and have an better sense of well being. Not surprisingly, they live longer too.

The challenge is to make breakfast a priority in your life – plan ahead and allow yourself the time to enjoy your meal without feeling too rushed. In less than 10 minutes, you can be eating a delicious meal that will brighten your whole day.

Breakfast is probably the meal that changes the least when you become a vegetarian. For the lacto-ovo vegetarian, breakfast is a breeze. Think about our traditional breakfast foods: cereal, toast, pancakes, French toast and eggs. Sure they are accompanied by meat on occasion, but it's just a side dish that can be easily eliminated. For vegans, breakfasts can be modeled after traditional fare (muffins and pancakes taste great without a speck of milk or egg) or they can take on a whole new shape – you are limited only by your imagination!

Wise Choices

A healthy vegetarian breakfast provides close to a third of your daily nutrient needs and a sizable portion of fiber and phytochemicals as well. By selecting a variety of foods from the vegetarian food guide, it's hard to go wrong. Begin by being choosy about the breads and cereals you eat. Look for those that are made with a whole grain, and even better, a variety of whole grains. Include a vitamin C-rich fruit or juice and some soymilk, nuts or nut butter, tofu or beans (why not?) with your meal. Lacto-ovo vegetarians may wish to add low-fat milk, cheese or cottage cheese, yogurt and eggs (in moderation).

If you are trying to reduce your intake of eggs and dairy products, you'll be pleased to know that there are all kinds of great alternatives. Non-dairy beverages made from soy, tofu, nuts and rice can be used as a direct substitute for cow's milk on cereal and in most recipes. Look for varieties that are fortified with calcium, vitamin D and other nutrients. You may also enjoy some of the non-dairy cheeses and yogurts in your morning meals. Tofu makes a delicious substitute for scrambled eggs (see recipe on page 212) and can even be used as an egg substitute in some recipes. Ground flaxseed, or commercial egg replacers also work wonders in pancakes, muffins and other baked goods.

The following breakfast suggestions are all fast, nutritious and delicious.

- hot cereal using a combination of grains and spices (top it off with some sliced fruit, wheat germ, nuts or ground flaxseed and a milk of your choice)
- English muffins with tomato sauce, cheese (non-dairy or dairy) and peppers
- ready-to-eat cereal or granola with wheat germ, berries and soymilk
- multigrain toast with tahini or almond butter and blackstrap molasses plus grapefruit juice
- whole grain pancakes or waffles topped with fresh fruit or fruit sauce and maple syrup
- scrambled tofu or leftover savory beans served with cornbread, muffins or chapati and a glass of orange-pineapple juice

Breakfast in a Flash

If you can't seem to get it together, don't give up. There are many ways of becoming part of the breakfast crowd without sacrificing the better part of your morning.

1. Postpone it a little.

Breakfast doesn't have to happen at 7:00 a.m. sharp. Ten o'clock will do just fine. So if you don't have much of an appetite first thing in the morning or can't seem to make the time, simply postpone it a little, such as during your coffee-break at work. Portable breakfasts don't need to be fancy or time-consuming to prepare. How about packing along:

- a muffin, some almonds and an orange;
- granola with sliced apples and yogurt (leave a bowl and utensils at work);
- a bagel with peanut butter and bananas, and a glass of grapefruit juice;
- some rye crisps, cheese (soy or dairy) and pineapple juice;
- leftover bean burritos.

2. Get it ready the night before.

Simplify your morning by getting things ready the night before. If you have a crock pot, cook some grains overnight (see Whole Grain Pudding on page 215–16). For other meals, take out non-perishables like cereal. Mix up the juice, set the table and do whatever else you can manage.

3. Get up earlier.

When it boils down to an extra 10 minutes of sleep or breakfast, breakfast wins hands down. When you get into the breakfast habit, you'll never regret it.

LET'S DO LUNCH

Whether you have a row of brown bags to fill for hungry family members or are faced with frequent business lunches, there are many things that you can do to make lunch more interesting.

Business or Restaurant Lunch

With the tremendous boom of interest in health, it has become much easier to find appealing vegetarian meals in restaurants. Well-established family restaurants offer veggie-burgers, steak houses carry vegetarian stir-frys and fast food establishments sell vegetarian pizza and salads. If you are at the mercy of the nearest lunch wagon, you may want to consider bagging part of your meal. Bring some hummus and pita, and buy a salad to go with it.

Those who live in a larger city and have the the time to explore can expect to find a number of very inviting places. For a speedy meal, try ordering a sandwich and salad at a veggie-friendly deli. Ethnic restaurants offer amazing meals at very reasonable prices (you may wish to check to see if lard is used in cooking). Here's a sampling of some of the options available:

Ethnic Restaurant	Vegan Choices	Lacto-Ovo Vegetarian Options
Middle Eastern	Falafel Baba ghanoush Meatless stuffed grape leaves Hummus and pita	Eggplant moussaka Greek salad or spinach pie
Mexican	Beans and tortillas Burritos, tacos, enchiladas	Any of the vegan choices with cheese
Italian	Pasta and tomato sauce Pasta primavera Pasta with pesto	Pasta with alfredo sauce or other cream sauce Eggplant parmigiana
Indian	Bean and vegetable curries with chapatis or other bread	Raita (yogurt)
Chinese	Rice, and noodle dishes Vegetable dishes with nuts or seitan (gluten) Tofu dishes	Stir-fries with egg Egg foo yong
Japanese	Tofu in sauces Miso soups with noodles Vegetarian sushi Spinach and seaweed salads	Same as vegan

Bag Lunches

If you have mainly bag lunches, you may think becoming vegetarian will leave you with little more than cheese or peanut butter sandwiches. After a year or so, lunch can seem pretty unappealing. The key to enticing vegetarian bag lunches is to move away from the traditional and experiment a little. Even sandwiches can be interesting if you use your imagination. Start with fresh, thick slices of whole grain bread, rolls, pita bread or bagels. Fill them with hummus and sprouts; thin slices of soy cheese, avocado slices and lettuce; veggie-burgers, green onions, tomatoes and pickles; or tofu salad, olives and red peppers. Consider the variety of "sandwiches" eaten around the world. The Japanese have nori rolls, the Chinese, rice rolls and the Mexicans, tortillas. All of these make a nice change from traditional Western-style sandwiches. For food safety, you can keep your lunch cold until noon by putting a small freezer pack or a frozen food item (frozen juice or a muffin) in your lunch bag.

If you aren't big on sandwiches, pack along something else. Bring rice and leftover vegetable or legume dishes for lunch. Carry soup, stew or chili in a thermos. Include cornbread and a piece of fruit. Mix and match lunch items from the combinations provided below – be creative!

Sandwich and Bag Lunch Ideas

Bread	Sandwich filling	Vegetables	Dessert
Multigrain bun	Almond butter or tahini with banana, blackstrap molasses or preserves	Carrot and green pepper sticks	Cranberry muffin
German rye bread	Tofu bologna and nayonaise	Sprouts and tomato	Homemade granola bar
Whole wheat pita bread	Hummus, falafel or veggie patty	Tabbouleh salad	Oatmeal cookies
Pita bread pizza	Soy or dairy cheese	Pizza toppings (in roll)	Pear
Rice rolls			Trail mix
12-grain bread	Cashew or peanut butter	Cherry tomatoes and celery	Yogurt (soy or dairy)
Nori rolls	Rice, vegetables and tofu with tamari	(in roll)	Molasses cookies
Pumpernickel bagel	Carrot-tahini filling	Waldorf salad (walnuts, apples)	Fruit leather
Sourdough whole wheat roll	Bean salad	Vegetable salad	Carrot cake
Tortilla	Refried beans	Chopped tomatoes, lettuce, green onion	Cantaloupe

WHAT'S FOR DINNER?

The difficulty with dinner is that it is traditionally centered around meat. That presents a bit of a challenge for the new vegetarian. To make dinner meals both simple and enjoyable, here are a couple of options:

1. MODIFY TRADITIONAL STYLE MEALS

Simply replace the meat in traditional meals with beans, meat analogs, tofu burgers, veggie wieners, nut loaves, patties or textured vegetable protein. You can still have all your favorite trimmings like mashed potatoes and gravy, corn on the cob, dressing and vegetables.

2. GO WITH ETHNIC OPTIONS

Borrow some ideas from the cultures that rarely use meat, or use it in very small quantity. Try Mexican, Lebanese, East Indian, Chinese or African dishes.

When you first begin preparing vegetarian dinners, you may find it easiest to make traditional meals most of the time, gradually incorporating ethnic foods into your repertoire. Before you know it, you'll be whipping up interesting dishes from around the world. Of course, if you have the advantage of growing up in a culture that uses very little meat, your task will be that much easier.

If you're concerned about the time it takes to cook vegetarian meals, relax. They needn't take longer to prepare than meals with meat.

Tools for Fixing Fast Dinners

Whether you like to prepare things from scratch or prefer to rely on ready-made convenience foods, there are many things that you can do to make your life easier and your meals tastier.

1. Decide on your menu in advance.
When you plan ahead, you can walk in the house at 6:00 p.m. to a nice, hot meal just waiting in the crock pot – how about a hearty soup, a thick bean stew or some spicy chili? It means soaking beans ahead of time and allowing time to cut up vegetables in the morning. Needless to say, it's well worth the effort.

2. Cook in batches of at least double what you or your family can eat in one meal.
Making double or triple batches means that you'll be able to enjoy an evening

or weekend off somewhere down the road. You can save leftovers for the next day or freeze a batch for later use. Cook grains and beans in large quantities too. Package them in meal-sized portions and freeze, or plan a couple of different dishes using them as a base. For example, you may serve a vegetable/cashew stir-fry with brown rice for supper one day, then some curried tofu with the leftover rice a day or two later.

3. Make up large quantities of baking mixes.
You can pre-mix flour and other dry ingredients to use in baked goods, pancakes, muffins and cookie recipes. Simply freeze or refrigerate and use as needed. To make the recipe, just add the liquid ingredients.

4. Stock your pantry and freezer well.
If you haven't tried any of the vegetarian convenience foods that are on the market, you're in for a pleasant surprise. You can have burgers, burritos, hot dogs or pizza ready in minutes. Here are some basic standbys you'll need to keep on hand to create great meals in a flash:

Beans and other legumes
Canned lentils and beans are available either plain or dressed up with sauces. Add them to soups, spaghetti sauces, chili or casseroles. Firmer beans such as garbanzos can be thrown into a stir-fry. Freeze-dried beans such as refried beans and bean soups are particularly useful for backpacking or camping.

Tofu
Tofu is a wonderful convenience food that can be made into a meal in a matter of minutes. It can also be stir-fried, baked and scrambled, or made into patties, sandwich fillings, desserts, puddings, cakes, tofu mayonnaise and creams. Tofu can be frozen and thawed to obtain a pleasant, chewy consistency. Some tofu is packaged in tetra-pack containers so that refrigeration isn't necessary.

Quick whole grains and mixes
Quick-cooking wild or brown rice and pastas are now available in most stores. Bulgar wheat, whole grain couscous, millet and quinoa all can be prepared in less than 30 minutes. Whole grain pancake mixes can be turned into dumplings or hot biscuits in a hurry.

Wheat gluten products (chai or seitan)
The concentrated protein in wheat flour is kneaded, seasoned and cooked to produce seitan or "wheat meat." Its chewy texture often resembles beef or

chicken, thus it is great in stews, soups and casseroles.

Seasonings

Flavor your foods with salsa, tamari, miso, nutritional yeast, seaweed powder, garlic powder, lemon juice (try the frozen variety), seasoned vinegars, canned tomatoes and instant vegetable broth powders.

Frozen foods

There are wonderful discoveries to be made in the frozen section of health food stores and supermarkets. In addition to frozen bread dough, pizza crust and vegetables, there are a wide number of vegetarian entrées available. Some favorites include:
- pizza (including soy cheese pizza) and burritos;
- Greek foods (spanakopita, tyropita);
- veggie pies and pockets;
- TV dinners (pasta with sauces, cabbage rolls and perogies);
- burgers, patties and wieners.

SNACKS

For most North Americans, eating between meals is an important part of life. The first snack of the day often comes during our coffee break or recess. Then there's the after-work or after-school snack, and finally the bedtime snack (or non-stop evening munching). Foods eaten between meals make up about a quarter of our daily calories. If these calories come from junk food, we get short-changed on nutrients.

The answer is not to eliminate snacks from our daily diet. In fact, eating snacks between meals, rather than eating three big meals a day, can be beneficial for the some people. This practice can help to increase mineral absorption and keep blood sugar levels even. Snacks are especially important for children with small stomachs who have trouble getting enough calories from meals alone and for those who are underweight. Instead of omitting the snack, we need to focus on choosing the right kind of snacks. Simply select your snacks from the five food groups of the vegetarian food guide. If it's not part of the guide, then chances are it's not a healthy snack. The following tips will ensure that your snack choices make a real contribution to your nutrient needs.
- *Choose snacks that aren't too high in concentrated sugars.* Some high sugar snacks can be quite nutritious, but they can also contribute to tooth decay. One of the worst offenders is dried fruits. When these are eaten

along with nuts or cheese, which can protect against cavities, they seem to be less damaging. It's a good idea to brush your teeth after eating sweet foods.

• *Choose a variety of foods from each of the food groups for your snacks.* For example, you could have a muffin for your morning snack, some trail mix on your way home from work, and some soy or dairy yogurt with apple slices before bed.

• *Pick foods that you don't generally include with meals.* For example, if you don't often include fruits at mealtime, eat them as snacks instead.

• *Keep your pantry and refrigerator well stocked with nutritious snack foods.* We tend to eat whatever is most convenient when we're hungry. If only healthy choices are available, that's what we'll choose.

• *If you want a snack while you're away from home, don't go for junk.* Stop at a produce place for an apple, at a bakery for a bagel, or at a natural food store for a muffin. Most corner stores carry fresh fruit and yogurt, and even vending machines carry trail mixes and fruit juice. Bring food from home when you know healthy options will be hard to come by.

Super Snack Suggestions

• Trail mix (use commercial trail mix or make your own)
• Fresh fruit salad or fruit kabobs
• Celery stuffed with nut butter
• Yogurt mixed with cut-up fruit
• Homemade muffins, cookies or loaves
• Whole grain pudding with fruit sauce or canned fruit
• Rye crisps or rice cakes with almond butter and banana slices
• Mini-pizza on English muffins or pita bread
• Blender tofu, fruit or yogurt drink
• Frozen juice popsicles
• Raw vegetables with tofu or yogurt dip
• Popcorn topped with grated cheese or seasonings
• Crispy tofu "fingers"
• Hummus and pita bread
• Hot or cold cereal topped with sliced fruit and milk
• Soy nuts
• Bagel with soy cheese or deli slices

RECIPES: SIMPLE TREASURES

Welcome to the wonderful, creative realm of vegetarian cooking! These recipes were carefully selected to enhance the nutrition of a plant-based diet and to introduce tasty ways of preparing highly nutritious foods. Each recipe has been designed for use by all vegetarians including vegans. You will find great ideas for food selection and preparation in our "Chef's Tip" boxes. For additional information on ingredients, consult the glossary on pages 252-254. Enjoy!

GUIDELINES FOR NUTRITIONAL NOTES

Under each recipe, the calorie, protein, fat, carbohydrates and fiber content is given for each serving. In the nutritional notes you will find comments about particular ingredients or nutrients which contribute to the healthful aspects of the recipe. Directly below the recipes, information is provided regarding minerals and vitamins that are discussed earlier in the book. Each of these nutrients in the recipe is rated according to the percent of Recommended Daily Allowances (RDA) for that nutrient and is based on the highest recommended intake for both age and sex (excluding pregnancy or lactation). For example, the RDA level for calcium (see Appendix 2) for people 11 to 24 years is 1200 mg, whereas the level for an adult above 24 years of age is 800 mg. In this case we use the higher figure because it is the highest recommended intake for all the age groups. Therefore the nutritional analysis of the recipes may underestimate the percent of nutrients recommended for your age.

If the recipe meets 10 to 20 percent of the RDA, it is considered a *good source* of that nutrient. If the recipe meets 20 percent or more of the RDA for a nutrient, it is considered to be a *high source* of that nutrient. So if a particular dish is a high source of iron and a good source of calcium, it would appear in the nutritional box as follows:

Per Serving:
High source: iron
Good source: calcium

The nutritional analysis of the recipes has been done using the basic ingredients, not the variations given. Fortified soymilk and regular fat tofu have been used in the recipe analyses. Optional ingredients are included in the analyses, *unless otherwise specified.*

Breakfast

Scrambled Tofu
Fruity Whole Grain Pancakes with
    Jiffy Fruit Sauce
Flax Egg Replacer (for baking)
Whole Grain Pudding

Spreads and Sandwich Fillings

Eggless Egg Salad
Carrot and Tahini Sandwich Filling
Hazelnut Pâté

Soups, Salads and Dressings

Green Sea Soup (Split Pea)
Non-Dairy Vegetable Cream Soup
Wild Garden Salad
Sesame Tahini Salad Dressing
Basic Flax Oil and Vinegar Dressing

Vibrant Vegetables

International Greens
Spicy Yams and Kale

Cooking Grains and Legumes

Cooking Grains
Perfect Pilaf
Legume Wizardry

Entrées

Chunky Red Lentil Tomato Pasta
    Sauce
Two Bean Stew
Red Star and Crispy Tofu Fingers
Vegetable Stir-fry

Patties and Festive Entrées

Millet Patties
Wheat Gluten "Cutlets" (Seitan)
Savory Roast/Patties–Vegan-Style
    (with TSP)
Mexican Feast

Desserts and Baking

Apple Spice Cookies
Almost Instant Candy
Multi-Purpose Muffin and Cake
    Batter
Old Fashioned Low-fat Ginger-
    bread
Berry Uncheesecake
Instant Creamy Chocolate
    Pudding/Pie

SCRAMBLED TOFU

This dish demonstrates one of the many ways tofu can be used as a convenience food. Whether for a hot breakfast or as a sandwich filling the next day, young children and adults love it.

Basic Ingredients:
- 1 lb medium-firm tofu (made with calcium)
- 2 tsp vegetable oil
- 2 tsp tamari, soy sauce or "chicken-style" vegetarian seasoning

Gourmet Options (include any or all as desired):
- 1 Tbsp Red Star T-6635+ nutritional yeast flakes
- 2 Tbsp green onion, chopped
- ¼ cup mushrooms, sliced
- 1 large clove garlic, minced
- 2 Tbsp fresh parsley, chopped

Drain the tofu well. In a heavy or cast-iron frying pan, sauté the vegetables in the oil until soft. Add the tofu, tamari soy sauce and seasonings. Scramble with a fork. Cook on medium heat for 2 to 3 minutes. Sprinkle with parsley and serve immediately.

MAKES 3 SERVINGS (½ cup each)

Per serving: Calories: 150, Protein: 8 gm., Fat: 7 gm., Carbohydrates 5 gm., Fiber: 2 gm.

High source: folate, niacin, riboflavin, thiamin, vitamin B_6, and vitamin B_{12}

Good source: calcium, zinc

Nutritional Note: Red Star T-6635+ nutritional yeast is an excellent source of B_{12}.

FRUITY WHOLE GRAIN PANCAKES

You don't need eggs or cow's milk to make great pancakes. Ground flax seed makes a terrific egg replacer (see recipe pages 214–15). Use it in baking or sprinkle it on hot cereal. Load these pancakes up with additional fruit for a real taste treat.

> 2 Tbsp vegetable oil
> 1½ cups milk (non-dairy or dairy)
> 2 tsp sweetener (e.g., maple syrup, honey)
> 1 Tbsp ground flaxseed or commercial egg replacer (follow
>   package directions), or 1 egg
> ¼ cup wheat germ
> 1 cup fruit (blueberries, thinly sliced apples, bananas, peaches)
> 1 cup whole wheat flour
> ¼ cup other flour (e.g., oat, corn, buckwheat, spelt or more
>   whole wheat)
> 2 tsp baking powder
> 2 tsp cinnamon (optional)

In a large bowl, combine the oil, milk, sweetener and ground flaxseed. In a small bowl, mix together all the dry ingredients very well. Add the dry ingredients to the milk mixture, and stir gently. Fold in the fruit. (Note: If the batter is too thick, add ¼ cup liquid.) Heat a non-stick skillet over medium heat. The real key to a great pancake is to make sure the pan is hot before you pour on the batter. Add oil to coat the bottom of the pan. Pour the batter onto the hot skillet, and cook until the top begins to bubble. Flip the pancake and cook until the underside is golden brown. Serve with fruit sauce (given below), fresh fruit slices and/or maple syrup.

MAKES 3 SERVINGS (3 medium pancakes each)

Per serving: Calories: 415, Protein: 13 gm., Fat 14 gm.,
    Carbohydrates 63 gm., Fiber 9 gm.
High source: iron, zinc, folate, vitamin A
Good source: calcium

Analysis was done using fortified soymilk, apples, whole wheat and buckwheat flour.

FRUIT SAUCE IN A JIFFY

Fruit sauces are a refreshing change from sugary syrups. Dream up your own using whatever fruits you have on hand. Leftovers are wonderful on pudding, cake or yogurt.

  1 medium banana
  1 medium orange, peeled and quartered
  2 Tbsp raisins, apricots or other dried fruit
  2 cups fresh or frozen fruit (blueberries, raspberries or kiwi)

In a blender or food processor, purée the banana, orange and raisins until smooth. Pour into a medium bowl. Fold in the fresh or frozen fruit (thawed).

MAKES ABOUT 6 SERVINGS (½ cup each)

Per serving: Calories: 63, Protein: 1 gm., Fat: 0 gm., Carbohydrates: 16 gm.,
      Fiber: 2 gm.,
High source: vitamin C
Good source: folate, Vitamin B$_6$

Analysis was done using strawberries.

Nutritional Note: Fruit sauces are far more nutritious than the sugar-based pancake syrups they replace. The fresh fruit provides antioxidants such as vitamin C and beta-carotene.

FLAX EGG REPLACER FOR ONE EGG

Ground flaxseed works well as a substitute for eggs in pancakes, cookies, cakes and muffins. It helps to produce a moist, light product and provides essential omega-3 fatty acids. You can buy flaxseed already ground, or grind seeds in a blender and store in the freezer.

> 1 Tbsp ground flaxseed (grind 1 cup in a blender and store
>   the remainder in the freezer)
> 3 Tbsp water

Mix the flax and water in a small bowl. Let set 1 to 2 minutes. (It becomes very thick if left too long).

Chef's Tip: In some recipes, such as the one for fruity pancakes where there are plenty of liquids, ground flaxseed may be added directly to the wet ingredients.

WHOLE GRAIN PUDDING

This pudding is a great way to use whole grains. Cook overnight in a crockpot for an instant breakfast; leftovers can double as dessert. Try mixing a number of grains together for an interesting combination of flavors and textures. If you have a sensitivity to wheat or gluten, use brown rice, millet, buckwheat or quinoa (remember to wash quinoa before cooking).

> ¾ cup uncooked whole grains (barley, wheat berries, spelt
>   berries, millet, quinoa, rice or any combination of
>   grains)
> 3 cups boiling water
> 1 to 2 Tbsp maple syrup, honey or sugar (optional)
> ¼ tsp salt
> ½ tsp each: cinnamon, cloves and nutmeg or allspice
> ½ cup raisins or other dried fruit
> ½ cup milk (non-dairy or dairy)

If using a crockpot, combine the grains and water, and cook on low overnight. For the stove top method, place the grains and water in a heavy saucepan, cover, and cook for about 2 hours (adding extra water if necessary). Stir in all the other ingredients, and cook for ½ hour more. Serve hot or cold. Top with crunchy granola, fresh fruit, fruit sauce and/or milk.

MAKES 4 SERVINGS (1 cup each)

Per serving: Calories: 244, Protein: 6 gm., Fat: 2 gm., Carbohydrates: 54 gm., Fiber: 4 gm.

High source: folate

Good source: iron, niacin, thiamin

Analysis was done using fortified soymilk, barley, millet and wheat berries.

Nutritional Note: The nutritional content of this pudding varies according to the grains used in its preparation. To boost its nutritional value, use some quinoa (be sure to rinse it well before cooking), or amaranth with the other grains. Less than 5 percent of the calories in this recipe come from fat.

Chef's Tip: If you presoak grains for 4 hours, the cooking time will be cut in half.

EGGLESS EGG SALAD

This tasty sandwich filling is a snap to make and is a favorite lunch box item. Tofu is such a useful, satisfying convenience food; keep some on hand for those last minute meals.

Basic Ingredients:
- ½ cup medium tofu, drained
- 1 tsp tamari or soy sauce
- 1 tsp Dijon mustard
- 2 tsp tofunaise or mayonnaise

Gourmet Options (include any or all as desired):
- 1 tsp Red Star T-6635+ nutritional yeast flakes
- 3 olives, diced
- 1 Tbsp green onion, finely diced
- 2 Tbsp carrot, grated
- 1 Tbsp celery, finely diced
- 1 Tbsp fresh parsley, minced
- turmeric or other seasonings, as desired.

Crumble the drained tofu with a fork. Stir in all the other ingredients, including choices from the gourmet options list, and mix thoroughly. Use as a sandwich filling or cracker spread. Add lettuce and tomatoes or stuff pita bread and top it with sprouts.

MAKES FILLING FOR 2 SANDWICHES

Per sandwich: Calories: 85, Protein 7 gm., Fat: 4 gm., Carbohydrates: 5 gm.,
    Fiber: 1 gm.
High source: folate, riboflavin, thiamin, vitamin A, vitamin B_6, vitamin B_{12}
Good source: niacin

Analysis was done using all optional ingredients.

Nutritional Note: The Red Star T6635+ brand of nutritional yeast, adds a cheese-like flavor and provides an excellent source of vitamin B_{12}. Tofu contains essential fatty acids, isoflavones and high-quality protein.

CARROT AND TAHINI SANDWICH FILLING

This filling has a tuna-like texture. For the best effect, be sure to grate the carrots finely. Tahini is a nutritious and tasty seed butter. Flavors can vary, so you may want to try a few brands. Greek or Lebanese stores carry some great tahini at reasonable prices.

Basic Ingredients:
    1 medium carrot, finely grated
    2 Tbsp tahini sesame butter

Gourmet Options:
    1 tsp soy or dairy mayonnaise
    1 tsp Red Star T6635+ nutritional yeast flakes (optional)
    1 Tbsp onion, diced
    1 Tbsp celery, diced
    1 tsp each: kelp powder and lemon juice
    Salt and pepper to taste

In a small bowl, combine all the ingredients. Use as a sandwich filling or spread, and refrigerate in an airtight container.

MAKES FILLING FOR 2 SANDWICHES

Per sandwich: Calories: 115, Protein: 4 gm., Fat: 7 gm.,
    Carbohydrates: 10 gm., Fiber: 2 gm.
High source: riboflavin, thiamin, vitamin A, vitamin B_6
Good source: folate, niacin, vitamin B_{12}, vitamin C

Analysis was done using all optional ingredients excluding the mayonnaise.

Nutritional Note: Using Red Star T-6635+ nutritional yeast boosts the B vitamin content, including vitamin B_{12}.

HAZELNUT PÂTÉ

This is an innovative way to take advantage of the full flavor of hazelnuts and mushrooms. It's popular with vegetarians and non-vegetarians alike. Serve on crackers or use it as a sandwich filling.

> 1 cup raw hazelnuts (filberts)
> ½ medium onion, sliced
> 1 cup mushrooms, sliced
> 2 cloves garlic, sliced
> 1 tsp olive oil (optional)
> 1 Tbsp sliced black olives (optional)
> ¼ cup fresh parsley
> 1 Tbsp tamari or soy sauce
> 2 tsp Red Star T6635+ nutritional yeast flakes or your favorite
>   seasoning (Spike, Mrs. Dash)
> Salt and pepper to taste

Cook the hazelnuts in a microwave on medium-low heat, or roast in a 350°F oven for 3 to 4 minutes. Sauté the onion, mushrooms and garlic in the oil, or cover and cook in a microwave without oil for about 3 to 4 minutes until soft. In a food processor, purée the cooked vegetables. Add the nuts and all the other ingredients, blend until very smooth, and add a little lemon juice if the mixture is too thick. This pâté freezes well.

MAKES 8 SERVINGS (¼ cup each)

Per serving: Calories: 103, Protein: 3 gm., Fat: 9 gm., Carbohydrates: 4 gm.,
     Fiber: 1.5 gm.
Good source: folate, thiamin, riboflavin, vitamin B_6, vitamin B_{12}

Analysis was done using Red Star nutritional yeast flakes, olives and excluding the olive oil.

GREEN SEA SOUP

Simple! You don't need soup bones for great flavor. This soup freezes so well,
you may want to make a double batch and freeze portions for days when you
don't feel like cooking.

      1½ cups dry split peas
      5 cups water
      1 to 2 bay leaves
      1 tsp salt
      1 to 2 cloves garlic, minced
      1 stalk celery, chopped
      1 large carrot, sliced
      1 leek, sliced (1 cup)
      1 tsp each: marjoram, basil and cumin
      2 Tbsp dry hijiki or wakame seaweed (optional)

Combine all the ingredients in a large, heavy saucepan or a cast-iron Dutch
oven. Cover, bring to a boil, and simmer for 3 to 4 hours (this develops the flavor).

MAKES 6 SERVINGS (1 cup each)

Per serving: Calories: 211, Protein: 14 gm., Fat: 1 gm., Carbohydrates: 40 gm.,
     Fiber: 5 gm.
High source: iron, folate, thiamin, vitamin A
Good source: zinc, niacin

Analysis was done using hijiki.

Nutritional Note: The seaweed provides potassium, iron and other minerals.
With less than 1 gm of fat per serving, this soup is quite a contrast to the traditional higher-fat version of pea soup.

NON-DAIRY VEGETABLE CREAM SOUP

Broccoli, carrots or leeks are excellent choices for this recipe, but use any combination of vegetables. Prepare it as a thick soup for a meal with some whole grain bread on chilly days, or make a thinner version to introduce an elegant meal.

3 cups fresh vegetables (carrots, broccoli, celery, kale, rutabagas, etc.)
2 to 3 medium potatoes, quartered
1 cup onions or leeks, chopped
2 cups water or vegetable broth
2 tsp light miso or vegetable powder
1 tsp marjoram or thyme
¼ cup raw cashews
freshly ground pepper to taste
¼ cup fresh parsley, chopped

Cook the vegetables in water until soft. In a food processor, purée the vegetables with all the other ingredients except the parsley. Garnish with parsley.

MAKES ABOUT 5 SERVINGS (1 cup each)

Per Serving: Calories: 215, Protein: 7 gm., Fat: 5 gm., Carbohydrates: 36 gm.,
    Fiber: 5 gm.
High source: folate, Vitamin A, vitamin C
Good source: iron

Analysis was done using carrots, broccoli, kale and rutabagas.

Variation: Creamy Leek Soup: Use 2 cups potatoes and 3 cups chopped leeks, and omit all the other vegetables. Omit the marjoram and use a little grated nutmeg. Use ¼ cup of calcium-fortified, non-dairy milk powder instead of the cashews. Purée as above.

WILD GARDEN SALAD

Chef Michael Fisher from Vancouver, B.C., created this unusual salad with its combination of sharp and subtle flavors. Try it with the zesty tahini or flax oil dressings on the next pages. For visual appeal, arrange your salad in an interesting bowl, or spread it on a platter. To a base of romaine lettuce, add any of the following ingredients. The amounts given are only a guide; vary the quantities as desired.

6 cups romaine lettuce (1 large head)

2 cups high-calcium greens (kale, bok choy or collards), sliced matchstick thin

½ cup any of the following: sharp greens (mustard, radichio, watercress, endive, etc.), sliced matchstick thin

1 cup of any 2 or 3 of the following: orange sections, alfalfa sprouts, flower petals (chive flowers, kale flowers, nasturtium, pansy), chopped peppers (red, yellow and green), cubed cucumbers

¼ to ½ cup any of the following: chopped green onions, kohlrabi, sliced radishes or olives, nuts or seeds (almonds, sliced and toasted, pumpkin seeds, sunflower seeds or pine nuts)

2 Tbsp orange zest (small strips of organic orange rind) (optional)

Wash the greens well and tear or chop into bite-sized pieces. To prepare greens like kale, remove the ribs before slicing. Add the other ingredients and toss.

MAKES 5 SERVINGS (2 cups each)

Per serving: Calories: 88, Protein: 3 gm., Fat: 0 gm., Carbohydrates: 8 gm., Fiber: 3 gm.

High source: folate, vitamin A, vitamin C

Good source: iron

Analysis was done using kale, mustard greens, alfalfa sprouts, cucumber, almonds and green onions without dressing.

Chef's Tip: The secret to making sturdy greens appealing in salads is to finely slice them. If you have a food processor, roll the greens into a cylindrical shape, and slice with the machine. Without dressings, salads keep for up to 3 days refrigerated in a tightly covered container.

SESAME TAHINI SALAD DRESSING

This special, zesty dressing was developed by Joseph Forest, a professional vegetarian chef. The piquant flavor combination of tahini, Dijon mustard and fresh lemon juice is particularly appealing. Besides using it on salads, try this dressing on steamed vegetables or baked potatoes instead of using margarine or butter.

¼ cup lemon juice
½ cup tahini
1 tsp Dijon mustard
1 to 3 cloves garlic, chopped
2 Tbsp tamari or soy sauce
½ tsp pepper, or to taste
½ cup water

Combine all the ingredients in a blender and purée. You may prefer to add a little water for a thinner dressing.

MAKES 1¾ CUPS

Per Tbsp: Calories: 36, Protein: 1 gm., Fat: 3 gm., Carbohydrates: 2 gm., Fiber: 0 gm.

Variations: Replace half of the tahini with ¼ cup extra-virgin olive or flaxseed oil. Another option is to add ½ tsp sesame oil, 1 Tbsp toasted sesame seeds or 1 Tbsp chopped fresh herbs.

Nutritional Note: This dressing provides small, but significant, amounts of vitamins and minerals, including calcium.

Chef's Tip: If a small-mouthed Mason jar fits your blender, place all the ingredients in it, and purée. Use what you need, replace the lid and store the leftover dressing in the refrigerator.

BASIC FLAX OIL AND VINEGAR DRESSING

Here is a wonderful way of using cold pressed oil. For different flavors substitute other oils such as canola, hazelnut or pumpkin seed for the flax oil. Use on baked potatoes, pasta or stir-frys.

Basic Ingredients:
  ½ cup flaxseed oil
  3 Tbsp lemon juice or rice or cider vinegar
  3 Tbsp water
  2 to 3 medium cloves garlic
  ½ tsp sweetener (maple syrup or honey)
  1 tsp Dijon mustard

Gourmet Options (include any or all as desired):
  1 tsp light miso
  1 tsp tamari or soy sauce
  ½ tsp ground cumin or curry powder

Purée all the ingredients in a blender until smooth. Cover and refrigerate for up to 5 days.

MAKES ¾ CUP

Per Tbsp: Calories: 85 Protein: 0 gm., Fat: 9 gm., Carbohydrates: 1 gm.,
  Fiber 0 gm.

Variation: Add 2 Tbsp chopped fresh or 1 tsp dried herbs.

Nutritional Note: The flax oil in this recipe gives a pleasant, nutty flavor and provides an excellent source of essential omega-3 fatty acids in addition to the antioxidants vitamin E and beta-sitosterol.

INTERNATIONAL GREENS

Getting enough calcium from plant foods means you want to feature greens frequently on your menu. This is easy if you have simple and delicious ways of preparing them. This recipe provides a wide range of sensational seasoning options from around the world.

Basic Ingredients:

   2 lb (9 cups)★ greens (collards, kale or Chinese greens)

   2 tsp olive oil

   3 cloves garlic, minced

   1 lemon, cut into wedges

   Salt and pepper to taste

   ★ In cooking, greens shrink to about ⅓ the fresh amount, so 9 cups fresh = about 3 cups cooked.

Follow the preparation method below, then add one of the following seasoning combinations to the basic recipe:

Middle Eastern:

   1 tsp cumin

   2 tsp paprika (optional)

   ½ cup fresh parsley or fresh cilantro, chopped

Far Eastern:

   2 Tbsp tamari or soy sauce

   2 tsp freshly grated ginger

African:

   1 medium onion, chopped

   1 tsp each: cumin and coriander

   pinch cayenne (optional)

   1 tomato, cubed (add at the end of cooking)

   2 Tbsp each: peanut butter and water (combine and add when
      the greens are almost cooked)

Mediterranean:

    ¼ cup fresh basil, chopped, (or 1 tsp dried)

    ¼ cup fresh oregano, chopped, (or 1 tsp dried)

    ½ cup fresh parsley, chopped, (or 2 tsp dried)

East Indian:

    1 to 2 Tbsp mild curry paste

Wash the greens well and remove the tough ribs. Slice the greens in slivers or small cubes. Heat the oil in a very large skillet or Dutch oven. Add the garlic and your choice of seasoning combinations from the list. Cook for about 1 minute, stirring well (adding a few tablespoons of water to prevent burning or sticking). Add the greens and mix. Cover, lower the heat and simmer for 5 to 15 minutes or until tender. Serve hot with fresh lemon wedges. Squeeze lemon liberally over greens. Season with salt and pepper.

MAKES 4-5 SERVINGS (¾ cup each)

Per serving: Calories: 88, Protein: 4 gm., Fat: 2 gm., Carbohydrates: 12 gm.,
    Fiber: 12 gm.

High source: calcium, iron, vitamin A, vitamin C

Good source: folate, riboflavin, thiamin, vitamin B_6

Analysis was done for 4 servings using raw collards and Mediterranean seasonings.

Nutritional Note: Dark greens are elite among many vegetables because of their high nutrient content, including omega-3 fatty acids and calcium.

SPICY YAMS AND KALE

This simple vegetable dish offers many nutrients and great flavor. The orange and green colors make it very attractive.

    4 cups yams or sweet potatoes, peeled and diced in ½-inch
       chunks

    ½ cup vegetable broth or water

    1 tsp curry powder

    ⅛ tsp each: cloves, cinnamon, cardamom and cayenne

1 cup kale or parsley, finely chopped

2 Tbsp fresh lemon or lime juice

1 Tbsp hazelnut or olive oil (optional)

2 Tbsp hazelnuts or almonds, sliced or chopped (optional)

salt and pepper to taste

In a medium saucepan, combine the yams, stock and ground spices, and bring to a boil. Stir, cover and simmer 3 to 4 minutes until the yams are fork tender. Add the rest of the ingredients, and toss well to blend flavors. Serve hot or chilled as a salad.

MAKES 4 SERVINGS (¾ cup each)

Per serving: Calories 185, Protein: 2 gm., Fat: 0 gm., Carbohydrates: 36 gm.,
    Fiber: 3 gm.

High source: vitamin A, vitamin C

Good source: folate, vitamin B$_6$

Analysis was done without the oil or nuts.

GREAT GRAINS

There is a whole world of grains that can make your vegetarian meals interesting. They are high in complex carbohydrates, B vitamins, protein and trace minerals. Cooking in a cast-iron pot will also boost dietary iron. There are many ways to cook grains: simmer in liquid until tender, pressure cook or bake. Whatever you choose, remember to use a pot large enough to allow for the expansion of the grain. Millet and barley expand to 4 times their original size, while other grains usually expand 2 to 3 times.

Cooking Whole Grains in Under 25 Minutes

Sometimes people don't use whole grains, thinking they take too long (45 minutes to 1 hour to cook). However, some small whole grains such as quinoa and whole wheat couscous can be prepared in 15 minutes or less. To cut the cooking time in half, presoak larger grains such as pot barley, brown rice and whole grain berries (rye, wheat, spelt, kamut, oat groats etc.). Use the amount of water suggested in the table below. When you are ready to cook the soaked grains, cover and bring to a rapid boil. Stir, cover and reduce heat to a simmer. Cook without lifting the lid for 20 to 30 minutes (larger grains take longer).

When the initial cooking is complete, you can add cooked or raw vegetables, fruits, nuts and additional seasoning.

Cooking Grains in the Microwave Oven

You will be surprised how easy it is to cook grains in the microwave, especially if you have one with programmed cooking stages. Use a large glass casserole with a lid. Measure out the correct amount of water, and add your grain. Cover and bring to a rapid boil. Reduce to a simmer and cook for the suggested time from the cooking chart. If you are using programmed cooking stages, simply set the time for boiling on high heat, then the time for simmering on low heat. If you have presoaked the grain for a few hours, cooking will take half the time.

Cooking Times and Directions for One Cup of Whole Grains Without Presoaking
Grains are cooked by combining the grain with the measured amount of water, bringing to a rapid boil, covering and simmering for the recommended time.

Grain	Water	Time*	Special Directions
(1 cup)	(cups)	(minutes)	
Amaranth	2½	20 to 25	Toast in heavy skillet. Add water, bring to boil, cover, simmer.
Barley			
brown	3 to 4	50 to 55	
pot	2 to 3	40 to 45	
pearl	1 to 2	35 to 40	
Buckwheat groats,			
kasha	2	15 to 20	
Millet	3 to 4	20 to 30	**
Oats, whole (groats)	3 to 4	45 to 60	
Quinoa	2	15 to 20	Rinse well in fine strainer to remove the bitter resin.
Rice, brown			
long/short grain	2	45	
brown basmati			
or wehani	2	45	
Rice, white	1 to 2	25 to 30	
Rice, wild	3	60	
Rye, triticale	4	60	
Wheat			
whole berries	3 to 4	60	
bulgur	2	15 to 20	
cracked wheat	2	30 to 35	

* Cooking time will be longer if you have hard water.

** Cook millet for 30 minutes and allow it to set, covered, for 10 to 15 minutes or more for a fluffy product.

PERFECT PILAF

Pilafs are quick and easy to make. Freshly cooked grains or leftover grains come alive with color, flavors and nutrition.

Starting with Uncooked Grains

Lightly sauté a chopped, medium onion or some garlic in a little oil. Add seasonings (see ideas below) cashews, cubes of tofu, tempeh or chopped vegetables such as mushrooms and carrots. Add the grain and the required liquid. Stir, cover and cook for the suggested time. Before serving, add a few more vegetables such as fresh or frozen peas, chopped sweet red peppers or celery. Cover and simmer for a few minutes to heat throughout. Garnish the platter with additional vegetables, fruits or nuts.

Reviving Leftover Grains

Sauté onions, garlic and desired spices, in a little oil. Add chopped, colorful vegetables, such as carrots, mushrooms or okra. Stir, cover and cook a few minutes. Add the cooked grain and simmer 3 to 5 minutes until everything is almost soft and the flavors are mixed. Place on a platter and garnish with chopped nuts or cherry tomatoes, fruits or parsley.

Seasoning Ideas

Oriental:
soy sauce, seaweed powder, sesame seeds, grated ginger
Use all or any combination.

Mediterranean:
fresh parsley, chopped, marjoram, sweet peppers, oregano, basil

Asian:
curry powder or ground cumin with chopped cilantro, hot or sweet peppers, green onion, orange sections

LEGUME WIZARDRY

One important secret of vegetarian cooking is stocking your freezer with a wide variety of cooked legumes to use for quick food preparation. These include adzuki beans for pasta sauce, chick-peas for hummus or a stir-fry, kidney beans for a big batch of chili or several different beans that can be made into a wonderful stew. So whenever you cook beans, make extra, then freeze them in freezer bags or plastic containers for later use.

Below there are two categories of legumes requiring different cooking methods.

Cooking Beans in a Snap

Legumes in Group 1

Presoaking is not required with this group; however, it always speeds up cooking time.

Group 1 Legumes	Cooking Time	Legume:Water Ratio
Lentils, red	25 to 35 minutes	1:2 cups
Lentils, brown or green	45 to 60 minutes	1:2 or 2½ cups
Mung beans	40 to 50 minutes	1:2 or 2½ cups
Split peas	30 to 50 minutes	1:2½ cups

Legumes in Group 2

This group includes all other beans, such as adzuki, kidney, lima, pinto, garbanzo and black bean which take a longer time to cook so they need to be presoaked.

Presoaking and Cooking Legumes in Group 2:

Sort the beans carefully to remove any small stones, and soak overnight with three times the volume of water. Discard the water and rinse the beans thoroughly. Cover the beans with 3 inches fresh, unsalted water and boil hard for 1 minute. You may wish to add fennel seeds or kombu seaweed to reduce the gas produced during digestion. Cover and simmer for 1 to 3 hours. The cooked beans should be very soft so that you can mash these beans with your tongue against the roof of your mouth.

Add seasonings and continue to cook for 10 minutes more. The cooked beans are ready for eating as they are, or you can use them in recipes.

If your next step is to bake the cooked beans in tomato sauce, cover the beans with 2 inches of liquid, and replenish it as it evaporates. Cover during cooking to minimize evaporation.

Chef's Tip for Reducing Presoaking Time: The long presoaking time of 8 to 10 hours can be shortened by bringing the beans to a boil, and soaking for one hour. Then discard the liquid, rinse, cover with fresh water, and cook for the recommended time or until tender. Don't add salt, tomatoes or other highly acidic foods to dried beans until they are cooked tender, or they will not soften and become digestible. Very hard water (high in minerals) can increase bean cooking time.

Cooking Beans in a Slow Cooker

Many people prefer to cook beans all day or overnight in a slow cooker. For every cup of dry beans, add 3 cups of water. You may also add bay leaves, peppercorns or your favorite herbs. Cover, turn on the slow cooker in the morning, and by dinner your beans will be perfect. Remember to add tomatoes and salt near the end of the cooking time.

CHUNKY RED LENTIL TOMATO SAUCE

Red lentils are the fastest cooking of all dried legumes. This sauce can be prepared in about 20 minutes and simmered in a crockpot all day or cooked on the top of the stove for about 1 hour. "Chunky" refers to the vegetables; you can use those listed here, or select others. The lentils almost dissolve into the sauce, and add protein. Use more or less lentils, depending on your taste preferences.

   1 onion, diced
   2 to 3 cloves garlic, minced
   1 large carrot, sliced diagonally
   1 stalk broccoli, chopped
   1 cup mushrooms (fresh or canned), sliced
   ½ cup sweet green pepper, diced
   1 small zucchini, sliced or grated
   28 oz (3 cups) stewed tomatoes, whole or diced
   28 oz (3 cups) prepared tomato sauce

1 cup water

½ to 1 cup dried red lentils

2 Tbsp each: fresh basil and oregano, chopped, (or 2 tsp dried)

Place all the ingredients in a crockpot or saucepan, and stir. If using the stove top method, bring the ingredients to a boil, turn the heat down and simmer the sauce for about 1 hour or more. If using a crockpot, cook on low for 6 to 8 hours, or on high for about 4 hours. Serve with your favorite pasta, or spaghetti squash.

MAKES 8 SERVINGS

Per serving: Calories: 163, Protein: 8 gm., Fat: 1 gm., Carbohydrates: 35 gm.,
    Fiber: 6 gm.
High source: iron, folate, thiamin, vitamin A, vitamin C
Good source of: niacin, riboflavin, vitamin B$_6$

Analysis was done using ¾ cup dried lentils

Variations: Try other vegetables in this recipe; chopped cauliflower, celery, spinach or kale work well. For an extra-fast sauce, use precooked lentils, a prepared pasta sauce and frozen vegetables. Sauté the vegetables in 1 Tbsp olive oil until tender. Add the lentils, the prepared pasta sauce and additional seasonings, and cook for 15 to 20 minutes.

Chef's Tip: Be adventurous with pasta! Try quinoa, spelt, kamut, vegetable or other varieties. Fresh pastas make a meal extra special.

TWO-BEAN STEW

Any two kinds of canned beans, your choice of cooked vegetables, dumplings or a slice of good bread make this flavorful stew a quick, nutritious meal. We like to make it with new potatoes, sweet carrots, peas, rutabagas and cabbage. If you want to freeze leftovers, omit the potatoes.

2 (19 oz) cans beans (or 4 cups cooked) beans (chick-peas,
    kidney, lima, etc.)

1 cup water or vegetable broth

2 medium potatoes, scrubbed and chopped

2 medium carrots, chopped

2 medium onions, chopped

2 cups other vegetables, chopped (rutabaga, cabbage, celery,
    kohlrabi, okra, etc.)

2 Tbsp tamari or soy sauce

2 to 3 bay leaves

2 tsp each: thyme, marjoram and garlic powder

1 to 2 tomatoes or sweet red peppers, chopped (optional)

½ cup flour

¾ cup water

½ cup fresh parsley, minced or frozen green peas

Salt and pepper to taste

Place the drained liquid from the beans in a large Dutch oven or heavy saucepan. Set the beans aside. Add the water, cover and bring to a boil. Add the vegetables, tamari and herbs. Cover, bring to a boil, reduce heat, and simmer for about 8 minutes, or until the vegetables are still a little crunchy. Add the beans and tomatoes to the cooked vegetables, cover, and bring to a boil. Combine the flour and water in a jar with a tight fitting lid. Shake well then slowly add the mixture to the hot stew, stirring while it thickens. Add the parsley, cover, reduce the heat, and simmer for 3 to 4 minutes. Adjust seasonings to taste.

MAKES 6 HEARTY SERVINGS (1½ cups each)

Per serving: Calories: 355, Protein: 16 gm., Fat: 1 gm., Carbohydrates: 73 gm.,
    Fiber: 12 gm.,
High source: iron, folate, niacin, thiamin, vitamin A, vitamin B_6, vitamin C
Good source: calcium, zinc, riboflavin

Analysis was done using cabbage, rutabagas, adzuki and Great Northern beans

Variation: For a very quick dinner, substitute 4 cups frozen vegetables for fresh vegetables. For additional minerals, 1 to 2 tsp kelp powder may be added instead of the salt.

Dumplings:

1 cup whole wheat flour

1 tsp baking powder

¼ tsp salt

⅓ cup milk (non-dairy or dairy)
1 Tbsp vegetable oil (optional)
½ tsp dillweed (optional)

Mix the flour, baking powder and salt thoroughly. Add the remaining ingredients, stirring lightly just to mix. Using a tablespoon, place small mounds of batter the size of a walnut over the thickened stew. Cover and cook on low heat for 15 minutes without peaking.

RED STAR TOFU FINGERS

These two recipes are favorites of the authors. More than any other recipes we know, these two recipes have succeeded in turning people (including children) onto tofu. They're super simple too! The nutritional yeast gives the tofu slices a cheesy savory flavor.

2 Tbsp tamari or soy sauce
½ cup Red Star T-6635+ nutritional yeast flakes
1 tsp seasoning (garlic powder, curry, Mrs. Dash, Spike, paprika
    or other)
12 oz firm tofu, cut into ¼ inch slices
vegetable oil for coating the baking sheet

Pour the tamari into a small bowl. In another small bowl, mix together the yeast and seasoning. Dip the tofu slices into the tamari, then into the seasoned yeast. Place the tofu slices on a baking sheet, lightly wiped or sprayed with oil. Bake at 350°F for 20 minutes, flipping once to brown both sides, or fry the coated tofu in a little oil until both sides are browned.

MAKES 3 SERVINGS (4 oz each)

Per Serving: Calories: 181, Protein: 22 gm., Fat: 10 gm.,
    Carbohydrates: 7 gm., Fiber: 3 gm.
High source: iron, folate, niacin, riboflacin, thiamin, vitamin B6,
vitamin B_{12}
Good source: calcium, zinc

Analysis was done using tofu fingers baked in the oven

Nutritional Note: Tofu, with its low fiber and high fat content, helps to balance the higher fiber foods found in many vegetarian diets and supplies additional calories which are particularly important for growing children. Although other brands of nutritional yeast powder or flakes taste just the same, the brand Red Star T6635+ is a reliable source of vitamin B_{12} for vegans.

CRISPY TOFU FINGERS

Tofu can be used as the protein part of a dinner, as an appetizer or in sandwiches. When you go out for dinner with a non-vegetarian group and want to take along the ingredients for your "meat alternative," this simple recipe works well. Some people like tofu soft, others like it crisp, so experiment with the cooking time.

    vegetable oil for coating the baking sheet
    12 oz firm tofu
    ½ cup thick sauce (vegetarian oyster-style sauce, sweet and sour
        sauce, BBQ sauce or other favorite thick sauce)
    salt, garlic powder or other seasonings to taste

Coat the cookie sheet with oil. Slice the tofu lengthwise, about ¼ inch thick, and pat dry. Put the sauce in a dish, and dip each piece of tofu into the sauce, coating it well. Place the tofu on the cookie sheet in a single layer (pieces can be touching but should not overlap). Sprinkle on the seasoning, and bake at 350°F for 20 to 30 minutes, depending on how crisp you like your tofu. Halfway through the cooking time, flip to brown both sides.

MAKES 3 SERVINGS (4OZ. EACH)

Per serving: Calories: 191, Protein: 13 gm., Fat: 10 gm.,
    Carbohydrates: 15 gm., Fiber: 1 gm.
Good source: calcium, iron, zinc, folate, thiamin

Analysis was done using firm tofu coated with barbecue sauce.

VEGETABLE STIR-FRY

If you're getting tired of your same old stir-frys, the two easy but interesting combinations here will wake up your taste buds! The first seasoning mixture adds a sweet and gingery taste; the second is more exotic. Hijiki, a seaweed high in calcium, is included as an optional ingredient; this is a good way to introduce seaweed into your menus.

Basic Recipe:

> 3 Tbsp tapioca flour or cornstarch
> 3 Tbsp water
> 1½ cups chick-peas, firm tofu, tempeh or seitan pieces
> 1 Tbsp vegetable oil
> 1 medium onion, sliced
> 2 medium carrots, sliced diagonally
> 3 cups broccoli florets with stems, peeled and sliced
> 2 Tbsp dry hijiki seaweed (optional)
> ⅓ cup very hot water (optional)

Follow the preperation method below, then add seasoning mixture no. 1 or no. 2 to the basic recipe.

Seasoning mixture no. 1:

> 2 Tbsp tamari or soy sauce
> 1 Tbsp freshly grated ginger
> 1 Tbsp rice syrup or honey

Seasoning mixture no. 2:

> 2 to 3 Tbsp tamari or soy sauce
> 2 to 3 tsp rice vinegar or white wine vinegar
> 1 tsp ground cumin
> 2 cloves garlic, minced
> 1 tsp minced or freshly grated ginger
> 2 Tbsp fresh cilantro (optional)

If you are using hijiki, combine it with hot water in a small bowl, and set aside to soak for 15 minutes. From the basic recipe, mix the tapioca flour with the water, and set aside. Choose a seasoning mixture, and combine it in another bowl. Add the seasoning to the chick-peas. Heat the oil in a wok or deep, cast-iron skillet on high, and sauté the onion until golden brown. Add the carrots and broccoli, and cook until tender-crisp. Add the chick-peas and hijiki, and cook an additional 2 to 3 minutes. Thicken by stirring in the tapioca and water mixture and cooking a few minutes. Serve with brown rice, noodles, other grains or pasta.

Variation: Replace the oil with 3 Tbsp vegetable broth water.

Makes 3 servings (2 cups each)

Per serving: Calories: 365, Protein: 12 gm., Fat: 7 gm., Carbohydrates: 60 gm.,
    Fiber: 12 gm.
High source: iron, folate, thiamin, vitamin A, vitamin B_6, vitamin C
Good source: calcium, niacin, riboflavin

Analysis was done using seasoning no. 1, chick-peas and hijiki.

Chef's Tip: The secret of having an attractive, sparkling appearance to a stir-fry is to use tapioca starch (found in Oriental groceries), instead of cornstarch, to thicken the cooked mixture. Cornstarch needs more cooking (5 minutes) and has a duller appearance. Mix tapioca starch with a little water or broth, and add slowly to the cooked stir-fry. Stir and cook for a quick 30 seconds until thick and shiny.

MILLET PATTIES

Cooked millet is moist and has a slightly buttery, sweet flavor, making it an ideal base for patties. The beans or soy flour in this recipe add extra protein while the cornmeal gives a fine texture. This patty is wheat-free and provides a wide variety of optional seasonings to please many palates.

    1 cup dry millet
    2 cups boiling water

¼ cup onions, finely chopped

1 tsp ground oregano or thyme

2 tsp vegetable oil

1 cup cooked beans, drained and mashed, or ¼ cup soy flour

¼ cup corn meal or oatmeal

2 Tbsp tamari or soy sauce

1 Tbsp Red Star T-6635+ nutritional yeast flakes

½ tsp garlic powder

½ cup fresh parsley, minced fresh

1 tsp oregano or thyme

3 Tbsp sesame seeds (optional)

seasoned cornmeal for breading the patties

In a medium saucepan, cook the millet in boiling water, covered, for 45 minutes. Meanwhile, in a small frying pan, sauté the onions and spices in the oil until soft (add a little water if necessary to prevent sticking). In another large bowl, thoroughly combine the cooked millet, sautéed onion mixture and remaining ingredients. Form into patties or balls. Coat each patty with the seasoned cornmeal. Bake at 350°F on a greased baking sheet until browned, approximately 25 to 35 minutes (flip over once to brown both sides). Another option is to fry them in a little oil until golden on both sides.

Serving Suggestion: Place in a casserole dish and cover with gravy (see pages 241–42 and double the recipe). Bake in the oven for about 10 minutes more.

MAKES ABOUT 6 PATTIES (3 oz each)

Per patty: Calories: 134, Protein: 5 gm., Fat: 2 gm., Carbohydrates: 24 gm.,
     Fiber: 4 gm.
High source: folate, thiamin, riboflavin, vitamin B_6
Good source: iron, niacin, vitamin B_{12}

Analysis was done using cooked navy beans and cornmeal.

NUTRITIONAL NOTE: In contrast to traditional burgers, these patties are low in fat and contain no cholesterol.

WHEAT GLUTEN CUTLETS (SEITAN)

If you haven't tasted products made with vital wheat gluten (instant gluten powder),* you're in for a wonderful surprise. These cutlets are made of a savory, vital wheat gluten mixture that is boiled in a flavorful broth. The broth can then be thickened and served as gravy for the cutlets and potatoes, creating a more traditional meal, especially for festive occasions.

Broth for Boiling the Cutlets:
- 4 cups water
- 2 tsp vegetable seasoning powder
- 1 onion, chopped
- ¼ ~~½ tsp cumin~~ *or*
- ¼ tsp each: ground sage, thyme, garlic powder, celery seed and turmeric, *celery salt*
- ⅛ ts. paprika

Making the Gluten Cutlets:

Dry Ingredients:
- 1 cup vital wheat gluten
- ¼ cup defatted soy flour — *garbanzo flour*
- 2 Tbsp Red Star T6635+ nutritional yeast flakes
- 1½ tsp each: garlic powder and vegetable seasoning
- 1 tsp ground thyme

Wet Ingredients:
- 1 cup water
- 2 Tbsp tamari or soy sauce

Preparing the broth for boiling the cutlets:
In a large sauce pan, combine all the broth ingredients, cover, bring to a boil, and simmer.

Making and boiling the cutlets:
Mix the dry ingredients thoroughly. Add the wet ingredients and knead a few

*See glossary, page 254, for sources.

times until smooth. Form into a roll about 3 inches in diameter. With a sharp serrated knife, cut into slices ¼ inch to ⅜ inch thick (see Chef'sTip below) and drop into the boiling broth. Stir gently to prevent sticking together. Cover and boil gently for 15 to 20 minutes or until cooked. Using a slotted spoon, remove the patties from the broth. Choose one of the serving suggestions below and proceed.

Baking or frying the cutlet:

American Style with Gravy:

> To make gravy, combine ¼ cup white flour with ½ cup water in a jar with a lid. Shake to form a very smooth paste. Add the flour mixture to the hot broth, and stir briskly. Cook on low heat until thickened. Place the boiled cutlets in a casserole dish, and cover with the gravy. Bake in 350°F oven for 15-20 minutes. Garnish with cranberry sauce or applesauce.

European Style:

> Dip the boiled cutlet into seasoned breading meal (1 cup flour, 1 cup corn meal, 2 tsp sage) and brown them on both sides in a frying pan with a little oil. Serve with applesauce.

Spanish Style:

> Place the boiled cutlets in a casserole dish with a lid. Add tomato sauce with chopped green peppers, cilantro or parsley. Bake covered in a 350°F oven for 15 to 20 minutes.

MAKES **10** SERVINGS (3 oz each)

Per Serving: Calories: 71, Protein: 7gm., Fat: 0 gm., Carbohydrates: 10 gm.,
   Fiber: 2 gm.
High source: riboflavin, thiamin, vitamin B_6
Good source: folate, niacin, vitamin B_{12}

Analysis was done using the boiled cutlet.

Chef's Tip: To make a uniform cutlet, roll out the uncooked gluten slices to ¼ inch thick with a little flour, bake in a 350°F oven for 5 minutes, and then boil in the broth. Unused boiled patties can be frozen or refrigerated right in the broth. When ready to use, thaw, remove the cutlet, and thicken the broth for gravy.

350 – 3 hrs.
325 – 4.5
300 – 5
275 – 7.5
250 – 9

or - bake 20-40 min.
pour broth over +
continue 30-60 min.

SAVORY VEGAN TSP ROAST OR PATTIES

Textured soy protein (TSP) is a versatile, convenient soy food that can broaden your recipe repertoire. It is high in protein but very low in fat compared to most other soy products. This recipe can be made into a festive center piece surrounded with roasted vegetables and served with cranberries and gravy or shaped into delicious patties for a quick everyday dinner. For a crowd, double the recipe.

> 1½ cups onions, finely chopped
> 2 cloves garlic, minced
> 1 Tbsp vegetable oil
> 2 cups unflavored TSP granules (textured soy protein)
> 2 cups hot vegetable broth (made from water and vegetable season
>   ings)
> 1 Tbsp tamari or soy sauce
> 2 cups bread crumbs
> 2 Tbsp Red Star nutritional yeast T6635+ flakes
> 2 Tbsp vital wheat gluten
> ¼ cup tomato sauce or catsup
> ½ tsp each: ground thyme, rosemary and sage
> 1 cup fresh parsley, finely chopped (optional)
> potatoes, carrots, parsnips, etc., quartered and lightly brushed with
>   oil to be roasted (optional)

Sauté the onions and garlic in the oil, and cook until the onions are soft. In a large bowl, mix all the other ingredients and add the cooked onions and garlic. Mix very well. Allow the mixture to set for 5 minutes to absorb moisture and flavors and to improve the texture.

Making a Roast:
Preheat the oven to 350°F. Form the roast mixture on an oiled cookie sheet or place it in a loaf pan. Bake for 1 hour or until nicely browned and firm. If desired, roast the vegetables the last half hour of the cooking time. Place the roast on a platter, surrounded with brightly colored vegetables or parsley, and serve hot with gravy (double the recipe given on the next page). If you are doubling the recipe and making 1 large roast, cook for 1½ hours.

Making Patties:

Form into patties about 3 inches across and ½-inch thick★. Fry in a little oil, or bake on a cookie sheet in a 350°F oven for 10 minutes or until golden brown. Serve with condiments on a whole wheat bun or pita bread, or cover with your favorite gravy or tomato sauce, and cook in a microwave or oven for a few minutes.

★For crispy patties, try coating them in seasoned cornmeal before frying.

MAKES 6 SERVINGS (3 oz. each)

Per serving: Calories: 244, Protein: 21 gm., Fat: 4 gm., Carbohydrates: 32 gm., Fiber: 6 gm.

High source: iron, folate, niacin, riboflacin, thiamin, vitamin B_6, vitamin B_{12} and vitamin C

Good source: calcium

Analysis was done using parsley without the roasted vegetables.

Chef's Tip No. 1: TSP is frequently the main ingredient in commercial meat analogs such as veggie burgers and deli slices. Some TSP is natural and unflavored while some is colored and flavored with hefty amounts of undesirable additives, fat and salt, so check the label. The granules can be used to replace ground meat in recipes, and the larger chunks are good in stews, fajitas, kebabs or pot pies. TSP has a long shelf life making it especially handy for using at home or on camping trips.

Chef's Tip No. 2: It's important to add the right amount of water to TSP. One cup dry TSP + one cup boiling water or broth will make two cups hydrated TSP. After adding the water, stir and allow to soak until all the water is absorbed and the TSP is soft (5 to 10 minutes depending on the size of the TSP).

When browning, stir often to avoid sticking and burning. When shaping into various forms, keep your hands wet so the mixture won't stick to them.

SIMPLE BROWN GRAVY

This rich gravy is delicious over a roast, loaves, veggie patties, potatoes or cooked grains. For gravy lovers, double the recipe.

⅓ cup flour

½ cup cold water

2 cups boiling water (vegetable water can also be used)

1 Tbsp tamari or soy sauce

1 Tbsp miso *or* vegetable soup seasoning *or* vegetarian oyster
   sauce

2 tsp vegetarian or chicken-style seasoning

½ tsp ground rosemary, sage or thyme

1 bay leaf

1 tsp garlic powder

2 tsp Red Star T6635+ nutritional yeast flakes

Salt and pepper to taste

Put the flour and cold water in jar with a lid. Shake until a smooth liquid is formed. In a small saucepan, make the broth with boiling water, tamari, miso and 2 tsp yeast. Add the seasonings and stir in the flour mixture. Continue stirring 2 to 3 minutes over medium heat until the mixture thickens. Serve hot. Add a little water if the gravy becomes too thick.

MAKES 5 SERVINGS

Per serving: Calories: 43, Protein: 2 gm., Fat: 0 gm., Carbohydrates: 8 gm.,
   Fiber: 0 gm.
Good source: vitamins B_6 and B_{12}

Analysis was done using miso.

Variation: For a mushroom or onion gravy, sauté ½ cup finely chopped onions or sliced mushrooms (or both) in 1 tsp oil. Add to broth, and proceed as directed above.

Nutritional Note: This quick, savory and very low-fat sauce offers a wonderful option to the traditional gravy made from high-fat, cholesterol-laden roast drippings.

MEXICAN FEAST

For building your next taco or burrito, this recipe offers three great alternatives, based on tofu, TSP (textured soy protein) as well as the familiar bean filling. For a real feast, prepare two or three fillings and double the basic recipe.

Tortillas:
8 soft whole wheat or corn tortillas or taco shells, heated

Filling:
one of the following:
– 2 cups cooked pinto beans, drained and mashed
– 1¾ cups TSP granules, unflavored, combined with 1¾ cups hot
     broth or water
– 2 cups crumbled firm (hard) tofu

plus the following:
1 clove garlic, chopped
½ cup onion, finely chopped
¼ tsp each: paprika, cayenne, cumin and salt
2 tsp chili powder
2 Tbsp water, or 1 Tbsp vegetable oil
½ cup tomato sauce or crushed tomatoes
2 Tbsp fresh lemon or lime juice
¼ cup cilantro, finely chopped

Saute the garlic, onion and spices in the water. Add the beans, TSP or tofu. Stir frequently and cook for 5 to 10 minutes. Add the tomato sauce, lemon juice and cilantro. Cover and cook for 5 more minutes. Spoon into a serving bowl. To serve, place 3 to 4 Tbsp of the mixture into a soft tortilla or taco shell, and garnish with suggestions below.

Garnishes for 8 Tacos or Burritos:
    2 cups lettuce, shredded
    2 large tomatoes, chopped
    1 ripe avocado, mashed
    1 cup taco sauce or salsa
    1 cup cheese (non-dairy or dairy), grated (optional)

Top with lettuce, tomatoes, avocado, cheese and your favorite taco sauce or salsa.

MAKES 4 SERVINGS

Per serving (2 burritos each) using bean filling: Calories: 269,
    Protein: 11 gm., Fat: 9 gm., Carbohydrates: 39 gm., Fiber: 11 gm.
High source: iron, folate, thiamin, vitamin B_6, vitamin C
Good source: zinc, niacin, riboflavin

Analysis was done omitting cheese and vegetable oil.

Per serving (2 burritos) using textured soy protein filling: Calories: 222,
    Protein: 21 gm., Fat: 9 gm., Carbohydrates: 17 gm., Fiber: 10 gm.
High source: iron, folate, vitamin A, vitamin B_6, vitamin C
Good source: calcium, zinc, niacin, riboflavin, thiamin

Analysis was done using unfortified textured soy granules.

Per serving (2 burritos) using tofu filling: Calories: 283, Protein: 18 gm.,
    Fat: 18 gm., Carbohydrates: 18 gm., Fiber: 6 gm.
High source: iron, folate, vitamin A, vitamin B_6, vitamin C
Good source: calcium, zinc, niacin, riboflavin, thiamin

ALMOST INSTANT CANDY

This no-bake recipe is so easy and delicious, it's sure to be a hit with you and your family! Peanut butter, almond butter or hazelnut (filbert) butter all work well.

> ½ cup nut butter (almond, peanut, hazelnut or cashew)
> ¼ cup blackstrap molasses
> ¼ cup liquid sweetener (maple syrup or honey)
> 1 cup milk powder (non-dairy or dairy)
> 1 tsp vanilla
> ½ cup chopped dried fruit (optional)
> crushed cereal flakes, coconut or sesame seeds (optional)

Stir together the first 5 ingredients. Add the dried fruit. Pat into an 8" x 8" pan, or form into 1" balls. Roll in crushed cereal flakes, coconut or sesame seeds, if desired.

MAKES 18 SERVINGS (2 balls each)

Per serving: Calories: 141, Protein: 4 gm., Fat: 3 gm.,
        Carbohydrates: 23 gm., Fiber: 1 gm.
High source: calcium, vitamin B12

Analysis was done using fortified tofu beverage, peanut butter and dried apricots

Nutritional Note: These are the kinds of candies you can give your children guilt-free! Blackstrap molasses is the most nutritious of all sweeteners. Just 2 Tbsp provide as much calcium as a glass of milk and as much iron as an 8 oz steak.

APPLE AND SPICE COOKIES

These soft, flavorful cookies are sure to please your whole family.

    ½ cup dark brown sugar
    ¼ cup oil
    1 Tbsp ground flaxseed or 1 egg
    ⅔ cup milk (non-dairy or dairy)
    1 tsp vanilla
    1 carrot, finely grated
    2 small apples, grated
    1½ cups whole wheat flour
    ½ cup wheat germ
    2 tsp baking powder
    1 tsp each: allspice and cinnamon
    ½ tsp nutmeg
    ½ cup raisins or coconut (optional)
    ½ cup walnuts or pecans, chopped (optional)

In a medium bowl, thoroughly mix the first 7 ingredients. In a large bowl, mix the dry and optional ingredients well. Add the wet mixture and mix well. Drop 1 Tbsp of batter per cookie onto a greased cookie sheet, placing the cookies 1 inch apart. Bake in 375°F oven for 10 to 15 minutes.

MAKES 15 SERVINGS (2 cookies)

Per serving: Calories: 138, Protein: 3 gm., Fat: 5 gm.,
     Carbohydrates: 23 gm., Fiber: 3 gm.
High source: vitamin A
Good source: folate, thiamin

Analysis was done using ground flax, raisins and fortified soymilk.

Nutritional Note: This cookie is a powerhouse of wholesome ingredients including apples, carrots and whole grain flour. The addition of soymilk boosts the protein and gives a soft, melt-in-your-mouth texture.

MULTI-PURPOSE FRUIT MUFFIN AND CAKE BATTER

This versatile batter makes moist and delicious muffins or cake. Don't let the list of ingredients fool you, they're really very simple to make. If you use mashed banana or grated apple in the recipe, you may wish to reduce the sweeteners.

Muffin Batter:
2 cups whole wheat flour
1 cup wheat germ or oat bran (or a combination)
2 tsp baking powder
½ tsp baking soda
2 tsp cinnamon
½ tsp each: allspice and cloves
1½ cups mashed bananas, pumpkin, grated apples, carrots or
     zucchini
¼ cup vegetable oil
1¼ cups milk (non-dairy or dairy)
1 Tbsp ground flaxseed + 3 Tbsp water, or 1 egg
¼ cup blackstrap molasses

⅓ cup liquid sweetener (maple syrup or honey)

½ cup raisins or dates (optional)

½ cup walnuts or pecans, chopped (optional)

In a large bowl, combine all the dry ingredients. In a small bowl, stir together the wet ingredients including the flaxseed egg replacer. Add the wet to the dry ingredients, and stir until just blended. Add the raisins and nuts. Fill greased muffin tins (vegetable or lecithin spray works well). The trick to big, moist muffins is to load the tins right to the top. For muffins, bake at 375°F for 15 to 20 minutes or until done. For cake, use a greased 9" x 13" cake pan, and bake in a 350°F oven for 50 to 60 minutes.

MAKES **12** MUFFINS

Per muffin: Calories: 232, Protein: 6 gm., Fat: 7 gm., Carbohydrates: 40 gm., Fiber: 5 gm.

High source: iron, folate, thiamin, vitamin A

Good source: zinc, niacin, vitamin B_6

Analysis was done using fortified soymilk, wheat germ, ground flaxseed, carrots and raisins.

Nutritional Note: These muffins or cakes are nutritional powerhouses, and when served with some fresh fruit, they make a great dessert or substantial snack.

OLD FASHIONED LOW-FAT GINGERBREAD CAKE

This moist, dark, nutritious favorite is so easy to make, and it's low in fat.

¼ cup vegetable oil

¼ cup milk (dairy or non-dairy)

2 Tbsp ground flaxseed or 2 eggs

¾ cup maple syrup or honey

½ cup blackstrap molasses

⅛ tsp salt (optional)

2½ Tbsp ground ginger

1 tsp each: cinnamon and cloves
2 tsp baking soda
1 cup boiling water
2 cups whole wheat flour

In a large bowl, mix all the ingredients well except for the baking soda, water and flour. In a small bowl, combine the baking soda and boiling water, and immediately stir into the other bowl, mixing well. Using a spoon or whisk, gradually and lightly blend in the flour, to prevent lumping. Pour into a greased bunt pan (cooking spray works well) or a 9" x 9" cake pan. Bake in 350°F oven for 35 to 40 minutes or until a toothpick inserted in the center comes out clean. Cool and glaze with lemon icing if desired.

MAKES 12 SERVINGS

Per serving: Calories: 200, Protein: 3 gm., Fat: 6 gm., Carbohydrates: 35 gm.,
    Fiber: 3 gm.
High source: iron
Good source: calcium, folate

Analysis was done using fortified soymilk and ground flaxseed.

Lemon Icing:
¾ cup sifted icing sugar
½ tsp grated lemon rind
1½ Tbsp lemon juice

In small bowl, combine the ingredients, and mix until smooth. Spread on cooled gingerbread.

BERRY UNCHEESECAKE

Virginia McDougal, a creative cook from Oregon, developed the filling for this special recipe. The beautiful appearance of this dessert will make it a conversation piece at festive occasions. For those with soy or dairy allergies, this will be a welcome treat.

Oatmeal Cinnamon Crust:

> 1¼ cups whole wheat flour
> ¾ cup oatmeal
> 2 tsp cinnamon
> 3 to 4 Tbsp brown sugar
> ¼ cup vegetable oil
> ⅛ tsp salt
> 2 Tbsp ground flaxseed
> ¼ cup very cold water (make using ice cubes)

Filling:

> ⅔ cup millet, uncooked
> 2½ cups water
> ½ tsp salt
> ½ cup unsalted cashews
> ⅓ cup each: lemon juice and maple syrup (or honey)
> 1 tsp grated lemon rind
> 1 tsp vanilla
> 1 to 2 tsp lemon extract (optional)

Quick, Elegant Fruit Topping:

> 2 to 3 cups berries or sliced fruit (strawberries, kiwis, peaches,
>   plums, etc.)
> 2 to 3 Tbsp all-fruit jelly or jam, melted (optional)
> 1 drop almond extract (optional)

Crust:

In a large bowl, combine the flour, oatmeal and cinnamon, and mix well. In a small bowl mix the sugar, oil, salt and ground flaxseed. Add the oil mixture to flour mixture forming a meal. Stir in the cold water until well mixed. Press firmly, thinly lining the sides and bottom of a 10-inch pie plate, a large spring-form pan or the bottom of a large cake pan. Bake in a 350°F oven for 9 to 12 minutes until lightly browned. Cool before filling.

Filling:

In a medium saucepan, place the millet, water and salt. Bring to a rapid boil, cover, reduce the heat, and cook for about 45 minutes until all the water is absorbed and the millet is soft. Meanwhile, in a food processor, add all the remaining ingredients, and purée for about 1 minute, until perfectly smooth.

Scrape down the sides if necessary. When the cooked millet is still *warm*, add it to the mixture and process for about 1 minute until creamy and smooth. Occasionally scrape down the sides of the processor with a rubber spatula. Pour into the cooked pie shell, and chill.

Topping:
Arrange the fruit over the filling and serve, or prepare a glaze as follows. Melt the jelly or jam. Add the almond extract and berries or sliced fruit. Gently stir and spread over the filling, and chill.

MAKES 10-12 SERVINGS (one-tenth of cake)

Per serving: Calories: 326, Protein: 8 gm., Fat: 13 gm., Carbohydrates: 46 gm.,
    Fiber: 6 gm.
High source: iron, folate, vitamin C
Good source: zinc, niacin, thiamin

Analysis was done including the crust, filling and a strawberry topping.

Nutritional Note: One serving of this delicious pie provides 8 gm of protein with less than half the fat of a traditional cheesecake.

Chef's Tip: Tapioca flour dissolved in fruit juice gives that wonderful glaze to fruit toppings for garnishing cakes or pies with very little cooking. This preserves both the flavor and vitamins.

INSTANT CREAMY CHOCOLATE PIE OR PUDDING

A rich, dairy-free tofu dessert that is too good to be true! Even those who have never tasted tofu won't be able to resist this pie. The filling can be used as a pudding or as a chocolate dip for fresh fruit. Extra-firm silken tofu gives a velvety-smooth filling. Chilling at least 4 hours enhances the flavor.

Filling:
    2-10.5 oz packages silken extra-firm tofu
    3 Tbsp liquid sweetener (maple syrup or honey)
    1 tsp vanilla extract (optional)

1⅓ cups semi-sweet chocolate or carob chips
1 to 2 cups fresh or canned fruit (optional)

Pie Crust:
　　Use the Oatmeal Cinnamon Crust on page 249, or a crust
　　　　of your choice.

In a blender, combine the tofu, liquid sweetener and vanilla until very creamy.
Heat the chips in a microwave on medium heat for 3 to 4 minutes until soft.
Quickly add to the tofu in the blender, and combine until very smooth. Pour
into a cooked pie crust or individual pudding cups, and chill for at least 4
hours. Garnish with fruit. Fresh raspberries, strawberries, bananas and/or
sliced kiwi are particularly attractive.

MAKES 8-10 SERVINGS

Per serving: Calories: 260, Protein: 8 gm., Fat 10 gm., Carbohydrates: 38 gm.,
　　　Fiber 3 gm.
High source: iron
Good source: vitamin C

Analysis was done using raspberry garnish.

Variation: For butterscotch pie, substitute 1⅓ cups butterscotch chips for
the chocolate chips. Use maple syrup as the sweetener.

APPENDIX 1: GLOSSARY

Adzuki beans: Small, dark-red, mild-tasting beans, which cook quicker than most other beans. Available in Oriental groceries and natural food stores.

Agar-agar: A clear, flavorless substance from some red seaweeds. It is freeze-dried, sold in sticks, flakes or powder and used like gelatin. Use one-quarter less agar-agar when substituting in place of gelatin. Available in both natural food stores and Oriental markets.

Amaranth: Ancient Aztec grain with a buckwheat flavor. Available at natural food stores and Oriental markets.

Atherosclerosis: A buildup of fatty material (plaque) in the arteries, including those surrounding the heart.

Baba ghanoush: A Middle-Eastern dip made of eggplant, tahini, garlic and spices.

Black turtle beans: Small, black, oval-shaped beans that are a staple in South America and used widely in China. Available dried or canned in natural food stores and many supermarkets.

Blackstrap molasses: A dark, strong-tasting liquid by-product of sugar refining. It contains significant amounts of minerals, calcium and iron. Other types of molasses have very low mineral content compared to blackstrap molasses.

Bok choy: A crunchy, mild Chinese cabbage. It has pale oblong white stems with pale green top leaves. Rich in calcium.

Buckwheat: Technically not a grain, but a member of the rhubarb family; buckwheat is gluten free, and therefore excellent for those who have wheat allergies. It can be purchased as kasha, flour or groats.

Bulgar: Cracked wheat that has been hulled and parboiled. Available in coarse or fine-ground varieties.

Cilantro: The fresh leaves of the coriander plant. It also is called Chinese or Mexican parsley.

Control group: In a scientific study, this group goes untreated or receives a placebo treatment while the experimental group receives a treatment. This allows researchers to better determine the effects of the treatment.

Couscous: Crushed, steamed and dried durum wheat, popular in Moroccan and other Middle Eastern dishes. Available in refined or whole wheat varieties.

Daily Values (DV): An estimate of the daily nutrient requirement of an individual on a 2000 calorie diet; used on food labels. These figures were based on the 1968 RDA set by the National Science Academy – see Appendix 2 for the current edition with some modifications for cholesterol and dietary fiber.

Dulse: A purple-red, soft-textured seaweed with a unique spicy flavor used in soups and condiments. It is high in minerals, such as iron, potassium, magnesium, iodine and phosphorus.

Egg replacer: A substitute for eggs in cooked and baked foods. Some examples are ground flaxseed, arrowroot powder and tofu. Available in natural food stores and supermarkets.

Falafel: A spicy chick-pea patty that originated in the Middle East. Also often made into balls and served in pita bread with lettuce, tomatoes, onions and a creamy dressing.

Flaxseed (linseed): A small brown seed that is high

in omega-3 fatty acid (alpha linolenic acid) and the mineral boron. For maximum benefits, grind and use on cereals or in baking as an egg replacer. Also available in oil form. Once the seed coat has been broken, it becomes rancid very quickly, so it must be frozen or kept refrigerated.

Garbanzo beans (Chick-peas): Round, light-brown beans with a nutty flavor. Traditionally used in Middle-Eastern dishes such as hummus and falafel.

Gram: A unit for measuring weight. Commonly abbreviated as gm. (28 gm = 1 oz).

Hijiki: A black, string-like seaweed that expands to five times its dry volume. It should be soaked for about ten minutes before using. Available in Oriental and natural food stores. It is a good source of calcium.

Hummus: A Middle-Eastern spread or dip made of chick-peas, tahini, lemon juice, garlic and seasonings.

Hydrogenated fat: A process in which hydrogen is added to liquid vegetable oil changing it into a solid margarine or shortening. The fat that is formed becomes more saturated and contains trans-fatty acids.

Kamut: An ancient grain related to the wheat family, used in place of wheat in cooking and baking.

Kelp powder: A delicately flavored, salty-tasting, brown seaweed that is ground into a powder. It adds flavor and minerals, such as calcium and iron, to many foods. It contains less sodium than salt. To increase minerals in your diet, add it to the ingredients for making such foods as breads, muffins and stews, and omit the salt. Available in Oriental markets and natural food stores.

Kohlrabi: A root vegetable related to the cabbage family, similar in shape to a turnip but with a light green skin. It can be steamed, stir-fried or eaten raw with a dip.

Leek: A mild, onion-garlic-flavored vegetable that resembles a giant green onion.

Legume: A family of plants whose seeds are in pods (e.g., beans, peas, lentils and peanuts). Most legumes are low in fat and high in protein, minerals and fiber.

Meat analogs: Products made to resemble meat in taste, appearance and nutritional composition. They are often made with wheat gluten or soy protein.

Mg/dl: Milligrams per deciliter (1/1,000 of a gram per 1/10 of a liter).

Microgram: 1/1,000,000 of a gram. Commonly abbreviated mcg or μg.

Milligram: 1/1,000 of a gram. Commonly abbreviated mg.

Millet: A tiny, round, golden grain that becomes light and fluffy when cooked. Popular in India and Africa, it is very low in gluten, making it an ideal grain for those with sensitivity to gluten. Available in natural food stores and some supermarkets.

Miso: A salty paste made from cooked, aged soybeans and sometimes grains such as barley and rice. Thick and spreadable, it's used for flavoring and soup bases. It comes in several varieties; darker varieties tend to be stronger flavored and saltier than lighter varieties. Available in natural food stores and some Oriental grocery stores.

Mmol/l: A unit of measure expressing the amount of a given substance in millimoles (mmol) or 1/1000 of a mole per liter of fluid.

Non-dairy "milks": Any "milk" liquid that is made from plant foods such as nuts, seeds, grains and soybeans. Unless they are fortified, the calcium content is lower than that of cow's milk. They can be substituted for cow's milk in most recipes but must never be used in place of infant formula.

Nori: Thin, crispy sheets of pressed seaweed usually crumbled as a garnish or rolled around rice for sushi. It is also known as dried laver. Available in both natural food stores and Oriental markets.

Nut butters: Spreads made from finely ground nuts or seeds such as cashews, peanuts, almonds and sesame.

Nut "milks": Non-dairy beverages, such as almond milk, made by puréeing nuts with water in a blender. The calcium content of nut "milks" is considerably lower than cow's milk unless they are fortified. These beverages can be useful for people who are allergic to cow's milk or soymilk. However, they are not suitable for use as infant formula or as the primary milk for children under the age of six.

Nutrients: Chemical substances in food that nourish the body. Classified as protein, fats, carbohydrates, vitamins, minerals and water.

Nutritional yeast: A dietary supplement and condiment, rich in B vitamins, that has a distinct cheese-like flavor and a pleasant aroma. Although there are many brands of nutritional yeast powder or flakes, the Red Star T6635+, because it is grown on a B_{12} medium, is a reliable source of vitamin B_{12} for vegans. Nutritional yeasts are not leavening yeasts used in making bread. Available in natural food stores and some groceries stores.

Okra: Green, finger-like vegetable pods that have a slippery texture when cooked. Used in soups and stews and may be oven-fried; a source of calcium.

Omnivore: A person who eats plants and animals.

Organic food: Foods that have been grown without the use of synthetic fertilizers, pesticides, herbicides or fungicides. Certification codes vary from state to state.

Placebo: A fake, harmless supplement or substance given to the control group in a scientific study.

Quinoa (pronounced keen-wa): An ancient grain of the Incas, quinoa is nicknamed the "super-grain" because it contains more high-quality protein than any other grain. This round, sand-colored, quick-cooking grain has a light texture and a mild, nutty taste. Wash well before cooking to remove a natural, strong-tasting resin. It is very low in gluten, which makes it a good substitute for those who have wheat allergies.

Rice "milk": "Milk" made by puréeing rice and water and straining it. Although it can be used by those who have a sensitivity to cow's milk or soymilk, it is lower in protein, calcium and fat. Thus it is not suitable for use as an infant formula or as a primary milk for children under the age of six.

Rutabaga: A large, yellow-fleshed root vegetable with a sweet flavor. It can be cooked like a potato, added to winter stews or eaten raw.

Seed butters: Spreads made from finely ground nuts or seeds such as cashews, peanuts, almonds and sesame.

Seitan: A chewy, high-protein food made to resemble meat in taste and texture by boiling or baking flavored wheat gluten.

Soybean: A legume which has a higher percent of protein and fat compared to the others, making it more versatile. Can be made into products such as tofu, miso, tempeh, soymilk, soy sauce, soy flour, soy grits and meat analogs (TSP).

Soymilk: A non-dairy milky liquid made from soybeans. The fat and other nutrients, such as calcium, in these products vary considerably from brand to brand, therefore it should not be used as infant formula.

Spelt: A Middle-Eastern grain related to wheat.

Sucanat™: A natural, organic sweetener made from granulated sugar. Use equal amounts of Sucanat as required in recipes using white sugar.

Tahini: A thick, smooth paste made of raw, ground sesame seeds. Available in natural food stores, Middle Eastern or gourmet groceries, and some supermarkets. Rich in calcium.

Tamari: A type of soy sauce naturally fermented from soybeans.

Tempeh: A high-protein, highly digestible, cultured food made from soybeans and sometimes grains. Available in Oriental grocery stores and natural food stores.

Textured soy protein (TSP®): A fibrous soy product that resembles meat with a very low fat content and no cholesterol. Available dried in granules, chunks or flakes at natural food stores or through The Mail Order Catalog (see page 97).

Tofu (soybean curd): A highly versatile soy product made from the milk of soybeans and coagulated with nigari or calcium salts. Available in many textures from soft to extra-firm. Medium-firm tofu, when made with calcium salts, provides an excellent source of calcium, while extra-firm tofu made with nigari provides higher levels of zinc and iron. It is only an excellent source of calcium if it is made with calcium salts; read the label. It can be substituted for eggs in baking by using ¼ lb (50 mL) for each egg in many recipes. Many food products are made from tofu including non-dairy milks, cheese (Tofu Rella) and meat analogs.

Triticale: A hybrid grain developed by crossing wheat with rye, thus producing a grain that is higher in protein. It is often sold in flakes or flour rather than as a whole grain.

Triglyceride: The chemical structure of fats and oils in the body and in food. It is composed of three fatty acids bonded to glycerol.

Vital wheat gluten: A wheat powder with all the carbohydrate and starch removed. If you are unable to find this in your area, you can order it from The Mail Order Catalog (see address, page 97)

Wakame: A brown seaweed with a mild flavor. Used in soups and stir-frys. Rich in minerals such as calcium.

APPENDIX 2: NUTRITION RECOMMENDATIONS

Table 1 – *Estimated Safe and Adequate Daily Dietary Intakes of Selected Vitamins and Minerals[a]*

Category	Age (years)	Vitamins	
		Biotin (μg)	Pantothenic Acid (mg)
Infants	0–0.5	10	2
	0.5–1	15	3
Children and	1–3	20	3
adolescents	4–6	25	3–4
	7–10	30	4–5
	11 +	30–100	4–7
Adults		30–100	4–7

Category	Age (years)	Trace Elements[b]				
		Copper (mg)	Manganese (mg)	Fluoride (mg)	Chromium (μg)	Molybdenum (μg)
Infants	0–0.5	0.4–0.6	0.3–0.6	0.1–0.5	10–40	15–30
	0.5–1	0.6–0.7	0.6–1.0	0.2–1.0	20–60	20–40
Children and	1–3	0.7–1.0	1.0–1.5	0.5–1.5	20–80	25–50
adolescents	4–6	1.0–1.5	1.5–2.0	1.0–2.5	30–120	30–75
	7–10	1.0–2.0	2.0–3.0	1.5–2.5	50–200	50–150
	11 +	1.5–2.5	2.0–5.0	1.5–2.5	50–200	75–250
Adults		1.5–3.0	2.0–5.0	1.5–4.0	50–200	75–250

[a] Because there is less information on which to base allowances, these figures are not given in the main table of RDA and are provided here in the form of ranges of recommended intakes.

[b] Since the toxic levels for many trace elements may be only several times usual intakes, the upper levels for the trace elements given in this table should not be habitually exceeded.

All tables reprinted with permission.

Table 2 – Food and Nutrition Board, National Academy of Sciences – National Research Council Recommended Dietary Allowances,[a] Revised 1989

Category	Age (years) or Condition	Weight[b] (kg)	(lb)	Height[b] (cm)	(in)	Protein (g)	Fat-Soluble Vitamins Vita-min A (μg RE)[c]	Vita-min D[d] (μg)	Vita-min E (mg α-TE)[e]	Vita-min K (μg)	Water-Soluble Vitamins Vita-min C (mg)	Thia-min (mg)	Ribo-flavin (mg)	Niacin (mg NE)[f]	Vita-min B₆ (mg)	Fo-late (μg)	Vitamin B₁₂ (μg)	Minerals Cal-cium (mg)	Phos-phorus (mg)	Mag-nesium (mg)	Iron (mg)	Zinc (mg)	Iodine (μg)	Sele-nium (μg)
Infants	0.0–0.5	6	13	60	24	13	375	7.5	3	5	30	0.3	0.4	5	0.3	25	0.3	400	300	40	6	5	40	10
	0.5–1.0	9	20	71	28	14	375	10	4	10	35	0.4	0.5	6	0.6	35	0.5	600	500	60	10	5	50	15
Children	1–3	13	29	90	35	16	400	10	6	15	40	0.7	0.8	9	1.0	50	0.7	800	800	80	10	10	70	20
	4–6	20	44	112	44	24	500	10	7	20	45	0.9	1.1	12	1.1	75	1.0	800	800	120	10	10	90	20
	7–10	28	62	132	52	28	700	10	7	30	45	1.0	1.2	13	1.4	100	1.4	800	800	170	10	10	120	30
Males	11–14	45	99	157	62	45	1,000	10	10	45	50	1.3	1.5	17	1.7	150	2.0	1,200	1,200	270	12	15	150	40
	15–18	66	145	176	69	59	1,000	10	10	65	60	1.5	1.8	20	2.0	200	2.0	1,200	1,200	400	12	15	150	50
	19–24	72	160	177	70	58	1,000	10	10	70	60	1.5	1.7	19	2.0	200	2.0	1,200	1,200	350	10	15	150	70
	25–50	79	174	176	70	63	1,000	5	10	80	60	1.5	1.7	19	2.0	200	2.0	800	800	350	10	15	150	70
	51+	77	170	173	68	63	1,000	5	10	80	60	1.2	1.4	15	2.0	200	2.0	800	800	350	10	15	150	70
Females	11–14	46	101	157	62	46	800	10	8	45	50	1.1	1.3	15	1.4	150	2.0	1,200	1,200	280	15	12	150	45
	15–18	55	120	163	64	44	800	10	8	55	60	1.1	1.3	15	1.5	180	2.0	1,200	1,200	300	15	12	150	50
	19–24	58	128	164	65	46	800	10	8	60	60	1.1	1.3	15	1.6	180	2.0	1,200	1,200	280	15	12	150	55
	25–50	63	138	163	64	50	800	5	8	65	60	1.1	1.3	15	1.6	180	2.0	800	800	280	15	12	150	55
	51+	65	143	160	63	50	800	5	8	65	60	1.0	1.2	13	1.6	180	2.0	800	800	280	10	12	150	55
Pregnant						60	800	10	10	65	70	1.5	1.6	17	2.2	400	2.2	1,200	1,200	300	30	15	175	65
Lactating	1st 6 months					65	1,300	10	12	65	95	1.6	1.8	20	2.1	280	2.6	1,200	1,200	355	15	19	200	75
	2nd 6 months					62	1,200	10	11	65	90	1.6	1.7	20	2.1	260	2.6	1,200	1,200	340	15	16	200	75

[a] The allowances, expressed as average daily intakes over time, are intended to provide for individual variations among most normal persons as they live in the United States under usual environmental stresses. Diets should be based on a variety of common foods in order to provide other nutrients for which human requirements have been less well defined. See text for detailed discussion of allowances and of nutrients not tabulated.

[b] Weights and heights of Reference Adults are actual medians for the U.S. population of the designated age, as reported by NHANES II. The median weights and heights of those under 19 years of age were taken from Hamill et al. (1979) (see pages 16–17). The use of these figures does not imply that the height-to-weight ratios are ideal.

[c] Retinol equivalents. 1 retinol equivalent = 1 μg retinol or 6 μg β-carotene. See text for calculation of vitamin A activity of diets as retinol equivalents.

[d] As cholecalciferol. 10 μg cholecalciferol = 400 IU of vitamin D.

[e] α-Tocopherol equivalents. 1 mg d-α tocopherol = 1 α-TE. See text for variation in allowances and calculation of vitamin E activity of the diet as α-tocopherol equivalents.

[f] 1 NE (niacin equivalent) is equal to 1 mg of niacin or 60 mg of dietary tryptophan.

INDEX

Ask your store to carry these books, or you may order directly from:

Tofu Cookery
$15.95

Book Publishing Company
P.O. Box 99
Summertown, TN 38483

Or call 1-800-695-2241

Please add $2.50 shipping per book

Tofu & Soyfoods
Cookery
$12.95

Cooking with PETA
$14.95

The Uncheese
Cookbook
$11.95

Vegetarian Cooking for People
with Diabetes
$12.95

Vegetarian Resource Directory
$9.95

Vegetarian Cooking for
People with Allergies
$12.95

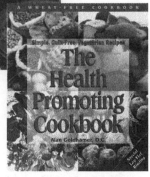

The Health Promoting
Cookbook
$12.95